Populism and Trade

Populism and Trade

The Challenge to the Global Trading System

Kent Jones

OXFORD
UNIVERSITY PRESS

OXFORD
UNIVERSITY PRESS

Oxford University Press is a department of the University of Oxford. It furthers
the University's objective of excellence in research, scholarship, and education
by publishing worldwide. Oxford is a registered trade mark of Oxford University
Press in the UK and certain other countries.

Published in the United States of America by Oxford University Press
198 Madison Avenue, New York, NY 10016, United States of America.

Library of Congress Cataloging-in-Publication Data
Names: Jones, Kent Albert, author.
Title: Populism and trade : The Challenge to the Global Trading System / Kent Jones.
Description: New York, NY : Oxford University Press, [2021] |
Includes bibliographical references and index.
Identifiers: LCCN 2020045695 (print) | LCCN 2020045696 (ebook) |
ISBN 9780190086350 (hardback) | ISBN 9780190086374 (epub)
Subjects: LCSH: Commercial policy. | Protectionism. | International trade—
Political aspects. | Populism—Economic aspects. | World Trade Organization.
Classification: LCC HF1411 .J624 2021 (print) |
LCC HF1411 (ebook) | DDC 382/.3—dc23
LC record available at https://lccn.loc.gov/2020045695
LC ebook record available at https://lccn.loc.gov/2020045696

DOI: 10.1093/oso/9780190086350.001.0001

1 3 5 7 9 8 6 4 2

Printed by Sheridan Books, Inc., United States of America

In memory of J. Michael Finger, 1939–2018
Trade Scholar, Visionary, Global Institutionalist

Contents

Preface and Acknowledgments

This book sets out to examine the impact of populism on national trade policies and international trade institutions, such as the WTO and regional trade agreements. It will argue that the implementation of populist trade policies by the United States has not only increased the implementation of protectionist policies, but has also damaged the basic rules-based framework of the global trading system. The economic nationalism it has inspired has severely undermined the principles of nondiscrimination, multilateralism, and peaceful dispute settlement that had previously established a predictable and stable trading order. The book project began as a response to a disturbing—but ultimately not surprising—trend in the evolution of global trade institutions. As a student of trade policy in Geneva in the 1970s, in the shadow of GATT (later WTO) headquarters, I learned of the disastrous legacy of a chaotic world economy between the first two world wars, including beggar-thy-neighbor tariffs, crippling trade wars, and the Great Depression, with the world descending into World War II. In 1947 the victorious allied countries, led by the United States, established a new system of multilateral trade rules designed to avoid the self-destructive policies of the interwar period. For several decades thereafter, the world economy enjoyed unprecedented economic growth alongside multilateral trade liberalization and a remarkably robust adherence to GATT-WTO rules, with leadership from the United States and the European Union. Yet as my early mentor, Jan Tumlir, impressed upon me, global trade policy tends to follow a long wave of sequential learning and un-learning. The long period of trade liberalization, sparked by the lessons of the turbulent times that preceded it, appears now to have run its course. The biggest shocks to the trading system occurred in 2016, with two populist surprises. In June of that year, the United Kingdom voted in a referendum to leave the European Union, giving up its membership in an economic agreement that it had joined in 1974 primarily for the trade benefits it offered. The Brexit vote represented a populist renunciation of a European trade and integration agreement that had begun in 1951 as a renunciation of war among former enemies, and served as the exemplar of successful international cooperation among its 28 member countries. The second shock came later that year, as Donald Trump, an avowed protectionist, won the US presidential election. In a few short years, the new populist US president began to dismantle the very global trading rules the United States had so strongly supported since

1947. His policies were not just protectionist; they were designed to overturn an entire system of global cooperation and return to an atavistic nationalist trade policy of mercantilism and unilateral tariffs. Understanding the origins of the global populist zeitgeist and its impact on trade policy is the goal of this book.

My acknowledgments begin with a tribute to my early mentors and influencers, now departed, who helped me to understand the nature and politics of trade and its global institutions: Jan Tumlir, Gerard Curzon, Robert Meagher, Rachel McCulloch, and J. Michael Finger, to whose memory this book is dedicated. More recently, I have benefitted greatly from observations and advice from Barry Eichengreen, Doug Irwin, Manfred Elsig, Gary Hufbauer, and especially Chad Bown, whose detailed and timely account of US trade policy in the Trump administration for the Peterson Institute has been particularly helpful in my research for this book. I am also grateful for critical reviews of earlier drafts of this book by my colleagues from various disciplines at Babson College, including Neal Harris, James Hoopes, and Martha Lanning, and by my sister, historian Jacqueline Jones of the University of Texas—Austin. I benefitted from additional helpful comments by participants in the International Trade and Finance Association Annual meeting in Livorno, Italy, in 2019, where I presented an early draft of parts of this book. My special thanks go to my colleague Yunwei Gai, whose help in preparation of the statistical study in chapter 6 was indispensable, and to my research assistant, Anna Saltykova, for help in the preparation of several tables and the bibliography. As always, I am eternally thankful for my wife, Tonya Price, whose patience and support served as essential inputs in completing this book.

1
Trade and the Roots of Disaffection

In the global trading system, the age of anxiety has given way to the age of populism. Since the financial crisis of 2008, voting for populist candidates in many countries has grown, and in recent years surged to levels not seen since the 1930s. Beginning in 2018, the United States imposed tariffs and other trade restrictions on a number of products and even initiated a trade war with China, echoing the tariff wars of the 1930s. Trade tensions have escalated to major confrontations among countries, even among long-standing allies. For the first time since the end of World War II, trade actions began to ignore the rules established by global trade agreements. In the United Kingdom the populist Brexit movement delivered a further blow to the trading system, setting in motion a reduction in trade and investment integration in Europe. Populist governments in many other parts of the world have had varying impacts on trade policy, depending on economic and political factors specific to the country. But in general, the populist-induced erosion of the rules of the game has already imposed economic costs on businesses and consumers around the world, through disruptions in consumer market and supply-chain linkages. Retaliatory tariff measures in response to the defiance of World Trade Organization (WTO) rules and norms have deepened the crisis. Reduced investment in trade-related businesses has dampened trade flows even more and amplified damage to the world economy. A continuation of such policies will compound the problem by imposing higher costs on businesses and consumers, and it could split the world into competing defensive trading blocs and cripple global economic growth.

Table 1.1 lists the trade restrictions imposed by the Trump administration, along with the retaliatory actions they provoked, from January 2018 to January 2020. Figure 1.1 focuses on the escalation of tariffs that took place in the US-China trade war through early 2020. Nearly all of the trade restrictions, including the foreign retaliation, defied WTO rules or long-standing practices. Thus Trump's unilateral protectionist measures, such as national security tariffs and the US-China trade war, not only attacked the trading system, but incited US trading partners to violate these disciplines as well. Together the exchange of tariffs represented a major erosion of the WTO as an institution.

Populism and Trade. Kent Jones, Oxford University Press. © Oxford University Press 2021.
DOI: 10.1093/oso/9780190086350.003.0001.

Table 1.1 US-Initiated Trade Restrictions and Retaliation, January 2018–January 2020

Date	Initiated by	Against	Action	Products
2018				
Jan. 22	US	Korea	Section 201 (safeguard)	Washing machines
		China		Solar Panels
Mar. 23	US	Most countries	Section 232 (nat'l security tariffs)	Steel
		Most countries		Aluminum
Mar. 28	US	Korea	Section 232 VERs*	Steel
Apr. 2	China	US	Retaliation	Steel/Alum tariffs
June 1		EU, Canada, Mexico	Extend Section 232	Steel/Alum
June 22	EU	US	Retaliation	Food, consumer goods
July 1	Canada	US	Retaliation	Steel/aluminum, Food, consumer goods
July 8	US	China	Section 301 trade war tariffs I	Various goods
	China	US	Trade war tariffs I	Various goods, food
Aug. 10	US	Turkey	Doubled tariffs (for currency manipulation)	Steel/aluminum
Aug. 14	Turkey	US	Retaliation	Cars, alcohol, tobacco
Aug. 23	US	China	Trade war tariffs II	Various
Aug. 23	China	US	Trade war tariffs II	Various
Sept. 24	US	China	Trade war tariffs III	Various
Sept. 24	China	US	Trade war tariffs III	Various
Aug. 27	US	Mexico, Canada	USMCA** VERs*, wage provisions	Autos
2019				
May 10	US	China	Raise tariff III rates	Various
May 30	US	Mexico	Tariff quid pro quo	Immigration policy
June 1	China	US	Retaliation: higher tariff III rates	Various
June 5	US	India	Withdraw GSP benefits	All Indian exports
June 15	India	US	Retaliation	Steel/alum
2020				
Jan. 15	US, China		Phase One trade war truce	Various trade quotas
Jan. 24	US	Several countries	Section 232 extension	Steel/aluminum derived products

*VER: voluntary export restraint, prohibited by WTO rules.

**USMCA: United States-Mexico-Canada Agreement, successor to the North American Free Trade Agreement (NAFTA).

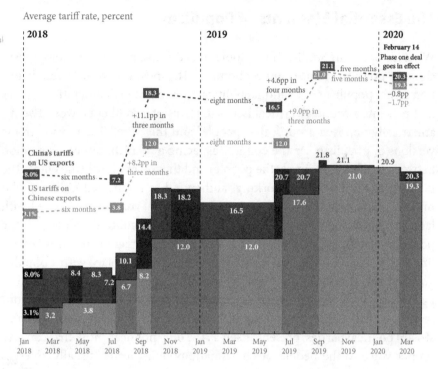

Figure 1.1 US–China Trade War: Escalation of Tariffs, January 2018–March 2020
Source: Bown (2020a).

Other actions, targeting smaller countries, were overt violations of specific WTO provisions. The negotiation of a voluntary export restraint (VER) agreement with the Republic of Korea on steel violated the WTO safeguards provision prohibiting such measures. The use of threatened tariffs against Mexico to change its immigration policy violated the tariff binding provision of General Agreement on Tariffs and Trade (GATT) Article 2, not to mention the regional North American Free Trade Agreement (NAFTA) provisions on market access between Mexico and the United States that existed at the time. The US-China Phase One agreement represented another major derogation of WTO rules and practices, establishing a discriminatory system of US export quotas to China. The list does not include other US assaults on WTO institutions, such as the veto of dispute settlement appellate body judges, to the point where panel decisions in dispute cases no longer had access to appellate review, crippling the entire system. These are some of the ways that populism is undermining the global trading system.

The Essential Elements of Populism

What is populism? Studies of this topic span the disciplines of sociology, psychology, political science, and economics.[1] The most widely accepted definition is that populism is a national political movement in democratic societies that presents a country's critical issues in terms of a conflict between two diametrically opposed groups: the "people" and the "elite." The most extreme versions of populism see the country as facing a Manichaean confrontation between the forces of good (the people) and the forces of evil (the elite). The people are genuine, hard-working, authentic but disaffected citizens, who must contend with a dishonest, aloof, exploitative, ruling elite aligned with larger, nefarious (and often foreign) economic and cultural influences. The populist scenario generally presumes a current elitist regime in control of political and economic institutions that the people must replace with a populist government. An important element of populism is that traditional political parties are either inadequate in representing the genuine people, or are conspiring with the elite. Thus a populist movement, operating outside mainstream political parties, presents itself as the only political entity that can give proper voice to the people. A charismatic populist leader usually emerges to channel the group's anger and maintain momentum to achieve political power. A successful populist movement then typically establishes itself as an insurgent force that overturns the status quo. Only then can the people create or restore their legitimate rights and benefits. The most distinctive feature of populism as a form of politics is therefore its polarizing nature. For supporters of a populist movement the status quo is not only unfair, it is outrageous, unnatural, despicable—an unjust situation that requires root-and-branch removal of existing policies and institutions. In most if not all cases, a charismatic leader heads a successful populist movement, winning support through resonating salt-of-the-earth rhetoric and "tough talk" against the elite, and focusing populist anger with slogans and anti-establishment policy goals. Yet even after a populist government comes into power, the basic conflict remains its animating force.

After President Trump's 2016 victory, former US President Barack Obama asked with some wonderment why Trump's supporters continued to be so angry—after all, they had won the election. But the reason lay in the nature of populism itself, which is essentially an expression of the perpetual politics of anger. The anger can have various roots, motivated by various sources of disaffection. It can come from humiliation when jobs are lost, dependency on government welfare increases, and retirement savings evaporate prematurely. It can come from the fear of losing one's job in the future, due to imports, technology, or other forces beyond a worker's control, based on current trends and the fact that one's neighbors have lost their jobs. Anger intensifies when the forces can be identified: politicians who support trade agreements that cause job losses, a multinational firm that relocates its factory to China, and EU directives from Brussels that dictate policies in the United Kingdom. Anger may grow when elites in the population are seen to be thriving, while the hapless people are left behind. City elites may often be pitted against country folk. Anger can well up among individuals, indirectly caused by havoc that disruptive market or social forces impose on the broader community and region, including poverty, drug abuse, and suicide. In this regard, a perceived demographic threat of immigrants and their unfamiliar cultures, languages, and religions may also instill anger based on resentment of the changing face of a neighborhood, and fear of displacement harbored by established native ethnic and cultural groups. Sociologists refer to this anger as a response to "status deprivation." Fears of crime and even terrorism can heighten anti-immigrant backlash. Restrictions on gun ownership may become a rallying cry against those who would deny the people's right to self-protection. The enemy within may be seen as those who undermine traditional social and religious mores: proponents of abortion rights, gay marriage, and gender equality. A successful populist movement typically emanates from a feedstock of mutually reinforcing discontents, which a populist leader can transform into potent, visceral anger focused on a culpable elite. A populist government sustains its political fortunes largely by stoking continuous angry energy needed among supporters in order to win the next election. In order to understand voting patterns and behavior under these circumstances, one must account for the role of emotions in the polling booth, where elections are transformed into life-and-death decisions on cultural and economic survival.

A key question surrounding populism is whether it is ultimately beneficial or detrimental to a country. This book will take up the question in terms of trade policy and its institutions. In principle, populism represents a political process, rather than an ideological set of policy prescriptions, although populist movements often adopt ideological frameworks to shape their political strategies. As a response to inadequate political representation, a major populist movement reveals a valid concern in democracies: the lack of political channels for a large portion of the population to express their grievances in a deliberative, pluralistic forum. Disaffected voters regard major political parties, or the controlling factions within them, as unresponsive to their concerns. In this regard, populism is the neglected—and resentful—stepchild of democracy. Populist movements seek to redress the perceived injustices and misdeeds of an untrustworthy regime and to implement needed changes.

On this point also, governments facing such resentment must consider what caused the populist movement to arise, and how it might have been avoided. Newly enfranchised supporters of US President Andrew Jackson in the 1820s and 1830s, for example, demanded replacement of land-holding elites who occupied most high government positions at the time and had allegedly favored elite interests in their policies. US populist movements in the Great Depression era of the 1930s demanded economic reforms, leading to the New Deal policies that still define many regulations and social safety nets in the United States today. These examples show that individual attitudes toward populism depend heavily on one's perspective. Many economic and political activists of the twenty-first century, for example, supported Occupy Wall Street and anti-globalization movements in order to overturn what they saw as an unjust, inequitable, political and economic power structure. On the other hand, many established ethnic, religious, racial, and cultural groups support nativist populist movements. They do so because these movements promise to protect or restore their dominant status, and also to restrict the intrusion or role of foreign or unfamiliar people or influences on society.

This book will approach the question of populism's impact with two criteria in mind, based on the fruits of a populist regime: how a populist government affects economic welfare for a country's entire population, and how it treats democratic institutions. Populist governments may implement short-sighted economic policies, designed to please their populist base but which instead lead to damaging inflation, significant trade welfare losses, market collapse, capital flight, price-gauging market concentration of industries, and corruption. Such policies are detrimental, regardless of the regime's original motivation to redress an unjust situation. Populist governments that implement lasting reforms, achieving support among the broader population beyond their term in office, are correspondingly beneficial, in terms of revealed preferences of the entire pluralistic society. Liberal democracy plays a crucial role in this assessment. The greatest danger of populism comes from the potentially perverse political dynamic it may create. Since by definition it is (or starts as) a democratic phenomenon, a populist government is subject to new elections. Populist leaders, having ridden a wave of anger into office, face the temptation of perpetually demonizing the elite, thus continuing the polarization of society, factionalizing government, and destroying the capacity for political deliberation and compromise. What is worse, populist leaders, fearing political opposition to their policies, may begin to dismantle democratic institutions in order to avoid giving up their office. Erosion of democratic institutions has occurred in many populist governments, through restrictions on freedom of the press and speech, seizure of the power of the judiciary, marginalization of the elected legislature, and the elimination of constitutional checks and balances. Studies of populism and democratic institutions show that all types of populist government tend to diminish democratic institutions, the longer they remain in power.[2] Populism exists on a political continuum; it ranges from governmental systems with well-established democratic traditions and institutions and protections for minority groups and opposing political parties, to authoritarian rule that concentrates power in a single ruler or party, with progressively weaker democratic traditions and legal protections for groups outside the populist base diminishing to zero. The starting position on the continuum for a new populist government in power is how well developed a country's democratic institutions are when a populist government wins the election. More critical is what happens during subsequent election cycles. The implications of this result are that strong and robust democratic institutions are required, with continued active support of the population, in order to discipline the temptation of authoritarianism that populist governments face. Both the economic welfare and the democratic criteria used in judging populism are reflected in the government's trade policy, through its impact on the population and on the institutional processes of its formulation and implementation. At the same time, the impact of an economically incompetent and anti-democratic populist regime will wreak havoc that goes well beyond the effects of its trade policy. The individual characteristics and ambitions of a populist leader play a crucial role in the policy outcomes for a country.

Populism in Global and Historical Perspective

Populism is a global phenomenon, even as it varies among countries according to their individual historical, cultural, and political environments. In addition to the United States and the United Kingdom, there were at least 23 other governments around the world with populist governments of various types in the years 2017–2021. In Eastern Europe, long-standing populist regimes in Russia and Belarus began under conditions of weak democracy, which have become more authoritarian. Serbia's government is also populist, but aspires to membership in the European Union, which tends to encourage softer, less confrontational, domestic and foreign policies. In the European Union itself, the populist government in the UK had the greatest impact, negotiating its final EU withdrawal by late 2020. However, Bulgaria, the Czech Republic, Hungary, Slovakia, and Poland also had populist governments, defined since 2015 in part by immigration restrictions and cultural issues.

Greece briefly had a left-wing populist government in the wake of its financial crisis, while Italy had several populist governments from the mid-1990s until 2019. Populist parties in that country remained strong in early 2021, also motivated by immigration and refugee concerns. In addition, populist parties throughout Europe garnered increasing shares of electoral votes from 2014 through early 2020, receiving approximately 25% of all votes in national parliamentary elections during this period. Norris and Inglehart (2019) tallied 135 active populist parties in European countries in 2014. In the Middle East, Turkey has a long-standing populist regime of authoritarian character, while Israel has its own brand of populism, defined by the Palestinian issue and regional hostilities. In Africa, the country of South Africa has had left-wing populist governments in recent years, fueled by land reform, failed stagnating economic development, and income distribution issues. Populism also plays a prominent role in Latin American countries. Venezuela remained technically populist in early 2021, although it had by that time become a failed state with highly eroded democratic institutions. Brazil and Mexico had recently elected populist governments in 2021, neighbors of a long-standing populist regime in Nicaragua. The populist government in Bolivia was deposed in 2019, but its future remained uncertain. Argentina's newly elected government in 2019 was Peronist, with historically populist roots, but the nature of the new regime was not yet clear. In Asia, India's populist government focused on ethnic and cultural divisions, and Sri Lanka's populist governments have been driven by outright civil warfare between ethnic populations. Indonesia's populist regime, on the other hand, was attempting to keep such divisions from boiling over. Populism in the Philippines in 2021 was strongly authoritarian. Among these populist governments, trade policies have varied according to the context of each country's "elite versus people" conflict and the role of trade in each economy.

Since populism as a political phenomenon is linked in principle to democratic electoral processes, populist movements can be traced back to the nineteenth century, with the ascendency of representative democratic systems of government (Eichengreen 2018). This definition excludes revolutions, coups d'états, and other violent or furtive means of overthrowing a government, even though such events may have popular support. Thus the French and Russian Revolutions of 1789 and 1917, respectively, may have involved popular insurrections but were not populist movements as such, since they occurred outside the realm of democratic politics. In this regard, countries such as Venezuela and the Russian Federation represent borderline cases of populism in the early twenty-first century. Their populist leaders— Hugo Chavez and later Nicolás Maduro in Venezuela, and Vladimir Putin in Russia—attained power initially through democratic elections, although democratic institutions may have been shallow or weak at the time. These administrations subsequently dismantled democratic institutions and gained control of the political process, to the point where it became extremely difficult for opposition candidates to gain power or even representation in the populist-dominated government. Yet a veneer of democratic elections appears to be part of an advanced populist regime's claim to political legitimacy, all the more so in order to reinforce its claim of representing the people.

Populism spiked dramatically in the two decades following the end of World War I in 1918. These were years of political and economic turmoil: many war-weary populations lost trust in their governments, empires fell or sank into decline, power relationships were realigned, new technologies disrupted the workplace and society, and the global economy descended into the Great Depression (Funke et al. 2016). The result was a corresponding rise in political extremism, a cautionary tale for the twenty-first century. While fascist, communist, and other authoritarian dictatorships during this period differed in principle from populist regimes, they sprang from similar political conditions. For example, Hitler's path to power in Germany went through the electoral process, as his National-Socialist party achieved a plurality in the 1932 German elections, after which Kaiser Wilhelm appointed him Chancellor. At this point, the Hitler government technically qualified as populist, despite lacking a parliamentary majority. Yet Hitler soon proceeded to claim emergency powers after his supporters allegedly staged the Reichstag fire. He then eliminated political rivals, decertified all parties other than his own, and eventually gained control over all domestic political, civil, and social institutions. Free elections did not return to (West) Germany until 1949, and during Hitler's rule, Nazi Germany was a fascist dictatorship. Other fascist dictatorships also took power in post–World War I Europe: Italy under Mussolini in 1922, and Spain under Franco in 1939. These dictators also once headed populist political parties, but without electoral success, and gained power through military means. This was also true in Japan, where a military dictatorship displaced weak democratic institutions through intimidation, aggressive foreign incursions, and assassination.

After World War II, populism receded as a major political force in most Western countries. Postwar recovery and reconstruction reinvigorated democracies, and robust economic growth and international trade helped maintain political peace at home and abroad. The Cold War conflict between the United States and Soviet Russia also helped to channel anxieties away from populist issues. This trend provides food for thought in understanding the environment in which populism can grow. Economic growth eventually slowed in most Western countries by the 1980s, as their economies matured and as developing countries began to compete in world trade. On top of disruptive trade and technological change, a powerful shock occurred with the global financial crisis of 2008, leaving a new populist surge in its wake. As we entered the third decade of the twenty-first century, many populist movements came to regard elites as the champions of globalization and of the multilateralism that grew out of postwar cooperation, integrating trade and financial flows among neighboring countries and around the world. Populist groups targeted elites as their tormentors across a variety of dimensions. In many countries, openness to trade has come with openness to foreign workers, immigrants, and even refugees. Diversity in racial and ethnic backgrounds then came with diversity in traditions and at times a collision of these traditions, which were often unfamiliar or strange to each other. Supporters of this type of populism tied their anger against the elite to diminished cultural, racial, social, or economic status. The populist agenda therefore combined various types of discontents into a larger platform for removing the incumbent elitist government. International trade may or may not have been a major part of the platform, but "globalist" trade policies remained an easy target of populist ire in that they could be linked to disruptions in the economy, especially in areas of diminished industrial output and employment. As the following pages will show, populism is by its very nature anti-establishment; once it undermines a trade regime with protectionist measures, domestic and global institutions of trade may weaken.

Organization of the Chapters

The rest of the book is organized as follows. Chapter 2 provides a conceptual framework for the link between trade and populism, based on anthropological and sociological research, examination of populist voting behavior, and current ideological profiles of populist movements. Chapter 3 describes the flashpoints of trade and populism: the hot-button topics and slogans of populist rallies, including national sovereignty, deindustrialization, trade deficits, tariffs, trade bargaining, China, the World Trade Organization, the European Commission, and immigration. Chapter 4 traces the development of populism in the United States, from Jacksonian populism in the first part of the nineteenth century to the post–financial crisis years of the early twenty-first century, including Donald Trump's successful presidential campaign. Chapter 5 explores the central issue of President Trump's populist assault on global trading rules and the pattern of protectionist policies he implemented during his presidency, culminating in the US-China trade war. Chapter 6 turns to Brexit and the populist surge in Europe, a reaction to centralized decisions by the European Council, Eurozone officials, and the European Commission regarding immigration, monetary integration, and regulations. While trade was not the main reason for Brexit, its trade implications will be of great importance for the post-Brexit United Kingdom, and perhaps for trade policy in the European Union in the future. Chapter 7 begins with a statistical study to determine if populist governments tend systematically to be protectionist, and then briefly profiles current and recent populist governments around the world in terms of their trade policies. The final two chapters assess the cost of populism and the outlook for addressing the root causes of populism. Chapter 8 summarizes economic research on the welfare cost of populist trade restrictions and the damage populism has inflicted on trade institutions, focusing on Trump's trade policies, the foreign retaliation they sparked, and the impact on the global system of trade policy rules. The final chapter presents the main conclusions of the book and discusses domestic economic policies to address underlying causes of the populist backlash against trade. It also addresses possible reforms at the World Trade Organization, and alternative ways to mend the fractures in multilateral trade cooperation that are likely to outlast the populist surge of the early twenty-first century.

2
Trade as a Source of Populist Conflict

What is the nature of populism from a behavioral point of view, and what is its connection to trade? This chapter begins with an examination of the individual behavioral reasons that a country's trade policy may be involved in a populist movement. Anthropological and sociological factors play a role in shaping individual attitudes toward either an open engagement with foreign trade, or a defensive, skeptical view. The role of national governments introduces an important political dimension in the linkage, as individual and group attitudes contribute to a sense of national identity and national sovereignty becomes a potent element in policies toward the outside world. The chapter then addresses the intermediate step of how populism affects voting behavior in a democratic society, with its distinctive appeal to emotions and presumption of deep, often irreconcilable divisions in society. Populist politics tends to upend traditional models of rational decision-making at the ballot box, requiring a new perspective on what motivates disgruntled voters. Unwanted social, economic, and cultural changes spark anger at the status quo, mistrust of existing elected officials, and a rejection of mainstream political parties. Trade effects may be either a major source of anger, or an associated issue that mediates populist anger. Finally, if populist candidates or parties win the election, the question arises as to how the new government will view the economy and trade. Does it matter what ideology—left, right, or "anti-establishment"—is attached to the populist movement?

Attitudes Toward Trade: Behavioral Elements

Trade developed as a form of social interaction, and attitudes towards trade with "outsiders" were shaped by human brain development, and the balance between the tendency to seek the advantages of such an exchange and the benefits of ingroup protection and security. As broader social groupings led to administrative control over trade, these attitudes were further mediated by a political process that would determine the group's policies towards interaction with foreigners, and institutionally, with foreign countries. This section addresses these two elements of trade policy formulation.

Populism and Trade. Kent Jones, Oxford University Press. © Oxford University Press 2021.
DOI: 10.1093/oso/9780190086350.003.0002.

Anthropological Origins

An understanding of human attitudes toward trade begins with evidence of human brain development regarding two critical psychological attributes.[1] The first is the human capacity for social interaction based on communication, task specialization, and exchange, an evolutionary development associated by anthropologists with advanced social organization, survival through cooperation, and the foundations of civilization. The second is the human tendency to identify with a group (at the level of the family, tribe, cultural community, or nation), internalize its interests, and exclude or resist outsiders when threats arise. The first of these attributes implies an affinity for "truck and barter," as Adam Smith put it, favoring an acceptance of exchange activity outside and beyond immediate social groups. The second attribute implies the primacy of group identity as a defining factor in social interaction, which under threats of external danger and disruption transforms into a defensive insider-outsider view of the world that can be associated with trade protectionism. These at times contrasting, at times complementary, human tendencies shape individuals' views toward trade and its impact in the larger community. In the twenty-first century, populist movements have typically shifted the balance in favor of insider–outsider politics, often including a backlash against globalization.

Trading provides the means for the individual to gain material benefits from new, different, or otherwise unavailable products, for acquiring them at cheaper prices or selling one's own products at better prices. It represents an outward engagement with unrelated and often unknown parties by going outside the known community. It shows humans as both inquisitive and acquisitive. Recent archeological evidence suggests that the long-standing human tendency to truck and barter beyond one's immediate community through long-distance trade may have begun as early as 140,000 years ago, and may furthermore be linked to the beginnings of human speech.[2] The exchange of goods and services, it seems, began in conjunction with the ability to exchange greetings and barter propositions. The economic incentives to trade find their motivation in neoclassical trade theory, which shows the benefits to both parties of specialization in production and exchange. At the level of the basic unit of social organization, specialization and exchange began within the family, the village, and the tribe, groups within which mutually reinforcing incentives to cooperate existed. The result was not only increased social development, but also, according to Hartwick (2010), the development of increased brain capacity. Productive activities within the group came to follow basic patterns of comparative advantage (hunting, cultivation, child-rearing, implement making, meal preparation, etc.), with corresponding internal exchanges of goods and services, institutionalized in assigned roles, and in the social organization of the group. In this regard, social organization facilitated further specialization and more distant travel to exchange goods and services.

The second element of human interaction, "in-group" identification, provides the means for social cohesion and the framework for culture, language, and typically a sense of safety among one's peers. The sense of safety in the in-group evolved from the immediate to the extended family, and then to the tribe and the nation. The individual's identity as a member, with distinctive customs and practices and a common history, also provides the security of membership in the larger group, and a way of establishing a boundary against members of the "out-group." It also imparts status to the individual, a benefit exclusive to the in-group. A compelling attribute of in-group identification lies in its attraction—particularly in times of stress or crisis—to those in search of transcendence, the individual's identification with and fulfillment through the larger national identity.[3] The notion of a unified, self-identifying nation later became the basis for today's system of territorial nation-states, which in turn placed great importance on the concept of *sovereignty*, the legal, political, and military control of a country's territory by its government serving to provide physical security as well as economic well-being of its population.

Regarding trade, the defensive reflex in primitive societies reflected the realistic fears about the dangers of venturing outside one's tribal homeland or familiar turf. Foreign trade was often a perilous activity, with the possibility of attack, robbery, piracy, and murder. One solution to the problem was to equip, train, and deploy armed escorts, or even armies, to protect the trading party. Such a security force could, if necessary or if the opportunity arose, further simplify the interaction through pillage and conquest, even though the result was not "trade" in the sense of a voluntary exchange. "If there are more of *them*, trade; if there are more of *us*, raid," would be the rule of thumb for an expeditionary force eagerly seeking access to foreign goods (Pinker 2011, p. 285). The history of trade thus paralleled, in part, the history of organized violence by social groups and governments, territorial aggression, and colonization (see Findlay and O'Rourke 2007). It was also certainly possible that a balance of power between potential trading partners, or a benevolent view and curiosity toward the interaction with foreigners, would lead to mutually beneficial reciprocal exchange, especially if territorial ambitions and xenophobia did not overshadow the transaction. Early trading expeditions of this sort represented the beginnings of bilateral trade diplomacy, another institutional response to the problem of transactions costs. Yet the suspicion that the trading partner harbored ambitions of domination often lurked just below the surface, and still affects trade relations today, as shown by the trade war between China and the United States. The nexus between trade and power may also be partly responsible for the tendency of countries, through their governments, to conclude preferential trade agreements with their neighbors and allies. To the extent that *trust* among the partners reduces the transaction cost of exchange, a stable trade relationship with predictable and reliable gains from trade was often more likely among countries with established cultural, linguistic, and political relations.[4] Populism, with its inherent distrust of international cooperation, tends to work against stable trade relations.

Politics and the Trade-versus-Protectionism Balance

The balance between the desire of individuals within a country to engage in international commerce, and their simultaneous desire to maintain a secure and unassailable group identity, is mediated through the political system and its process of policymaking. In democratic political systems (the focus of this book) voters choose governments that strike a balance between openness to foreigners, their investments, and their products, on the one hand, and the preferences for territorial security and for domestic rather than foreign influences, on the other. A desire among citizens and domestic businesses for a high degree of engagement with the outside world implies the implementation of open trade, investment, and immigration policies. Concerns about globalization, import competition, and job dislocation imply greater restrictions on trade, immigration, and international capital flows. Resentment by displaced workers may intensify as a result of their declining economic welfare, especially if elites are experiencing economic gains, presumably at the expense of the people (Algan et al. 2017). Such concerns are nothing new, and even open trade policies typically include defensive "safety valves" that allow some measured and circumscribed trade restrictions that serve to defuse flare-ups of protectionist sentiment. Such measures are based on rules and safeguards against disruptive or "unfair" trade. However, if more extreme cases of economic dislocation, sociocultural threat, and downward mobility cause group identity frustrations to reach a critical threshold of anger, support for a *populist* regime are likely to grow. The current wave of populist trade protectionism represents the latest reversion to a pattern of nationalist economic policies sparked by income shocks, often abetted by disruptive social and cultural change and a perceived loss of domestic sovereignty. Populism as a political force is best understood along a spectrum that spans a range from isolated

protests against prevailing economic, social, and political conditions, to democratically elected populist governments, all the way to authoritarianism and
even full-blown anti-democratic fascism. Similarly, the impact of populism
on trade policy ranges from focused protectionist sentiment in particular
industries to the subversion of domestic and global trade institutions.

Interpreting the trade policy balance between openness and protectionist
isolation often presumes that domestic consumers generally favor free trade,
while domestic producers favor protection if they compete with imports.
There are two main problems with this assumption in understanding the
link between populism and trade. First, the modern truck-and-barter motive
must take account of international supply chains, in which a domestic firm is
often both a producer and consumer of traded goods. The benefit of cheaper
imported inputs may therefore offset the agony of import competition in final
goods, and the same firm may be an exporter of related products as well. The
preferences of firms and their employees may therefore not be as predictable
as they would be under a simple scenario of strictly import-competing and
exporting industries. The second major problem is that consumer and worker
preferences, even if they appear to follow economic motives, may not trans-
late into corresponding pro- or anti-trade voting preferences if group identity
has a "resonance effect," influencing attitudes across issues. This may occur,
for example, if a voter who consumes imported goods is employed by an exporting firm, or otherwise benefits from trade, nonetheless sympathizes at the
voting booth with others in the community whose jobs have been displaced
by imports. Or if the same voter resents the growing immigrant presence in
the community or region enough to vote an anti-globalization, protectionist
ticket despite the apparent contradiction with his or her economic interests.
Such *expressive* or *sociotropic* voting behavior represents noneconomic and
often emotional motives that upset traditional voting models based on economic self-interest, which be discussed later.

If import disruption is the issue, the tariff is the typical policy measure to
restrict trade, although many other measures can effectively achieve the same
goal, such as domestic subsidies, regulations, and licensing requirements.
Nearly all countries now maintain immigration restrictions in support of policies that will ensure a desired demographic balance in the home population,
based usually on country of origin but implicitly also by race, ethnicity, religion, education level, and other factors that determine the desirability of the
immigrant. And while the protection of national identity and culture tends
to focus on immigration controls, restrictions on trade may often be closely
linked with the same concern. For example, if foreign imports lead to the closure of industries and displacement of jobs affecting politically influential

groups and their way of life, protectionist tariffs may serve a purpose similar to immigration restrictions in protecting the threatened domestic group.

Native identity-group animosity toward outsiders, fueled by a perceived threat of foreign incursion or displacement, may take the more extreme form of *xenophobia*—the fear or hatred of foreigners, strangers, or other out-group members—which often figures prominently in populism. When faced with a perceived threat from foreign intruders or influences, strident group identification may combine in-group solidarity, out-group xenophobia, subordination to a dominant and charismatic leader, and territoriality to create the conditions for aggressive anti-foreign sentiment, including war (Pitman 2011, p. 364; Aydin et al. 2014). These are also the typical conditions for most right-wing authoritarian populist movements, which can include elements of trade protectionism if imports can be linked to the threatened foreign incursion. Understanding the impulse for xenophobia is one of the key questions of research on populism. The lethal nature of xenophobic movements in the early twentieth century fueled populism, at first, followed by fascism and war. The perceived threat by native in-groups that an out-group is attempting to overturn the social, cultural, or religious order or racial balance of the country appears to raise existential fears of marginalization, lost social status, and political power, an indicator of how tenacious and entrenched such populist movements can be.

In the context of the truck-and-barter versus native group identity framework developed here, the trigger for a populist impact on trade policy would be revolt by the "people" against the current "elitist" government's policies. Theoretically, this can work either in favor of or against open trade. For example, established policies of heavy protection, such as raising prices and denying the population the benefits of trade, could result in a populist movement favoring trade liberalization. In the twenty-first century the more typical populist scenario, however, presents an advanced industrialized country's government tied into a system of open, rules-based trade, global capital mobility, and liberal (if not free) immigration. It suddenly confronts a global financial crisis, disruptive import competition, and unexpected surges in immigration by groups with ethnic and religious backgrounds different from the native population. At the same time, technological, cultural, and social trends are disrupting the settled expectations of many citizens. Many voters, disgusted with and distrustful of current government policies, turn against the traditional mainstream parties and support populist candidates who understand their pain and declare that they will throw the elitist rascals out, overturn their flawed policies, and finally protect the people's interests, "get back control" of the country and make it "great again." The main question of this book is: Will the populist government also undermine the trading system, as represented by the WTO and other trade agreements?

The Politics of Populism

The link between populism and trade policy is defined by the structure and dynamics of political processes in modern democratic societies. The key feature of trade policy in general is national sovereignty, which defines the legal control over trading activity within the territories of nation-states. Populist movements typically regard trade policy as a sovereignty issue, a confrontation between the country's "people" and its elites, who may allegedly cause trade to harm the people's interests. This confrontation plays out in the electoral process, which has become the subject of new behavioral models of voter behavior. Ideological factors may also enter the elector process, shaping the confrontation between the people and the elite. This section traces the impact of these factors on the ability of populism to influence trade policy.

Sovereignty

Assuming that trade plays a significant role in the populist movement, a final answer to the question regarding protectionism depends in large part on the populist government's assertion of sovereignty over trade access to its domestic market. Bernard Crick defines sovereignty as part of a theory of politics that requires every government to have within it a source of absolute power of final decision and the ability to enforce the decisions, but also notes that:

> Political theory has perpetually oscillated between stressing one or the other of the two primal functions of government—survival and betterment. Sovereignty sees the world in the light of survival alone and is most appropriate as a theory when the world of settled expectations seems urgently threatened. (Crick 1968)

Sovereignty can thus become a major issue "when the world of settled expectations seems urgently threatened," helping to trigger a populist movement. The breech of sovereignty may occur when imports, trade rules, or economic integration with other countries impinge on the country's control over trade flows, allegedly damaging the interests of the country's genuine people. A closer examination of the conflict in the present day usually reveals that the country has become part of an institutional structure of trade rules (such as the WTO), concluded by a treaty that makes its market access to trade part of an *exchange* of sovereignty. In contrast to a country free of any external trade commitments, with complete sovereign control over its trade policy and access to its domestic market, a country that is subject to international trade agreements accepts a reduction in its own sovereignty on these issues in a bargain to *gain* sovereignty over them from its trading partners. A country joining the WTO, for example, agrees to allow other WTO members to gain access to its domestic market through an agreed schedule of tariffs and other trade policy measures, in exchange for the new country's access to all other WTO members under similar terms. In another example, the European Union is an integration agreement in which the members sacrifice their individual trade-bargaining powers to a centralized customs union and trade-bargaining authority, in exchange for the benefits of bigger joint internal markets and greater collective bargaining power. Such bargains serve as the basis for regional and multilateral trading systems, and for further trade liberalization and changes in the rules.

Most WTO member countries accept such arrangements despite electoral changes in government, having freely concluded the required treaty commitments according to their own national economic self-interest. They allow larger gains from trade, with greater market access for their exporters balanced by a commitment to allow a greater availability of imports. As a WTO member, it is much easier to join the club with nearly universal market access than to negotiate separate trade agreements with each of the WTO's member countries.[5] The exchange of sovereignty in trade agreements is also a long-standing practice in international relations, which became common in the post-Westphalian period, beginning in 1648.[6] Furthermore, even populist governments will tend to value the trade and investment ties that come with international agreements such as the WTO and European Union when their economies depend on such reciprocal market access, and the alternative of quitting the agreements would leave them economically isolated. This will be true especially with small, open economies and indeed with most countries, unless they export oil or other valuable natural resources that increase their leverage on global markets or have access to large subsidies through supporting foreign aid and alliances.

A populist government, by its anti-establishment nature, may decide, on the other hand, to exit from or renege on international treaty commitments if it calculates that such a move will benefit its populist agenda, particularly its hold on power. The sanctity of treaties—*pacta sunt servanda*—does not stand in the way of an upstart populist leader bent on overturning the commitments of elitist predecessors.[7] The ability to assert sudden populist sovereignty over trade policy, overriding treaty commitments and institutional norms, typically comes down to bargaining power and ideology. Only a country as large as the United States in global trade could defy WTO provisions with impunity, for example. The United Kingdom, by the calculation of those choosing "leave" in the Brexit vote, regarded freedom from trade policy tyranny in Brussels as more valuable than whatever consequences would come from giving up EU integration, its gains from trade and cross-border investment, and its bargaining advantage. Some populist regimes in Latin America appear to be more openly hostile to the capitalist global trading system for ideological reasons, although only oil-rich Venezuela decoupled (if only informally) from the system of WTO rules. Other populist regimes have not gone that far, introducing protectionist policies through administrative or indirect means while avoiding major confrontations over WTO rules.

Populism, Trade, and the Election Process

A study of populist voting behavior must address the way emotional responses to issues of critical importance enter decision-making at the ballot box. To the extent that trade becomes a critical issue, its electoral impact therefore depends on if and how voters internalize it as part of an angry, populist renunciation of the status quo. There is a certain demand for trade policy preferences (and for other nontrade issues) among voters and a supply of trade and other policies offered by politicians in the election, and the nature and magnitude of these factors will vary according to the particular country, political culture, circumstances, and individual characteristics of the political leaders involved. The surge in electoral support for populist candidates has inspired a good deal of academic research. Why did voters cast their ballots for populist candidates? How did such an unlikely populist candidate get elected? The answers to these questions come down to what motivates voters upon entering the polling booth and how they evaluate the choices they face. In an election involving many disparate and multifaceted issues, with a voting population spanning many different points of view on them, voting outcomes may be difficult to predict.

In any electoral issue involving economic impact, the traditional approach among economists had previously been to analyze the voter as engaging in fully rational behavior (see Downs 1957). In this view, voters arrive at the election venue having completed calculations on how incumbents' past positions have translated into policies, and how these policies have affected the voter through changes in income, prices, and other economic variables. By updating their calculations based on the performance of politicians, voters can then generally assign expected values and risk levels to their next votes. Such models take the optimistic view that voters are cool, calm, and collected, calculator in hand, seeking all available information and then voting with the goal of maximizing their own welfare. The voter's calculations become more complicated when a new, populist candidate stands for election, proposing new and perhaps extreme or unprecedented policies, such as tariffs of 45%, which was US presidential candidate Trump's proposed policy for imports from China and Mexico. According to the economic theory of rational voting, each voter would estimate the expected impact on their economic welfare, compare the various candidates, and cast their vote for the candidate maximizing individual economic welfare. Over the next voting cycle, voters would pay attention to the winning candidates and reward those "honest" candidates whose policies result in the expected positive welfare effect. Otherwise, challengers might offer policies with greater expected welfare for the median voter in the next election. This process thus theoretically internalizes the costs of bad policy and broken election promises, as well the rewards of honest and good policies, in the election results over time.

The classic example of trade and rational voting behavior is the Stolper-Samuelson choice. This component of trade theory assumes that voters represent ownership of one of various factors of production used in making a country's output, generally represented as either labor or capital. More realistically, most voters reflect ownership of either *physical* labor or varying levels of *human-capital* (i.e., educated or highly skilled) labor. Some products—such as textiles, clothing, many production line-manufactured products, and retail, hospitality, and clerical services—require relatively more intensive inputs of physical labor, while others, such as high-technology, scientific and engineering products, and services, require workers with relatively greater degrees of human capital: education or other specialized training. The Stolper-Samuelson theory predicts that policies that increase the relative price of a labor-intensive product, such as an import tariff on textiles, will raise the wages of physical labor workers and reduce the wages of human-capital workers. A tariff on high-tech goods, in contrast, will raise human-capital worker wages and lower physical labor wages. Thus, economic theory predicts that textile workers will vote for textile tariffs and high-tech workers will vote against textile tariffs, and that these workers will take opposite positions on high-tech goods tariffs.[8] The typical case of a more advanced industrialized country is that it will tend to import clothing and export high-tech goods, hence factory workers will vote in favor a clothing tariffs and high-tech workers, who tend not to face import competition for their product, will simply oppose the clothing tariff.

If the surge in populism were simply the result of a backlash against globalization, one could explain it as the result of a backlash by factory workers against labor-intensive imports from less-developed countries. However, studies of electoral results in the 2016 US presidential race, and of recent European elections, do not indicate such a direct link, based on voter profiles, exit polling, and demographic patterns of populist support. Furthermore, behavioral studies of voting experiments indicate that few voters directly use Stolper-Samuelson reasoning in choosing candidates. A more likely explanation of voter behavior is that workers directly affected by import competition will take their cue from their union representatives or from the persuasion of specific candidates, in casting votes in favor of import tariffs. Even so, the relatively low proportion of factory workers in the United States and Europe would not be sufficient to tilt the election in favor of a protectionist populist platform. Yet populist policies tend in many cases to be economically damaging to those who vote for them, and to everyone else. What drives this sort of voting, aside from the votes of the minority that will benefit from the redistributed profits or benefits the populist candidate has promised them (see Ocampo 2019, pp. 7–10)?

Economic theory has sought to catch up with this issue. One possibility is that voters are ignorant: they don't understand or anticipate the damage that the candidates they choose will inflict (Rho and Tomz 2017). This assumption raises the obvious question, however, of why voters doesn't understand what they're voting for, which is inconsistent with the assumption that their voting decisions will seek to maximize personal welfare. A theory more charitable to such unknowing voters is that they are "rationally ignorant," that is, the information costs for each voter to discover the policy impact are prohibitive, so they remain "in the dark" when they vote. Related theories propose that voting decisions are based on "bounded rationality," in which voters do the best they can with limited information and resources. These theories suggest that Down's adaptive information model described earlier will both encourage and facilitate the gathering of information once the policy's damage is evident, allowing voters to throw out the populist in the next election. The problem in this case is that the damage has already been done, and may be difficult to reverse right away. Another problem is that a populist government, knowing its policies will fail and seeking to remain in power, may in the meantime undermine democratic institutions that will make it more difficult to have free elections in the future. An even more pessimistic theory is that voters are not ignorant at all; they are simply stupid or irrational, voting for politicians they know will decrease their economic welfare, despite their knowledge that this will happen.[9] This sort of departure from rational voting raises a difficult economic policy problem, since it implies a voting market "externality": if the majority is stupid, then the rest of the population is forced to suffer with it, and the degree of rationality needed to have an efficient democracy will tend to require some sort of government intervention. Yet in a democracy, who gets to determine what is really stupid, and how can this element be purged from afflicted voters?

Behavioral Economic Models

Further inquiries and research into the nature of populist voting have arisen in the field of behavioral economics, drawing on psychological and sociological elements of decision-making. Emotion plays a major role in populist voting behavior, especially through fear and anger (Gil 2016). Among voters with a low perceived ability to influence politics, a study by Magni (2017) suggests that anger tends to decrease trust in traditional mainstream parties and increase support for populist parties. Research by Salmela and von Scheve (2017) suggest that a fear of loss of social identity due to economic and cultural change transforms into anger directed toward immigrants and political elites and a retreat into stable religious, ethnic, and national identities. At a more fundamental level, neurobiological research has identified the sources in the brain for fear responses (LeDoux 2003) and anger responses (Blair 2013). Behavioral economists have linked these visceral emotions to extreme actions, such as the response to an act of perceived personal injustice in the form of an obsession with punishing the tormentor (Loewenstein 2000). Populism thus provides a channel for revenge at the ballot box. A threshold level of such anger in the population against a perceived enemy provides a particularly potent political force, as described by Friedrich von Hayek in the prelude to National Socialism in Germany:

> It seems to be almost a law of human nature that it is easier for people to agree on a negative programme, on the hatred of an enemy, on the envy of those better off, than on any positive task. The contrast between the "we" and the "they," the common fight against those outside the group, seems to be an essential ingredient in any creed which will solidly knit together a group for common action. It is consequently always employed by those who seek, not merely support of a policy, but the unreserved allegiance of huge masses. (Hayek 1944, p. 143)

The beliefs of individuals based on fear and anger have also contributed to new voting theories, in which emotional and noneconomic issues sway the voter to choose candidates in an expanded definition of rational choice. Caplan (2007) proposes the existence of "rational irrationality" in voting behavior, in which voters enter the election booth with systematically biased beliefs, which they regard as universal truths. Since voters know that their impact as individuals is small, there is little incentive to challenge their own beliefs, which in any case may be strongly held, such as "interaction with foreigners is bad for the country," "tariffs are good for the economy," or "the country is going to hell in a handbasket and regular politicians won't fix it." The prevalence of such views among the population provides the opportunity for populist candidates to offer a campaign package of goals and policies that will appeal to such voters (Jennings 2011). One might add that populist candidates knowledgeable of the sources of underlying dissatisfaction among these groups also have the opportunity to cultivate and reinforce such biases in their campaign rhetoric, increasing their chances to win the election.

A more subtle, but potentially revealing, variant of rational irrationality is "expressive" or "altruistic" voting (Jennings 2011; Weston 2007). Despite acting against their own material interest, some voters will cast their ballots for a protectionist candidate, for example, on the basis of identification and emotional attachment with a group or community that is harmed by import disruption. Colantone and Stanig (2018) refer to this phenomenon as "sociotropic" voting. These voters' economic interests may be neutral on trade issues, or they may in fact lie in pro-trade policies. They may also implicitly know that a vote for protectionist intervention in the economy will represent an inefficient welfare redistribution to displaced workers or communities that direct cash transfers or rational adjustment policies could accomplish more efficiently (Acemoglu and Robinson 2001; Mayda and Rodrik 2005). Yet another possibility is that the appeal for protectionism may resonate with voters otherwise not connected with the issue, but who see trade as part of a larger canvas of social disruptions afflicting the country. In any case, the expressive voters' emotional attachment to the interests of the identity group fosters voting with the afflicted community's anti-trade interests, especially when such individuals may regard their votes as insignificant in determining the outcome of the election. The vote for protectionism therefore becomes a relatively costless expression of solidarity. Such emotion-driven voting behaviors may be particularly sensitive to the appeal of a populist campaign that highlights the injustices imposed upon the victims of trade disruption. The populist leader's choice to use trade as a focal point for the electoral campaign may therefore be decisive in making such emotional linkages. In this manner trade issues may play an important mediating role in a populist campaign, extending the reach of dissatisfaction among voters beyond their own immediate economic interests.

In contrast, many studies of populism by sociologists and political scientists tend to minimize the impact of trade and economic factors in general as major explanations of populism. Regarding Trump's victory, Brexit, and the electoral gains of populists in Europe, this approach tends to focus more on sociocultural drivers of the people's anger against elites. Concerns over immigration, in particular, have led to populist fears of a threatened dilution of racial and cultural homogeneity, anger at lax immigration policies by elitist governments, and the growth of nativist demands to restore the traditional cultural, social, and even racial profile of the country.[10] The perceived threat experienced by many voters to their traditional social status is the sort of primal trigger for an emotional "us versus them" response stoking the populist call to oust the elitist politicians responsible for the mess. The leader is often a crucial element of the movement's success, creating a compelling narrative about the dire situation that only he or she can address, communicating goals in the plain and often rough language of the people, and focusing and personalizing constituent anger toward elites. Rallies featuring affective slogans such as Trump's "Build the Wall" and Brexit's "Take Back Control" create rallying cries for the populist group's identity and bandwagon effects to expand the movement's reach among the electorate (Wilson 2017).

Yet the sociological approach alone still begs an important economic question: Do populist voters rationally elect candidates who will predictably lower their own economic welfare? In principle, an economic evaluation of the populist platform can assign psychic value to implicit goals such as "the restoration of the country's previous ethnic/racial profile" and "the recapture of sovereignty from Brussels." However, the platform also has economic implications, such as immigration, trade, and foreign investment restrictions that may damage future economic growth. Specifically, Trump's campaign promises also included punishing China with massive tariffs, and Brexit's main purpose was to dismantle the United Kingdom's trade and investment integration with the European Union. So would soybean farmers of Iowa value lower immigration more than the lost export markets and lower soybean prices resulting from the president's trade war with China?[11] Would a Brexit voter value "taking back control" of the Britain's immigration and trade policies more than reduced EU trade and investment, with an estimated decline in GDP of 2% to 9%, based on most economic projections?[12] These trade-offs are further muddled by the fact that many—if not most—voters may be unaware of the economic cost calculations, or they may not trust them if they are aware. Models of expressive voting behavior suggest that emotions get in the way of economic reasoning on such issues, and the voters' perception of the insignificance of their individual votes give greater power to emotional impulses.

From an economic perspective, the value of achieving noneconomic goals may exceed the perceived cost of foregone income or national GDP for at least some voters, although many other voters may simply underestimate or ignore the possibility of such costs, or be persuaded by inaccurate campaign information. However, populist politicians do not typically acknowledge such costs in advance. Once any economic damage appears after the election, it is likely that they will become an issue for the next election cycle. The traditional assumption of voter rationality may then assert itself in a posthoc manner, as those hurt by the policy punish the incumbent next time at the polls. This "political market correction" may be of little consolation, however, if the populist outcome leads to fundamental institutional changes that are difficult to reverse, such as the erosion of longstanding trade rules or the termination of decades of economic integration. When the stakes are this high, the important role of confrontation, resentment, fear, and anger in the populist campaign raises the concern that such emotionally driven voting behavior may replace rationality with artful and possibly insidious psychological manipulation, with devastating and lasting economic and political consequences.[13] This book attempts to integrate the analysis of the two camps, representing the school of strictly rational voting behavior and the sociological school of purely cultural-political origins for populism. In the end, new theories of voter motivation suggest that the economic and sociological elements may interact with each other in the voting booth.

Ideological Varieties of Populism

The foregoing description of the populist bill of attainder against incumbent governments in the early part of the twenty-first century contains many disparate elements, from resentments and fears of immigrants and cultural change to distrust of government, loss of national sovereignty, and economic dislocation and diminished wealth and income. Unlike most political movements, ideology alone is not the primary basis of the populist platform (Stäheli and Savoth 2011). It is rather like an empty vessel with space that fills up with an angry and disaffected group self-identified as "the people"; a loss of trust in the "establishment"; a target of their ire, the "elite"; a triggering shock or crisis; and typically, a charismatic leader who finally provides a resonating ideological framework to focus the anger. Populism can therefore take various and ideologically contrasting forms. Left-wing populism typically arises when the underrepresented majority is pitted against a corporate or financial elite. Right-wing populism typically occurs when a formerly dominant national, racial, or cultural group clashes with a cosmopolitan or technocratic elite that is in legion with foreigners, immigrants, alleged social deviants, or "undesirable" racial minorities. Most of the discussion in recent years has focused on *right-wing* or *cultural* populism, for which the people typically self-identify as "native" to the country and as holding traditional religious and cultural views, and typically conservative political views. The elite, in this view, comprise an aloof and self-serving ruling class that favors the economic and political interests of educated and politically liberal segments of the population at the expense of the people. Right-wing populism often adopts a nationalistic ideology as the basis for policies to promote and protect nativist interests. In this view, the elite thus also favor internationalist over national interests, resulting in international agreements that allow imports to displace traditional (especially manufacturing) jobs, corporations to outsource jobs to foreign countries, and international rules to overregulate production and trade policy or to pursue global environmental goals. Major flashpoints for cultural populists often include overly generous immigration policies, the ceding of national sovereignty to foreign or global treaties, and the liberalization of abortion laws, all of which the elite has foisted on an unwilling people. Achievement of populist goals in this setting is entrusted to a strong and potentially authoritarian leader, such as Donald Trump (US), Vladimir Putin (Russian Federation), Rodrigo Duterte (Philippines), Recep Erdogan (Turkey), and Viktor Orban (Hungary). This form of populism is sometimes called exclusionary populism, based on how its supporters circumscribe membership in the ranks of the "authentic" people based on race, national, and cultural heritage, as well as language and religion.

The important distinction between the in-groups and out-groups in cultural populism contrasts with *left-wing* or *socioeconomic* populism, often called *inclusionary* populism. The "people" in this case are all those who suffer at the hands of a financial and economic elite, dominated by a wealthy plutocracy that controls the banking sector and large corporations and thereby wields political power. The long tentacles of the elite extend to the captains of global banking and industry, which have harnessed the forces of globalization to enrich themselves, to the detriment of the rest of the population. While this clash between the haves and the have-nots suggests Marxian class warfare, the populist version of the confrontation takes place within a democratic framework. In more economically advanced countries, it must therefore go beyond the poor and working class to count the broader middle class as victims, an important component of a democratic base needed to challenge the financial elite. Legal and illegal immigrants, as well as other oppressed and disenfranchised populations, are in principle also linked with the people as victims of corporate domination. Thus the populist Occupy Wall Street movement in the United States declared its struggle to be for the 99% vying to wrest control from the tiny minority of plutocrats controlling the government. Success in winning significant national political representation and control, however, has occurred mainly in countries with traditions and an existing base of left-wing support, particularly in Latin America. Recent populist leaders in this group include Evo Morales (Bolivia), Rafael Correa (Ecuador), Daniel Ortega (Nicaragua), and Hugo Chavez, succeeded by Nicolas Maduro (Venezuela).

In addition to ideologically distinct right-wing and left-wing types of populism, academic research often identifies a third variety, broadly based on "anti-establishment" motivations. This category includes populist movements that defy easy classification as either left-wing or right-wing in their resident ideologies. A common element in many instances of anti-establishment populism is opposition to the existing regime based on its corruption and incompetence. The "people" therefore regard themselves as the victims not so much of an unjust economic system or cosmopolitan elitism, but of a venal and self-aggrandizing maladministration, subject to capture by special interests. The regime treats critical national problems with benign neglect and rules by dishonesty. The elite in this sense includes those close to the government (the establishment) and their hangers-on, who pursue their own personal interests at the expense of the people. The conflict in this case pits the people against specific persons with access to power, and corrupt or unfit government officials themselves, rather than groups defined by racial or class identity, or economic status itself. The agenda for populist reform correspondingly focuses on booting out the current establishment, cleaning up corruption, and introducing reforms to improve governmental performance and accountability. Characteristic anti-establishment leaders since 1990 include Alberto Fujimori (Peru), Carlos Menem (Argentina), Joseph Estrada (Philippines), and Lech Walesa (Poland). Anti-corruption populism has been especially prevalent in some former communist countries in Central and Eastern Europe, where the transition to a well-functioning democratic system has been difficult.[14] Another example is Junichiro Koizumi, who led a populist reform movement in Japan to overcome the country's long period of economic stagnation. Italy's ruling Five-Star movement provides a different example, a coalition of left- and right-wing populist parties that has proven to be fragile.[15] In general, it is fair to say that the lines between the various types of populism are not always cleanly drawn, and each type may contain elements of the others.

Populism and the Ideological Link to Trade

The varieties of populism described in this chapter suggest that the role of trade policy in a given populist platform will depend on its specific ideological and economic context. Left-wing populism, for example, tends to identify neoliberal open-trade and economic policies as a major part of the problem, and therefore tends to advocate interventionist state control of trade. In Latin America, recent left-wing populism often follows the tradition of import-substituting industrialization policies that prevailed in the region from 1950 to 1980 (see Bruton 1998). Trade in this context is part of an exploitative system controlled by corporations and their governmental enablers that suppresses worker rights, despoils the environment, and concentrates social, political, and economic power in a complicit elite. Right-wing populism, while generally associated with capitalist regimes, often pursues policies of economic nationalism, associating imports with foreign disruption of national industries and displacement of jobs among the people. The associated view that immigrants threaten the native culture and jobs thus comes to include trade as a damaging foreign influence, whereby imports threaten wages no less than a large influx of immigrants. The Brexit version of this view (shared by many European populist parties) is that the European Union has usurped the national sovereignty of its members through bureaucratic economic and political control by Brussels. As a result EU members must accept not only unwanted immigrants, but also collectively imposed (from above) internal and external trade arrangements, as well as regulatory and (for Eurozone countries) monetary decisions. The common denominator in left- and right-wing populism thus lies in the view that trade is often a dangerous force associated with a ruling elite that the people must overturn in order to vouchsafe national sovereignty and protect their interests.

The operative principle in populist movements, in general, is to follow the contextual logic of an emotion-driven platform. Trade issues will be included to the extent that they represent a rejection of the incumbent elite's policies, resonate as a symbol of unjust treatment of the populist base, and act as a focal point of anger. Trade may be a separate source of disaffection, and the particular ideology adopted by the populist movement may call for protectionism as a matter of principle. But trade may also be swept up in an aggregation of disaffection represented by the populist platform. In this regard, it may become part of a larger referendum on the sins of the elite. Historically, populist movements have often preferred direct democracy, through simple up-or-down votes in referendums, as the most effective means of implementing populist agendas (Eichengreen 2018, p. 3). The Brexit referendum, which allowed the "leave" movement to gather all the collected grievances against Brussels into a simple yes or no vote, exemplified this approach. Trade, which was not a major anti-EU complaint, was nonetheless placed in the dock. Similarly, Donald Trump merged various discontents over numerous issues into a broad populist platform of protest against cultural and globalist elitism, and the 2016 presidential election became, for many, a yes-or-no referendum on what the candidates represented.

For other populist movements, the country may face external economic constraints that limit the country's ability to challenge the system, as in the case of small open economies. Populist governments may therefore not have the ability, or popular support, for a radical overthrow of the existing trade regime. In cases where the existing trade regime is highly protectionist, on the other hand, populist forces may advocate for lower tariffs or trade liberalization. In these cases the incumbent government is protectionist; it follows that the anti-establishment trade policy of the upstart populists is to favor freer trade. This principle may shed some light on the trade platforms for the broader category of anti-establishment populism, since the goal of cleaning up a corrupt, self-seeking, or inefficient government may be either pro- or anti-trade. To the extent that the existing regime's malfeasance involves bribery or rent-seeking lobbying to secure domestic monopolies, reduce import competition, or gain access to public funds, such a populist regime might favor a policy of more open trade as a corrective measure. The theory is that trade markets tend to discipline allocative processes and government policies. Weyland (1999) identified several examples of neoliberal populism in Latin America and Eastern Europe, usually sparked by crisis conditions of a failed government with widespread rent-seeking based on heavy market intervention. Menem (Argentina), Fujimori (Peru), Walesa (Poland), and Koizumi (Japan) are examples of populists whose reforms included significant trade liberalization. The New Deal policies of President Franklin D. Roosevelt, while not strictly speaking populist, nonetheless represented a response to populist grievances, rejecting the previous protectionist regime in favor of trade liberalization as part of a larger agenda of reforms. It is noteworthy, however, that these examples date from earlier times, including the period immediately following the collapse of the Soviet Union in 1991, which was marked by a perceived vindication of global capitalism and a widespread pursuit of market reforms. These examples predate the globalization backlash that has occurred since the financial crisis of 2008. Since then, the polarizing effects of globalization have led to populist movements that have tended to incorporate either left- or right-wing ideological frameworks—often, but not always, in opposition to trade liberalization. Anti-establishment populist regimes in this more recent period have tended to be neutral on trade issues; none of them were embracing pro-trade platforms as of early 2020.[16]

In considering the impact of populism on trade and trade policy, it is also important to recognize the difference between populist party platforms as espoused during election campaigns and the actual trade policies implemented if and when populist parties come to power. While left- and right-wing populist parties often tend to embrace economic nationalism and often propose greater control over imports, for example, populist governments often have to share power in coalition with other parties, and must often compromise on their policy platform proposals. In addition, populist governments must usually conduct trade policy in the framework of the country's existing international obligations, including WTO commitments and the terms of regional trade and integration agreements. Given the structure of these obligations, it is difficult for most countries to pursue unilateral trade restrictions, or to manipulate the rules, without triggering a WTO or treaty-based trade dispute. If the country refuses to recognize a third-party judgment in a trade dispute, it may ultimately face damaging trade retaliation. Governments do have recourse to certain contingency measures under trade rules, and may also legitimately take administrative measures that affect trade in a marginal way. But most countries are too small individually in global markets to disrupt trade flows and damage the world economy, aside from hurting their own populations. They are also unlikely to be able to abuse or defy the rules and disrupt the trading *system*, since the prospect of retaliation from other trading countries provides a strong deterrent. Multilateral trading rules, after all, tend to benefit all parties to the extent that they all follow them, and smaller countries are unlikely to defy them without a radical decoupling and isolation from the entire system.

Summary

This chapter has shown that throughout human history, people have been curious about the outside world and willing to engage in trade with those outside their homelands. Yet they also value the protection of their communities against outside dangers and foreign influences, and they furthermore derive status from their exclusive group identity. The balance of these two tendencies typically defines the way and extent to which a society structures its foreign trade relationships. Times of perceived cultural and social dangers to the society's in-group from foreigners and out-group members tend to trigger the protective impulse to assert sovereignty over the home territory, home culture, and possibly, by extension, over national markets through restrictive trade measures. In modern democratic countries, populism represents a type of electoral politics that channels such anxieties, fears, and anger into movements fueled by emotion-driven voting patterns. The societal divisions created by a populist movement tend to heighten the emotional nature of achieving an electoral majority, since the winners are assumed ready to overturn or reject policies and institutions promoted by their political rivals. Instilling division and inciting anger among its base therefore become strategic elements of a populist movement. The next chapter will explore several flashpoints of populist anger, and how they may be connected to a trade policy.

3

Emotional Flashpoints of Populism and Trade

The appeal and political success of a populist movement depends on its ability to motivate its supporters with compelling arguments that they are victims of a hostile elite. This chapter sets out to identify the main issues that populist leaders and movements have "weaponized" in their appeal to voters in the early twenty-first century. This has been a time of great change and upheaval in the global economy and in social and cultural disruptions of the status quo, an ideal environment for channeling popular fears and dissatisfactions into emotion-laden, anti-establishment platforms. Several key issues became the subject for populist rallying cries and campaign slogans. This chapter will explore the major populist flashpoints that came to be associated, directly or indirectly, with international trade and trade disruption. Each of these issues lends itself to an emotional appeal, particularly in terms of instilling fear or anger among target groups of voters. The political goal is to harness the anger of the populist base in focusing the movement on specific wedge issues, pitting the people against the elite. For right-wing populists the message is generally that the homeland is in peril, with the country's physical, cultural, and economic security at stake. For left-wing populists, the elite dominate the economic and class system, often in conjunction with malign global forces, requiring an often radical transformation of the country's social and economic structure. Anti-establishment populists tend to focus on the dangerous ineptitude and corruption of a hidebound ruling elite. While not all of the issues concern trade, together the flashpoints define a particular populist platform for upending the current regime and its institutions. Trade may therefore become part of a web of dissatisfaction that serves as the foundation of broader populist appeal. However, the weaponization of these issues as vehicles for populist outrage often substitutes emotional arguments for economic analysis, especially when it comes to a proper understanding of trade deficits, tariffs, and the gains from trade.

The chapter begins with a discussion of the central role of popular or territorial sovereignty in nearly all populist movements. Most flashpoints

Populism and Trade. Kent Jones, Oxford University Press. © Oxford University Press 2021.
DOI: 10.1093/oso/9780190086350.003.0003.

derive their emotional appeal from this concept. Trade policy, for example, was a prominent feature of President Trump's populist platform, which identified trade deficits as the source of US economic decline. Tariffs were his policy tool to fight back. The discussion will examine the populist appeal of the deficit argument, and provide an economic view of how it is based on false premises and endangers trade relations. Related to this issue is the president's demonization of the WTO as the framework for "elitist" multilateral trade liberalization and trade policy rules and the North American Free-Trade Agreement (NAFTA) that includes the US, Canada, and Mexico, special objects of President Trump's populist scorn. The president substitutes traditional trade bargaining, based on mutual gain from trade, for a populist, zero-sum nationalist economic strategy. In European populism, the main institutional targets are the prominent "elitist" centers of EU decision-making, including the European Commission, the Council of Ministers, and European Central Bank. The strains of advanced EU integration, flawed crisis management, and a democratic deficit have combined to foment Euroskeptic movements in many member countries, including Brexit. Another broad category of flashpoints centers on globalization. Populist politics has concretized this source of anger and anxiety by focusing on disruptive trading countries, such as China and Mexico, on immigration as an invasion and threat to domestic security and cultural traditions, and on international terrorism. The disruptive trifecta of trade, immigration, and terrorism sowed the seeds of populism in the United States, the European Union, and many other countries. All of these flashpoints, in turn, served to emphasize the supposed policy failures of the incumbent domestic elites, which in conjunction with malign foreign forces threatened the homeland's economic and national security.

Conceptual Flashpoints as Emotional Triggers

Populism seeks to transform conceptual sources of national pride into concrete rallying cries attacking the elite. The primary example is national sovereignty, which appeals to the populist base's sense of belonging to a larger collective identity that the elite has betrayed. Trade becomes a flashpoint to the extent that import disruption represents an attack on the nation's sovereignty through deindustrialization, the loss of economic security. Especially in the case of President Trump, tariffs then become the weapon that can protect the homeland from this danger, a symbol of assertive, even military-like strength.

National Sovereignty

"We want control back!" "Make America Great Again!" "If you don't have steel, you don't have a country!" As noted in the previous chapter, populist trade policies typically invoke the primacy of national sovereignty over access to the domestic market. A major taproot of populism is the fear of foreign threats, creating a powerful emotional response. The issue of sovereignty therefore underlies most populist slogans targeting the malign nature of foreign influences. The threat may relate directly to the incursion of foreign imports threatening domestic jobs, or foreign immigrants threatening traditional national culture and demographics, or commitments to foreign rules and agreements compromising control over the domestic economy, or even foreign visitors, who may threaten the nation's security through terrorism. The populist strategy is to make the foreign threat concrete by linking it to a particular country (China, Mexico), a particular institution (the WTO, the European Commission), a particular issue ("unfair" trade deficits), or particular groups (immigrant rapists, terrorists, and criminals). The foreign threat is amplified by the collaboration of domestic elites with the foreign intruders, or facilitation of their influence. The internal division of loyalties gives rise to conspiracy theories on both sides of the populist issues, a particularly toxic formula for political gridlock, paralysis, and perpetual conflict. The following flashpoints comprise variations on the populist theme of sovereignty, in which trade plays a leading or a supporting role.

Deindustrialization and the Trade Deficit

In both the United States and Europe the secular decline of employment in old-line manufacturing industries has played an important role in populist movements, and empirical evidence suggests that this factor has also tended to interact with cultural factors to support populist candidates at the polls. President Trump's populist narrative included trade because he maintained that trade deficits are a sign of the country's weakness, increasing unemployment and destroying the US manufacturing sector, and acting as a source of national humiliation, insisting that they made the United States into a global laughing stock. According to his view, trade deficits are the result of unfair treatment by foreign countries, representing a sum of money "stolen" from the US by foreign trading partners. Uncaring global elitists in the United States have foisted this problem on hard-working Americans by concluding flawed trade agreements, which Trump promised to rip up and renegotiate through his superior bargaining skills. It is therefore essential to understand his view of trade deficits—and his misunderstanding of this concept—in order to understand his populist views on trade policy and the WTO. In the populist playbook, national trade deficits are easy to link rhetorically with industrial decline, since a surge in manufacturing imports will often displace domestic manufacturing jobs. Yet the underlying problem is one of adjustment to economic change and how to manage it, a long-standing issue in national economic policy. Displaced workers need to move to new jobs in expanding sectors, and this is the challenge that governments must address. In the United States many workers have lost jobs over the years due to imports, but also from technological change, increased domestic competition, and changes in consumer tastes. In earlier years, finding new jobs was not usually difficult, due to the availability of other jobs in similar sectors and greater worker mobility between regions. The fact that such adjustment has become more difficult is a major concern for public policy.

However, Trump's obsessive focus on trade balances is uninformed, and his mercantilist understanding of trade deficits is clearly wrong. It is not true, for example, that an overall trade deficit is a sign of economic weakness, or foreign exploitation, or malign intent among the country's trading partners. Trade deficits are not the result of unfair trade practices by other countries or US trade agreements. The United States has run trade deficits for many years, typically during years of economic growth, and improvements in the trade balance are most often associated with recessions when domestic consumption, including consumption of imports, falls. The implication that Trump falsely draws is that foreign countries exploit the home nation whenever its payments for imports of goods and services exceed its export revenues from selling to the foreign country. A homespun comparison casts doubt on this proposition. Trump's argument is equivalent to saying that paying more money to your grocery store for food than the money you receive from the grocery store (perhaps as an employee or contractor) represents an amount of money that the grocery store has stolen from you.[1] From the point of view of the customer, the trade (or grocery) transaction merely represents a free exchange of money for the goods purchased—there is no exploitation here, and the customer has no concern if he or she runs a "trade deficit" by purchasing groceries. In fact, the pattern of consumer purchases in trade and at the grocery store tend to reflect the relative advantages of the seller in offering items the buyer prefers. The underlying benefit of trade lies in the comparative advantage of the foreign seller in producing the item that the customer prefers over comparable domestic products.

Yet one might argue in response that a problem would arise if a country's (or individual's) overall external spending exceeded external purchases. Wouldn't a country be in trouble if its consumers spent more money on imports than its producers earned on exports, just as an individual would face financial difficulty if he or she consistently purchased more groceries and other goods and services than were earned through "exports" of the individual's labor services and other items of value to pay the bills? The answer is that countries, as well as individuals, must finance the difference between external consumption expenditures and income earnings somehow. An individual might have to take out a bank loan (if his or her credit rating is good enough), sell property, or perhaps hock some belongings at the local pawn shop. Over an individual's lifetime, it is in fact common to have periods of net borrowing and net saving, exemplified by acquiring and discharging student loans, home mortgages, and loans for family weddings, and saving for retirement. An earnings deficit is not necessarily a sign of serious trouble, unless the borrowing pattern is unsustainable and a *default* occurs, when a more serious and often painful structural adjustment must occur, such as personal bankruptcy. A country, on the other hand, typically finances a trade deficit through the attractiveness of holding its currency through promises to pay in the future (IOUs), borrowing, or asset sales to the creditor. If these options become unattractive, then the country's currency (or its central bank stock of foreign reserves) is likely to depreciate, bearing the brunt of the correction.

Foreign companies typically export goods to the United States in exchange for dollar deposits in banks. The sellers can then exchange the dollars for their home currencies, or they can keep the dollars to earn interest on US financial assets, or invest in US stocks or in building factories or acquiring properties and other assets in the United States. The country's trade deficit is sustainable as long as the foreign holders of US assets prefer to hold these financing instruments rather than sell them and earn more interest or returns in alternative assets in their home or other countries. By liquidating their US assets, the foreigners would cause the value of the US dollar to decline. Such a depreciation would be a signal that foreigners doubt the competitiveness or attractiveness of US assets on global markets. The depreciation itself, however, would tend to correct the trade deficit, as a cheaper dollar would make US exports more attractive and imports more expensive. In general, trade deficits will be a sign of trouble for a country to the extent that its assets do not offer attractive financing opportunities, or if foreign creditors do not trust in its financial system. If a country's financial system is weak or vulnerable to corruption or sudden shocks, a large trade deficit could spark capital flight and a collapse of the currency. At that point the country will often need to turn to emergency external borrowing, such as through the International Monetary Fund (IMF), which in turn will often require the borrowing country to submit to conditionality requirements by the lender, limiting the government's economic policy independence.

As Lawrence (2018) and others have noted, trade deficits are inherently neither good nor bad in terms of the health of the economy. Trump's view is to regard the trade balance like a company's income sheet: imports are like company costs and exports are like company earnings, so the company strives to maximize the positive difference between exports and imports. Yet the country is not like a company, and the mercantilist view of trade balances is invalid. Individual independent consumers and producers buy and sell goods and services on the global market, and the payment is either exchanged for foreign currency or held as cash, investments, or asset purchases in the deficit country. A deficit will be a danger signal if it occurs as the result of country's unsustainable spending or distorted financial markets, such as artificially cheap borrowing conditions or inflated asset prices with underpriced risk. The trade deficit in this case would be a warning signal requiring correction to remove the trap of overspending and overborrowing. A trade surplus, on the other hand, can sometimes be a sign of weakness, as with highly indebted developing countries, which must often run trade surpluses, reducing consumption goods for the domestic population, in order to finance their debt. The absence of further foreign borrowing opportunities, efficient domestic financial markets, and attractive investment opportunities place the financing burden on their trade accounts.

Another critical element of Trump's misunderstanding of the trade balance is that it is subject to an identity: the difference between total public and private savings and investment, which is equivalent to the difference between domestic production and consumption of goods and services (see Lawrence 2018).[2] In other words, a country will run a trade deficit if it is consuming more than it produces, and a surplus if the opposite is true. Raising tariffs, for example, will not lower a trade deficit unless it can somehow raise national savings relative to investment; it will tend instead to readjust the source of imports and the level of exports. If tariffs increased significantly against *all* sources of imports, the reduction in consumption would tend to reduce consumption without increasing exports (and perhaps even by lowering exports), thus lowering national income, which is hardly a politically attractive outcome.[3] An examination of the US trade balance over the years shows its relationship to national income. The most reliable ways to lower a trade deficit include a recession and a real depreciation of the dollar, both of which tend to lower investment more than savings, and consumption more than production. One prominent reason that the US will continue to have large trade deficits is that the Trump's 2017 tax cut bill increased the federal budget deficit, lowering net public savings and creating a larger trade deficit in 2018, despite all the tariffs Trump imposed in 2018. Put another way, trade deficits by themselves do not reduce output, GDP, and economic growth. It is very likely that the leaders of potential trading partner countries know this relationship better than Trump, who began to offer bilateral "fair and reciprocal" trade agreements in 2017. Yet a set of such bilateral agreements can never result in a stable system because the US would always reserve the right to define fairness in its favor, and arbitrarily impose unilateral, discriminatory tariffs when facing continuing trade deficits, in a vain effort to redress the imbalance in its own economy.

Tariffs and Trade Bargaining as Weapons

Tariffs are Trump's trade weapon of choice, and he has declared himself a "tariff man." US trade laws, combined with compliant Republicans in Congress, have made it easy for him to impose them and then to raise them at his own discretion. His trade representative, Robert Lighthizer, knows the trade laws well and can advise Trump on how far he can extend their use. Tariffs are also a populist symbol for Trump, the renegade trade instrument that punishes foreign exporters for taking advantage of WTO rules in penetrating the US market. In addition, he asserts that he must impose or threaten unilateral tariffs in order to renegotiate trade agreements and rebalance trade bilaterally. The populist image is one of Trump manning the barricades at US ports, firing fusillade after fusillade of tariffs at incoming imports, saving the US economy from attack. Yet Trump's view on tariffs, like his view on trade deficits, is seriously misinformed. In promoting the populist mystique of tariffs, Trump has made the false claim that they impose little or no damage on the US economy, and force the foreign exporters to pay "billions and billions of dollars" in tariffs, enriching the US Treasury. The implication is that the tariffs redress the foreign "theft" from US trade deficits through the collection of tariff revenue from foreigners. He regards tariffs as a weapon to extract revenue from foreigners, when it is more likely that they will tax US domestic consumers and businesses. On this point his misperception appears to be based on his assumption that tariffs will radically improve the importing country's terms of trade, forcing foreign exporters to absorb the entire amount of the tariff. In this extreme scenario, the foreign product enters the domestic market at the same price as before, with the tariff amount being "paid" by foreign exporters forced to lower the import price by the amount of the tariff in order to clear the market. While it is possible that foreign exporters will absorb a portion of the tariff when selling to a large country, it is very unlikely that it will absorb the entire tariff. In fact, if the exporter can sell the product to other markets, much, if not all, of the tariff can be passed through to the importing country consumer.[4] One remarkable result of economic research on Trump's tariffs is that the import prices have largely held firm, with the entire brunt of the tariff falling on US import consumers, imposing heavy economic damage particularly on US firms that lost cost competitiveness because of input cost increases (Amiti et al. 2019; Fajgelbaum et al. 2019).[5] In any case, tariff revenues are collected at the importing country's border and paid by the importers or their agents, not the exporter. Whatever billions of dollars have flowed into the US Treasury have come out of US import consumers' pockets. Another major miscalculation in Trump's tariff policy was the assumption, as stated by his trade advisor, Peter Navarro, that foreign countries would not dare retaliate against US tariffs with tariffs of their own against US exports. Yet many retaliatory tariffs imposed additional burdens on US farmers and businesses, increasing the domestic cost of the tariffs. The incidence of the tariffs therefore fell on US domestic consumers and industries purchasing imports. Trump's disinformation on tariffs serves his populist narrative that trade restrictions punish foreign countries alone, justify unfettered tariffs, improve the US trade balance, and legitimize the dismantlement of trade rules that would limit their use.

President Trump's misplaced confidence in tariffs as his ultimate trade policy weapon also misinformed his view of international trade negotiations. In general, his approach to appears to have been shaped by his experience as a real estate developer. His self-proclaimed "art of the deal" rests on an assertion of superior bargaining power in a negotiation, in which the key is to achieve a dominant position in the presentation of alternatives and confront the counterparty with a take-it-or-leave-it decision that he (Trump) alone can control. In bargaining theory, this situation describes a "distributive" (zero-sum) strategy, in which one party wins and the other loses. Trump thus believed that unilateral tariffs would bring US trading partners to their knees, because he was convinced that any country with a US bilateral trade surplus would run out of retaliatory trade restrictions before the United States. Supporters of populist policies are drawn to this description of their leader's skills, since it allows them to participate vicariously in the thrashing of their political opponents and tormentors, foreign and domestic, a compelling transference of empowerment to them through identity with the populist cause. Trump's relentless assertion of strength in dealing with foreigners is a reflection of his self-image as a master dealmaker. However, trade relations differ significantly from bargaining with real estate contractors and clients. In trade, the mutual gains from trade suggest an integrative strategy, in which bargaining leads to an improvement in welfare for both (or all) sides, a pattern followed in all GATT-WTO era trade negotiations. At a political level, foreign leaders have their own patriotic and prideful domestic constituencies to satisfy, and any perceived capitulation to the aggressive, unilateral terms of a Trump deal would in many cases result in political suicide for them at home. A one-sided distributive bargain is typically available only to an all-powerful hegemon, and US economic power in the world economy, while still large, is not what it used to be. Furthermore, trade is not the zero-sum game that Trump appears to believe, as all participants in trade negotiations typically stand to gain from mutually agreed trade liberalization. Similarly, as described earlier, trade restrictions also hurt domestic consumers and businesses as well as foreigners.

Institutional Flashpoints as Objects of Derision

Populism seeks to demonize institutions associated with the elite, and international institutions, including trade organizations and treaties, as well as supranational bodies such as the European Commission, therefore become useful objects of derision. These institutions, negotiated by domestic elites and presumably administered by an unelected global elite, create externally imposed foreign rules and obligations on the victimized people, yet another attack on the member nation's sovereignty.

The WTO and Postwar Institutions of Global Trade

President Trump's focus on trade deficits and insistence on direct control of trade policy make him particularly disdainful of the WTO and any multilateral trade cooperation in which broad consensus dominates decision-making, reducing the bargaining power of larger countries. During his presidential campaign the WTO became a populist punching bag, an easy target for claiming that US membership in it gave global elitists control over US trade policy. Ironically, the current global institutional structure of trade policy began with strong US leadership and support after World War II, with the intention of preventing the sort of unilateral tariff escalation that plagued world trade in the 1930s and that that Trump was now advocating. The system began with the General Agreement on Tariffs and Trade (GATT) in 1947.

Rules included the principle of nondiscrimination in trade policy and the binding of maximum tariffs at negotiated levels, and the behavioral norm of peacefully settling disputes among members. The original GATT sponsored eight rounds of trade negotiations between 1947 and 1994, lowering tariffs from an average of about 22% to 11% for its signatories (Bown and Irwin 2015). Participating GATT countries negotiated the establishment of the WTO, a new organization with greater product and trade policy coverage, as well as a new, more formalized dispute settlement system during the last of these negotiations, the Uruguay Round, in 1994. The GATT-WTO system introduced a novel institutional framework for trade negotiations (Searle 2005; North 1991). Specifically, the WTO enhances economic welfare for its members by reducing transaction costs of negotiation, extending trade liberalization through the network of MFN treatment, and providing rules of discipline that anchor the members to more efficient policies (Anderson 2014, part V; Bagwell et al. 2016). Its main functions—a forum for negotiations, a repository of rules of participants' trade policies, and a system of dispute resolution—depends on both the written provisions of the treaty among its members and the behavioral norms of following these provisions. The GATT-WTO system itself is not a free-trade agreement, but rather a framework for regulating trade policies and relationships among its members in a predictable, nondiscriminatory manner. There are numerous provisions in the WTO that allow (while regulating) the use of tariffs, anti-dumping and countervailing duties, safeguard measures, and domestic regulatory measures that may affect trade. These measures are part of its institutional structure, acting as safety valves that isolate protectionist pressure and allow broader trade flows to continue. Countries participating in the GATT-WTO system thereby pledge to give up the right to unilateral tariff changes, discrimination in the application of tariffs, and unrestrained retaliation when a dispute arises with a trading partner. The underlying concept of such an arrangement was that if all the members follow the rules, all of the members would reap the benefits of a stable trade policy environment and increased trade. Not least among these benefits was the environment of *market access certainty* that firms relied on to plan their investments both at home and in foreign countries.

As globalization progressed, however, developed country economic growth rates tapered off while developing countries grew more rapidly and began to displace developed country jobs in textiles, clothing, and other labor-intensive goods. The emergence of China as a major exporter of a wide range of manufactured goods was particularly disruptive. Most developing countries joined the GATT (or later the WTO) in order to take advantage of the system's market access trading rules. China's accession the WTO in 2001 became a touchstone for many populist politicians, who portrayed the WTO as the center of either globalist elitism or global corporate exploitation. Until the populist surge and the election of Donald Trump as US president, it was easy to take for granted that members would generally follow the WTO rules, based on evidence that they valued the resulting gains from trade and global systemic stability in trade relations. This is no longer the case for the United States, as chapter 5 will illustrate. On top of this problem, WTO membership has now grown so large and diverse that its ambitions for further trade liberalization have encountered deadlock over an inability to achieve consensus. It therefore also finds itself unable to implement needed updates to its rules and dispute settlement procedures.

Regional Trade Integration Agreements

The GATT-WTO system allows member countries to form regional trade agreements (RTAs), based on GATT Article 24. These agreements promote varying degrees of economic integration among their participants. Some are strictly free-trade agreements, striking down trade restrictions but leaving external tariffs, regulations, and other economic policies to the individual members. Other agreements promote deeper integration by creating customs unions, mobility among the members of labor and capital, regulatory harmonization, and even monetary union. RTAs are essentially smaller versions of multilateral agreements such as the WTO, with jointly determined trade rules, based on negotiated compromises and trade-offs. From a populist perspective, they are therefore subject to the same sort of fear of foreign intrusion on the homeland, through import competition, immigration, and unwanted, externally mandated regulations. RTAs also typically bind neighboring countries in an integration agreement, which tend to magnify the conflict through the effects of familiarity and proximity, breeding populist contempt. Provisions or opportunities for immigration among members are often especially explosive.

RTAs that have been subjected to populist backlashes include the North American Free Trade Agreement (NAFTA), now the US-Mexico-Canada Agreement (USMCA) and the European Union (EU), from which the United Kingdom declared independence in the 2016 Brexit referendum. Populist campaigns against RTAs tend to be particularly divisive because they involve both increased competition and increased cooperation and integration with close neighbors. The close proximity of the partner countries gives rise to the outsourcing of supply-chain activities based on production logistics, low transportation costs, or lower wages, creating resentment among displaced workers across the border. Neighboring countries are thus portrayed as brazenly stealing well-paying domestic jobs. Yet the same cross-border investment, production, and market linkages create advocates for the arrangement, in opposition to the populist naysayers in their midst. The stakes of an RTA relationship tend to be higher the greater the degree and scope of integration, which increases the variety of potential complaints and allows populist leaders to foment public outrage on individual issues, in a strategy of generating opposition to the entire agreement. More advanced stages of integration can also stoke concerns that foreign control of politically sensitive policies compromise national sovereignty, a particularly potent emotional issue in populist movements.

The European Commission as a Lightning Rod

For many its member countries, the European Commission has become a special focus of populist anger. It is the executive arm of the European Union, responsible for the day-to-day implementation of EU policies. The original visionary plan of the European Union to unite member countries through "ever-closer union" has passed from hopeful beginnings at its launch in 1957, through largely prosperous years of reconstruction and growth after World War II, into an increasingly complicated era of advanced integration and crisis that has left the entire EU project open to populist challenges. For the United Kingdom the Commission became an object of scorn, resented by many for its regulatory intrusion into UK economic and social issues, and the subject of the rallying cry "Take back control" in the Brexit referendum. Other European populist movements have focused their ire on the Commission for its management of the 2015 immigration crisis, in which three million refugees arrived in the European Union from Africa, the Middle East, and Asia. The Commission attempted to allocate refugee arrivals through a quota system by EU member country. This plan was roundly rejected by several of the member governments and faced public disapproval in most EU member states, fueling mainly right-wing populist opposition to EU efforts to manage the situation by fiat. Another populist flashpoint arose from the Eurozone debt crisis, in which the Commission, in conjunction with the European Central Bank and the International Monetary Fund, implemented a series of bailouts for indebted EU countries along with harsh austerity measures, especially against Greece. These policies sparked right-wing populist backlashes against the bailouts in northern-tier countries, especially Germany, and left-wing populist backlashes against austerity in southern tier countries such as Greece and Spain.

Aside from ideological considerations, the vulnerability of EU decision-making institutions to populist surges lies largely in the fact that its institutions of EU-wide democratic deliberation have not kept pace with its ambitions of achieving a full economic—and eventually political—union. The European Parliament plays at best a supporting role in legislative initiatives and high-level policy decisions. In addition, the EU member states have not shed national identities and claims on policy autonomy in sensitive political issues. Thus a proud nationalism still exists among them, preventing them from developing a collective and unified European identity that would facilitate more coordinated fiscal, banking, and immigration policies, for example. In the meantime, the European Commission has become a symbol of bureaucratic overreach. Populist opposition to EU crisis management reflects frustration over both a lack of sufficient specialized institutional development to support advanced economic integration and a lack of responsive political channels to keep EU member state electorates involved in critical policy debates.

Countries and Groups as Scapegoats

Populist leaders typically scapegoat domestic elites for their alleged attacks on the people, and their names, often associated with the populist leader's political opponents, are familiar to the audience. Scapegoating often extends, however, to foreigners, who are easier to identify for populist audiences through national caricatures and stereotypes that describe their villainous and unfair acts. Similarly, the perceived threats to the homeland by foreign "invaders," such as immigrants and terrorists, become easy targets and instruments for populist rhetoric.

China and Mexico

China, as recently as 40 years ago, was a country with a large population but a small and seemingly inconsequential economy. Its rapid and dramatic emergence as the world's largest exporter and by some measures the largest economy imposed both and economic and a political shock on the rest of the world. The economic reforms of Deng Xiaoping in the 1980s, combined with foreign investment, eventually unleashed the massive potential of the Chinese economy. Deng's new policy of Chinese engagement with the world economy meant that several hundred million Chinese workers joined the global labor force, increasing its GDP sixty-fold from 1980 to 2018 and its share of world trade from little more than zero to 13%. While economic growth brought 800 million of its own population out of poverty, China's export-oriented development strategy imposed a significant adjustment problem on many countries across a large range of import-competing industries. China joined the WTO in 2001, with the support of the United States, the European Union, and most other WTO member countries. Consumers and many businesses, tied into supply chains with China, gained from the new trade opportunities, while many workers in importing countries suffered lower wages, lost jobs, and displacement. Rust Belt communities declined and a populist backlash against Chinese imports emerged, finding resonance also with those concerned with immigration and terrorist threats to the homeland.

As a member of the WTO, China was expected to move toward fully market-oriented policies, but its communist government remained heavily involved in many aspects of the economy. A review of the history of China's WTO accession shows that the United States negotiators had in fact taken a hard line during the lengthy accession talks on "traditional" GATT-WTO trade policy issues, such as tariffs, subsidies, and other direct government policy measures affecting imports and foreign intellectual property protection (Blustein 2019, ch. 4). The negotiators had tried to anticipate as many problems as possible that could arise once China became a WTO member. Its protocol of WTO accession therefore was the most detailed of any member. In the early years of its membership, from 2004 to 2010, China was the subject of 21 formal WTO disputes, brought mostly by the United States and the European Union (Blustein 2019, p. 144). In nearly all of the cases that it lost, China complied with the WTO panel rulings. However, the US negotiators had not anticipated the increasingly pervasive and embedded influence of the Chinese government, as well as parallel Communist Party structures, on its economy, especially on the activities of its state-owned enterprises. Wu (2016, pp. 261–265) refers to the unique features of Chinese involvement with its industries regarding production, technology, and access to intellectual property as the problem of "China, Inc." Many WTO trade disputes since 2010 have arisen because of issues related, for example, to China's overcapacity in traded goods and acquisition of foreign technology that cannot be easily documented in a dispute settlement proceeding. The result is that there is a gap in WTO rules coverage needed to hold the unique Chinese system of trade governance accountable. WTO members generally agreed that China's opaque system of state-run capitalism had become a major problem for its trading partners, and that an update of the WTO rules would be required to address the gap in coverage. This issue would erupt during the Trump administration, which claimed that the lack of rules coverage gave the United States the right to deal with Chinese policies unilaterally, without recourse to the WTO dispute mechanism. The populist message was that China was a threat that required severe unilateral action by the United States, outside the boundaries set by WTO rules.

Similarly, Mexico has played the role of disruptor in the US economy through the NAFTA (now USMCA), as a low-wage country that is also a source and a route of transit for immigration to the United States. The increased economic engagement of Mexico with the United States, Canada, and other countries has made it an attractive location for foreign direct investment, with much of its production exported to the United States. Its proximity to US territory and markets amplifies its double threat of import disruption and immigration. Mexico therefore became a useful populist target for Donald Trump, representing the dangers of maintaining an open trade and immigration relationship with a developing country at the homeland's doorstep.

Immigrants

Immigration is a major issue in many populist movements, especially if the associated ideology is nationalist, and it can be linked with trade protectionism. Over the centuries both the United States and Europe have experienced large inflows of immigrants, but those "native" (usually earlier immigrant) groups considering themselves culturally dominant have always had a fraught relationship with new waves of immigration. In the United States, immigration has variously stoked fears of cultural inundation by Catholics, German socialists, the Chinese and other Asian groups, southern Europeans, east European Jews, and, most recently, Hispanics from Mexico and Latin America. Within the European Union, movements of other native European workers across member state borders has sometimes created a backlash. Large Muslim immigrant populations live in many Western European countries, many of whom arrived from former European colonies in northern Africa and Asia. The large and sudden influx of largely Muslim refugees in the European Union beginning in 2015 created a major flashpoint for European populism. In general, the strong negative reaction among native citizens to immigrants—especially when their religion, ethnicity, or culture differs from those of the destination country—often emanates from the perceived threat to the native groups' status. "Status deprivation" can come from fears of ethnic and religious displacement, the erosion of native culture, increased crime, lost jobs, and lower wages. In the twenty-first century, Muslim immigration in particular has sparked fears of its association with international terrorism. The connection between xenophobia against immigrants and views on trade is more subtle, but in principle exists in the perceived link between the invasion of foreign people threatening native culture and the invasion of foreign goods threatening native jobs. Anti-immigrant populists may therefore oppose imports because of their contributing role in undermining traditional domestic jobs and communities, even when imports do not threaten their own jobs.

International Terrorists

Most citizens of the United States vividly recall the attacks of September 11, 2001, on New York and Washington, DC, carried out by the Islamic jihadist group Al-Qaeda. Europeans similarly recall the shock of major attacks by Islamic terrorists in Madrid (2004), London (2005), Paris (2015), Brussels (2016), and Nice (2016). The fear of Islamic terrorism has reinforced anti-immigrant sentiment in the United States and especially in the European Union, where the attacks in 2015 and 2016 coincided with a large influx of Islamic refugees. The strong public reaction to the refugee surge in many EU countries was a potent political force, and energized populist parties there. President Trump banned travel into the United States from seven Islamic countries (Iran, Iraq, Libya, Somalia, Sudan, Syria, and Yemen) as part of a broader anti-terrorist and anti-immigrant policy. The potential impact of terrorism on populist trade policy comes from its connection with the fear of immigration, but also from its reinforcement of negative sentiment against foreign malign motives in trade, as espoused by Trump's condemnation of allegedly unfair US trade deficits at the hands of its trading partners.

Summary

The success of a populist movement usually depends on the ability of a charismatic leader to energize a voting base and follow the populist formulation of conflict between the people and the elite. Easily identifiable targets that stoke anger, fear, and resentment, along with vitriolic rhetoric, often in public venues, are intended to establish effective communication between the leader and the base, and to stimulate the sort of emotional response that motivates enthusiastic support and large turnouts at election polls. The flashpoints described in this chapter were chosen and developed to allow the populist leader to portray the people's anger as his or her own, instilling loyalty among the base to the populist cause. The following chapter highlights this element of Donald Trump's successful presidential campaign in 2016. Chapter 6 will then pick up this strategy during the Brexit referendum in that year.

4

Populism, Trade, and Trump's Path to Victory

Under presidential candidate Donald Trump, trade became a potent populist issue and an important component of his 2016 victory. This chapter will show that populism has permeated US presidential politics at least since 1824, and while trade was not always a central issue, it always played a role in defining the difference between the political elites and the populist opposition. The chapter begins with a brief historical review of the roots of populism in the United States and the role of trade policy, beginning with President Andrew Jackson. Immigration subsequently became a populist issue in the "Know Nothing" anti-immigrant movement of the 1850s, and it has remained an important political issue since then. In the 1890s, agrarian issues related to debt, monetary policy, and railroad freight pricing led to the foundation of the short-lived Populist Party. The populist movement of the Great Depression years in the 1930s played a role in generating the New Deal policies of President Franklin Roosevelt, including important trade reforms. The postwar years of economic growth suppressed populism in the United States and most other parts of the world, driving it underground, where it remained politically dormant but still active psychologically. Renewed social and economic tensions led eventually to a cultural and anti-globalization backlash, culminating in the election of Donald Trump as president in 2016. Over the years, the populist view of trade did not consistently reflect an unwavering economic ideology of either free markets or protectionism, but instead tended to vary according to whatever the governing political party's view was on the tariff issue at the time. After the postwar era of global trade expansion under the GATT-WTO system led to a series of trade adjustment crises, however, the battle lines were clear. Trade expansion, multilateral cooperation, and global trade rules had become the policies of the establishment and therefore the targets of populist opposition. While popular opinion was not always against trade itself, trade became part of a populist narrative that held a globalist establishment responsible for unwelcome economic and social change. Despite his own international property and branding empire, Trump used the trade issue to vilify "global elites" as well as foreign trading partners, especially China and Mexico.

Populism and Trade. Kent Jones, Oxford University Press. © Oxford University Press 2021.
DOI: 10.1093/oso/9780190086350.003.0004.

US Populism in Historical Perspective

The evolution of democratic institutions in the United States gave rise to the first manifestations of populism as a political phenomenon, and this evolution reveals distinctive American traits for populist movements. It is important in this regard to note that the US two-party system has put certain constraints on populist politics throughout its history. The dominance of the two-party system has tended to moderate each major party's platform, causing a "reversion to the mean" in order to capture the most votes across a broader target spectrum of political preferences. A radical populist idea might find a home as a faction within one of the major parties, but its influence would typically wane as various factions reach compromises on the party platform. When an erstwhile populist idea does come to dominate the mainstream of the party, then the party's adoption of the idea would mean that it had become, ironically, part of the party's "establishment" position, giving it traditional representation among the electorate. In the absence of a claim of a people-versus-elite rift that lacked a proper political voice, what was formerly populist would no longer fuel an independent populist movement.[1] This phenomenon has occurred, for example, in the mainstreaming of immigration and trade issues within Republican and Democratic platforms. The constraint also helps to explain how populist movements could remain dormant over long periods of time, until circumstances change and mainstream parties fail to address the issue.

The motivation for populism in the United States began with a dramatic change in the size and profile of the electorate, upon elimination of property ownership as the basis for voting rights among white men in the early 1800s. This democratic extension of the voting franchise would eventually spark resentment—especially among new voters—against governing elites and their control of land, financial markets, and domestic industry. The growing sense of national identity in the young American republic also strengthened nativist views toward foreign immigrants, especially toward those of different racial, ethnic, and religious backgrounds, which created conflict in colonial times that continue to the present day. This feature provides evidence, described in chapter 2, of xenophobic tendencies of self-identified communities to defend their social and economic status against outsiders. The gains from economic growth also created a counterpoint to xenophobia, supporting the human tendency to truck and barter, and to seek the gains from both internal and foreign trade. The incidence of populism throughout US history has thus corresponded to periods of the fears and threats perceived by large, politically underrepresented groups from ruling governments regarding their social status and economic welfare. Periods of broader national unity have corresponded to the rising tides of economic growth and the existence of common external enemies in wartime. Trade has played a role to the extent that it has represented a flash point in times of populist division.

Jacksonian Populism

The administration of President Andrew Jackson (1828–1836) is considered the earliest touchstone for populism as a national political movement. It resulted from the gradual expansion of suffrage to all adult white men by the late 1820s, after most states removed property ownership as the basis for voting rights. The expanded franchise increased voter participation in presidential elections from about 1% of the total population in 1820 to more than double that in 1824, which doubled again in 1828.[2] This trend ushered in a backlash against the outgoing system of less participatory democracy, controlled largely by the landholding class of wealthy and educated elites. Jackson had actually won a plurality of the popular vote for president in 1824, but much to the chagrin of his supporters, he was denied the presidency because a four-way race had split the Electoral College vote, with no one receiving a majority. Backroom dealing in the contingent Congressional vote to break the deadlock delivered victory to his rival, John Quincy Adams.[3] Such elitist machinations became a political issue in the next presidential election cycle, in which Jackson defeated Adams in a landslide. Jackson, a frontiersman and military hero from the War of 1812, well-known for his volatile temper, was popularly viewed as a rough-hewn "man of the people," in stark contrast to the blue-blooded cosmopolitan diplomat John Quincy Adams. *Jacksonian populism* was associated with the unfettered boisterousness of many of his newly enfranchised supporters; Jackson famously hosted a public, postinaugural party at the White House that resulted in a drunken melee (Gordon 2009). Yet it ushered in a historical shift toward a more direct democracy, closer to the voters, in contrast to the earlier elitist democracy entrusted to a privileged, homegrown nobility. Throughout Jackson's presidency, he enjoyed a reputation among his supporters as an advocate for the common man against corrupt elites and their political enablers in Congress.

Jackson's populist views are now principally associated with his opposition to the Second Bank of the United States, the US central bank of its day, which he regarded as a corrupt financial monopoly favoring the interests of wealthy Americans and foreigners, to the detriment of the general population. He vetoed a Congressional bill to recharter the Second Bank, beginning a long US populist tradition of opposition to government banking and mon-etary institutions, including Donald Trump's frequent criticism of Federal Reserve policies.[4] Jackson made it a major issue in his 1832 reelection cam-paign, which he won decisively.[5] It is also worth noting that his brutal "Trail of Tears" resettlement of Native American tribes has also become part of his populist reputation, although widespread public support for this policy at the time suggests it was a bipartisan rather than a populist issue. Yet Jackson went further, openly defying an 1832 Supreme Court decision protecting Cherokee property rights in Georgia, a populist assertion of extra-constitutional power that reverberated in President Trump's disdain for court decisions unfavor-able to his administration. Trump prominently displayed Jackson's portrait in his oval office as an early model of a populist leader.[6] Yet on many sensitive political issues Jackson sought compromises, especially on tariffs (Irwin 2017, p. 168).

Jacksonian populism in its day did not have a clear-cut association with trade policy. At the time tariffs were a major source of government revenue, and all presidents, including Jackson, acknowledged their fiscal necessity. However, Jackson generally opposed high tariffs as *protectionist tools* favoring manufacturing industries in the North, which conflicted with the interests of his constituents in the southern states. Northern manufacturing lobbies had secured high protective tariffs against British clothing and textile imports, which in turn suppressed southern cotton exports to Britain, the main input for clothing production. Protectionism was therefore a source of internal US political conflict because of international supply-chain economics, nearly two centuries before this issue reemerged in Trump's trade war against China. In fact, Jackson's earlier defeat in the 1824 election was the result of an agreement between pro-tariff candidates Henry Clay and John Quincy Adams, one goal of which was to deny the presidency to an opponent of protectionist tariffs.

Jackson did not immediately challenge the high tariffs inherited from his Whig predecessor, but his efforts to expand US trade relations with other countries during his administration revealed his favorable views toward trade in general. The biggest trade policy issue during his term in office, however, arose when his sympathies with southern anti-tariff sentiment clashed with the attempt by South Carolina to declare unilaterally null and void the high "Tariffs of Abomination," passed in the previous administration by Congress in 1828, and hated by Southern cotton interests. Jackson vehemently opposed South Carolina's attempt to defy Congressional authority over national trade policy and its challenge to the federal constitution. In the end he agreed to a compromise legislative package that lowered tariffs somewhat while autho-rizing force against South Carolina if it continued its rebellion against federal tariff authority. Despite Jackson's populist reputation, his efforts promoted a distinctly nonpopulist compromise between two diametrically opposed political forces. Jackson, elected as a populist but now a member of the establishment, imposed a solution designed to preserve the union that extremists on both sides were forced to accept. Thus his presidency itself was not, strictly speaking, populist in terms of trade policy. This episode showed in fact the constraints on an elected *populist government*, as opposed to an aspiring *populist insurgency*, when higher principles of the country's legal institutions are at stake. If Jackson had attempted to impose a solution clearly favoring his southern supporters, he would have violated the constitution and exacerbated the growing rift between North and South. One can argue that his action as president of the entire country, rather than as a populist partisan, delayed the Civil War by 29 years.[7]

President Jackson himself showed his ability to assert presidential power in resolving a national crisis, independent of the interests of his populist constituency. Jacksonian populism, in contrast to the current connotation of populism as a deliberate political strategy of people-versus-elite divisiveness, came to represent an historical transition, the spirit of a newly enfranchised public. It did contain elements that would characterize later episodes of populism: a broader and lasting American tendency to distrust financial elites, foreigners, and big government, and the embrace of a plain-speaking leader by his supporters. These populist characteristics would continue to evolve, with changing circumstances of disruption and crisis, up to the present day.

Know Nothings and Anti-Immigrant Sentiment

Another important historical dimension of US populism, closer in its impact to current political conflict, began with the domestic backlash against the arrival of millions of new immigrants in the middle of the nineteenth century. The annual inflow of immigrants grew from 100,000 in 1842 to more than 400,000 in 1854, increasing the US population by three million (about 14.5%) during that period (Formisano 2008, p. 202). Arrivals from Ireland and Germany were particularly numerous from 1830 to 1850 (Betz 2017, p. 339). Most of the Irish and many Germans were Catholic, which triggered a native anti-Catholic resentment inherited from the mostly Protestant settlers in colonial times, fearful of inundation by—in their terms—misbelievers with their strange ways and fealty to a foreign pope. In addition, many of the Germans, refugees from the revolutions of 1848 in their homelands, were thought to have brought dangerous socialist ideas with them. Many Americans also feared that the mostly poor immigrants would cause wages to fall and jobs for native-born Americans to disappear. In this regard, it is important to note that the United States was undergoing major structural change in its economy during this period, with technological progress improving transportation and manufacturing efficiency, and financial markets developing quickly across the country. These developments introduced new economic opportunities but also threatened the established livelihoods and way of life for many tradesmen and artisans. The fear was that the relatively unskilled immigrants would accelerate the introduction of mass factory production, displacing traditional craft industries and trades.

Anti-immigrant sentiment began as a loosely organized Know Nothing movement in the 1840s, leading eventually to its formal national organization as the American Party in 1855, the first US political party with an openly populist platform.[8] It received widespread support in several American states and fielded a presidential ticket which won 22% of the popular vote in 1856, headed by former President Millard Fillmore and Andrew Jackson Donelson, adopted son of former President Jackson. Their supporters suspected that the growing Democratic Party machines in large cities were organizing immigrants as a voting bloc, securing jobs, housing, and services for them in exchange for their votes. Formisano (2008) notes that Know Nothing supporters rioted on several occasions in the mid-1850s in an attempt to prevent alleged voting fraud by immigrants.[9] The most violent of these incidents was the August 6, 1855, "Bloody Monday" anti-immigrant riot in Louisville, Kentucky, in which 22 people died (Harrison et al. 1997, p. 123).

The Know Nothing Party did not highlight trade policy in its platform, as its political focus was generally on state-level policies, but its members had largely come from the defunct Whig Party, which had strongly advocated protectionist tariffs. It is therefore not difficult to understand the Know Nothing view of immigrants as a sort of unwanted import, requiring protectionist measures

against the thousands of half-starved laborers from Europe, admitted *duty free* into the American labor market, there to compete with native industry by offering to do the work for half the price paid the American laborer.[10]

The Know Nothing Party disbanded soon after the 1856 election. It was unsuccessful in gaining national influence, partly because of the absence of a strong, unifying, and charismatic political leader, which would prove to be essential in providing a voice and political representation for any populist cause. The Party's membership had also split over the slavery question, which had intervened as the major political question of that era. The Civil War and its aftermath subsequently dominated political activity for several decades, overshadowing immigrant and other issues as focal points for populist protests. After the surge in Know Nothing anti-immigrant sentiment, US territorial expansion and growing prosperity tended to suppress organized populist activity based on this issue, as a growing economy tended to alleviate anti-immigrant anxieties. In addition, government-enacted restrictions on immigrants had become part of the establishment, pre-empting populist insurgencies over this issue. A new group of Chinese immigrants arrived to work on the transcontinental railroad in the 1850s and became the target for special government restrictions and discrimination. Informal and clandestine anti-immigrant sentiment would continue through organizations such as the Ku Klux Klan, proxies for populist political parties.[11]

German and Irish immigration continued throughout the nineteenth century, followed by large numbers of Jewish and other immigrants from eastern and southern Europe in the early twentieth century, all of whom faced both discrimination and intimidation by vigilante groups, as well as growing governmental restrictions and anti-immigrant policies. Potent anti-immigrant sentiment would reemerge in the early twenty-first century, based on new fears of immigrants from Latin America and Islamic countries. Know Nothing nativism would thus echo in similar times of rapid economic change and social division 160 years later, when the immigration issue converged with trade issues in the twenty-first century to divide the US electorate along populist fault lines.

Agrarian Populism and William Jennings Bryan

As the nineteenth century drew to a close, the next major episode of US populism emerged among farmers for somewhat different reasons. Unlike the cultural focus and economic fear of immigrants represented by the Know Nothing Party, US farmers' anger generally came from depressed prices for their crops, the result of deflationary monetary policies after the US Civil War. Farmers also opposed high freight prices charged by railroads to transport their crops, as well as corporate and financial elites in general, whose monopoly practices harmed agricultural interests. High tariffs supported by large industries and the Republican Party raised prices for most American consumers on items such as clothing and household goods, and in particular on farm implements and equipment. In 1892, a group of agrarian reformers founded the People's (Populist) Party. Its defining political issue was advocacy for bimetallism, the use of both gold and silver as constituent parts of the monetary base, and fiat ("soft") money, which would allow government more flexible management of the money supply beyond the limits of the "hard" monetary base. Together these tools were intended to increase the money supply and the price level, boosting farm revenues and alleviating the farmers' debt problems. The People's Party came closest to power when it endorsed the Democratic Party's presidential candidate, William Jennings Bryan, in 1896. Bryan's populist credentials, aside from his commitment to many populist issues, included his outstanding skill as an orator.[12] His "cross of gold" speech at the 1896 Democratic convention, invoking biblical imagery to denounce the prevailing gold standard as "a cross upon which the common man was being crucified," was emblematic of classic populist rhetoric. Bryan's speech electrified the convention and led to his nomination as the Democratic presidential candidate.

The People's Party was ideologically close to the Democratic Party of its day, which also opposed the high protective tariffs imposed by the Republican Party. The Democratic Party had, beginning with Andrew Jackson, favored moderation in tariff levels. This position was consistent with factor-based comparative advantage theory, with relatively abundant US farm labor (as well as manufacturing labor) standing to benefit from lower tariffs and more exports of agricultural goods, compared with the interests of the owners of relatively scarce capital, represented by the high-tariff Republicans. Bryan and the People's Party did not make trade a central issue in the 1896 presidential campaign, since the previous Democratic president, Grover Cleveland, had embarrassingly mismanaged the opportunity to reduce tariffs in 1894 (Irwin 2017, pp. 292–293). Bryan focused instead on the bimetallism issue. However, the Populist/Democratic goal of winning over urban workers to join farmers in a broad coalition failed, and Bryan lost to Republican (and staunch protectionist) William McKinley. Bryan, who went on to lose two more presidential races as a Democrat, nonetheless argued in favor of lower tariffs for the rest of his political career. The People's Party, for its part, eventually disbanded after Bryan no longer carried its banner. Yet some important Populist Party proposals were ahead of their time, eventually winning legislative support and implementation, such as women's suffrage, the direct election of US senators by popular vote, and the introduction of an income tax, which would replace tariff revenues as the main source of government revenue. In addition, lowering tariffs was a natural populist issue for its time, as it was a protest against the ruling Republican elite and corporate interests. The systematic reduction of the Republican tariff regime would require another, greater economic crisis and a new populist movement 40 years later.

The Great Depression and Franklin D. Roosevelt's Response

The crisis came with the Great Depression of the 1930s. Republican President Hoover had signed into law the infamous Smoot-Hawley tariffs in June 1930, fully convinced, along with most of his Republican supporters, that the protective tariff would secure US prosperity (Irwin 2017, ch. 8). Tariffs were, to be sure, not the primary cause of the stock market crash, 25% unemployment, and 36% fall in GDP during the early 1930s. It was rather the 1932 banking failures, followed by restrictive monetary and financial policies and globalization of the crisis, that provided the proximate cause of the collapse. At the same time, the heavy tariffs and ensuing retaliation by US trading partners did nothing to promote recovery, and would surely put a drag on future growth if the global trade war continued.

Facing this economic disaster, the United States was ripe for a major populist surge. Populations in many European countries, as well as Japan, reacting to bad economic times and unstable political environments after World War I, succumbed to populist influences that morphed into outright fascist dictatorships. In the United States the Democratic Party, led by Franklin D. Roosevelt, trounced the Republicans in the 1932 presidential election. Roosevelt, born into one of the wealthiest families in the United States, was not a populist but pursued populist-inspired policies. He focused in his first term on the beginnings of his New Deal regulatory reforms designed to provide relief for unemployed workers. Prominent populists of the day, such as Governor Huey Long of Louisiana and Father Charles Coughlin, a Catholic priest, initially supported Roosevelt, but later joined forces and turned on him, dissatisfied with what they considered his half-baked reforms within the existing capitalist system. Long, for example, presented a more openly anti-elitist platform focused on aggressive redistribution policies. Coughlin, in addition to redistribution, proposed centralized government control of industries and the elimination of an independent Federal Reserve System. Roosevelt, for his part, faced judicial and legislative opposition to his establishment in 1933 of the National Industrial Recovery Act (NIRA), which the Supreme Court declared unconstitutional, based on its violation of the Congressional mandate over commerce regulations.[13] Like some openly populist leaders, Roosevelt pushed the envelope in implementing his reforms, and subsequently attempted to pack the Supreme Court with judges friendly to his ideas. Bipartisan congressional opposition stymied this effort. The pushback by coequal judicial and legislative bodies provided a check on populist reforms, maintained by democratic processes in the United States, in contrast to the authoritarian response to the economic crisis in many European countries and Japan. Roosevelt continued his reform plan under these constraints, however, and defused the appeal of more radical and impractical populist programs by introducing Social Security and minimum wage legislation in his second term (Judis 2016, pp. 28–32). As a member of the patrician, establishment elite, he was an unlikely promoter of populist ideas. Yet his most significant accomplishment as a reformer was that he recognized the necessity of introducing government policies and programs to address the causes of the populist uprising, while managing to adapt these measures to the existing economic system and within a constitutional framework. Groundbreaking as his economic policies were, they represented ambitious but still incremental measures that forestalled a more radical erosion of democratic institutions. Unlike many populist leaders, he won reelection by wide margins without tampering with the electoral process, and his reforms continue to define many US regulatory and social welfare policies to this day. He was a populist in his sympathies, but an establishmentarian pragmatist in his actions.

As with other US populist irruptions, trade was not the centerpiece of the New Deal, but Roosevelt also recognized the opportunity to reform trade policy as part of his economic plan, as the country was ready for relief from high Republican tariffs. Roosevelt's plan resulted in a major change in the conduct of US trade policy, the 1934 Reciprocal Trade Agreements Act (RTAA), which delegated significant trade policy powers from Congress to the US president (see Irwin 2017, pp. 423–443). Congress had to approve this change, since the US Constitution gives Congress the authority to regulate foreign trade (Article 1, Section 8). This landmark act set out to facilitate a more cohesive, nationally focused US trade policy through the executive branch, replacing the district-by-district log-rolling protectionism that gave rise to the 1930 Smoot-Hawley tariffs. The delegation of trade powers to the executive branch, specifically to levy tariffs and negotiate bilateral trade agreements without prior Congressional approval, would play an unexpected role later in President Trump's protectionist trade policies; in 1934, however, it loosened the Congressional grip on the details of tariff policy, paving the way for general tariff reductions and multilateral trade negotiations.

Postwar Trade, the Globalization Crisis, and Renewed Populism

The RTAA was a turning point in the history of US trade policy. It set up the framework for broader trade cooperation, negotiation, and liberalization after the Second World War under the GATT-WTO system. It is noteworthy that populism during most of the first 40 years of the postwar period remained dormant as a national political force. Mead (2011) argues that the external threat of the Soviet Union kept populist challenges to the government establishment at bay during the Cold War. Yet continuing US prosperity and economic growth during this period played at least as important a role, in no small part the result of global economic stability provided by the GATT itself. However, George Wallace, pro-segregationist governor of Alabama, raised early signals of populist unease and distrust of government in 1968 when he ran for president and won 45 electoral votes and five states in the South. Wallace's populist appeal targeted the New Deal establishment and racial desegregation, which the mainstream portion of caucuses in both the Republican and Democratic Parties had accepted. His geographic and demographic patterns of support, as well as his blunt and provocative rhetoric,[14] foreshadowed those of later populist presidential candidates including Donald Trump, but his third-party campaign gained only 13.5% of the national vote. His platform did not challenge existing US trade policy or global trade agreements.

As the postwar cycle of global economic growth ran its course, however, import competition was increasingly disrupting large US manufacturing markets and displacing American jobs, and trade became a flashpoint of populist anger. US trade policy measures, especially anti-dumping law and voluntary restraint agreements, had provided safety valves for protectionist sentiment, especially in the steel, textile, and auto industries, from the 1960s to the early 1990s. But by 1992, populist presidential candidates were using trade and globalization as anti-establishment issues. In 1992 and 1996, billionaire Ross Perot ran as an independent candidate on a protectionist platform, made famous by his warning of the "giant sucking sound" of US jobs leaving for Mexico that he alleged the proposed NAFTA would create. He combined elements of both right-wing and left-wing populism and drew support from both Democratic and Republican voters. In 1992 he received 19% of the popular vote, the highest for any third-party candidate since Theodore Roosevelt in 1912, but his support was spread across the country and he received no Electoral College votes. When he ran against incumbent Bill Clinton in 1996 his voter share declined to 8%, but his two campaigns showed that an anti-trade candidate could draw from a broad swath of the electorate on a national scale. Green Party candidate Ralph Nader ran a left-wing populist presidential campaign in 2000 and focused squarely on an anti-trade platform, but received only 3% of the national vote.[15] Right-wing conservative, ex-Republican Pat Buchanan ran a much less successful Reform Party campaign in 2000, having eventually won the Reform Party nomination from a field that included first-time candidate Donald Trump. Yet Buchanan's appeal to anti-immigrant sentiment, to those opposing abortion rights, and to anti-globalization anxiety would provide the template for Trump's populist strategy in 2016.

Growing Populist Anxieties

Even with growing anxieties regarding trade and globalization, the circumstances for strong populist support at the national level would not ripen until 16 years after the Reform Party campaign. Several factors fed growing dissatisfaction among large portions of the US population during this interval. China joined the WTO in 2001, giving it permanent nondiscriminatory access to the US market and others. Its massive exporting capacity created disruptive import competition for several manufacturing sectors in specific regions of the United States, making it difficult for displaced American workers to find new jobs. Autor, Dorn, and Hanson (2016) found that import competition from China had particularly strong and concentrated impacts on regions with larger shares of manufacturing employment. Many factories in these regions were labor-intensive in production, especially in certain subsectors of the furniture, wood, textile, and toy industries. Chinese import penetration was so broad that it occurred across several industrial sectors in these regions, reducing the ability of laid-off workers in one affected sector from finding another similarly skilled job locally. Such a concentrated trade shock was unexpected because earlier instances of import competition in the postwar period had generally taken place under conditions of mutual trade expansion and specialization, lessening the severity of regional impacts. Previously, workers who had lost jobs due to import competition in a declining sector could expect to find new work in an expanding sector, often without relocating their residence.

Government policies were ill-designed and ill-prepared to adjust to this new problem of widespread job displacement, leaving laid-off workers with sharply reduced income, unpaid debts, reduced access to healthcare, and in many cases increased rates of drug dependency and suicide, leading to a sharp increase in "deaths of despair" (Dean and Kimmel 2019; Pierce and Schott 2020). These negative effects of trade shocks highlighted the inadequacy of health, social, and vocational infrastructure in US regions hard-hit by job losses in general, while government policies tended to discourage worker mobility and access to new job opportunities (Dolan 2016). It is important to emphasize that trade was not the only disrupter: over the years, concentrated job losses also came from technological change and changes in consumer tastes. In general, tariffs tend not to address the underlying problem of trade-based job displacement, as they often cause job losses elsewhere and often in greater numbers than for the jobs they save. However, foreign imports provided a potent rallying cry for workers directly suffering job loss or reduced wages, and these people were therefore likely to be receptive to populist calls for trade restrictions.

And yet other disruptions amplified populist anxiety over economic globalization. The terrorist attacks on the United States of September 11, 2001, killing nearly 3,000, created persistent fears of lethal threats from abroad, especially from organized jihadist groups in the Middle East; and they undermined the sense of safety from foreign attack that most Americans had come to take for granted. A knock-on effect of these anxieties was renewed anti-immigrant sentiment and calls for tighter controls on both legal and illegal immigration. The direct fear was that Muslim terrorists would enter and even "invade" the United States[16] and stage attacks domestically, even though Muslim immigrant participation in subsequent US terrorism was miniscule. Of 980 individuals who planned, attempted, or carried out terrorist attacks in the United States from 1975 to 2017, only 192 (20%) were foreign-born. Of the 257 who actually carried out lethal terrorist attacks, 139 were native-born US citizens and 54 were foreign-born. From a broader perspective, of the 801,000 total murders committed in the United States during this time period, foreign-born terrorist attacks were responsible for just 0.38% of the deaths. Of these 3,037 deaths, 84% (2,977) occurred on September 11, 2019, at the hands of 19 jihadist terrorists (Nowrasteh 2019). A more subtle effect of the terrorist fears was that the associated anti-immigrant anxiety appeared to stem from cultural and economic insecurity. While Muslims represented just 1% of the US population, for example, anti-Muslim sentiment was often associated with Muslim religion, dress, and customs. Other unfamiliar immigrant cultures stirred similar concerns. The larger political issue was that legal immigration to the United States had increased since 2001. Those obtaining permanent legal resident status averaged 1.1 million per year from 2005 to 2017, although earlier waves of immigration had been historically larger as a proportion of the US population. The majority of US-bound immigrants in the early twenty-first century had come from Mexico and other Latin American countries, and their large numbers had a political impact. Most were younger than the average age in the US population and worked in lower-wage labor markets such as agriculture, light manufacturing, and construction. Their presence became increasingly visible in American cities, often changing the ethnic profile of communities. A November 2016 poll of white working-class respondents indicated that 68% agreed with the statement "The American way of life needs to be protected from foreign influence" (Cox, Lienesch, and Jones 2017). In their most extreme form, fears of cultural displacement fueled white supremacist opposition to immigration in particular, based on conspiracy theories of white genocide.[17] The fear that immigrants were undermining wages for American workers was generally unfounded, in that they worked at jobs most Americans did not want and contributed positively to the national economy. Yet fear of their demographic and cultural impact was no less potent politically when the stress of economic change through globalization and technology gripped the local economy.

The United States, like most of the rest of the industrialized world, was experiencing many other social changes during this period, increasing and reinforcing populist anxiety, especially among those most exposed to the economic and cultural adjustment described earlier. Racial diversity, secularism, environmentalism, feminism, and LGBTQ and abortion rights were changing the workplace, economy, and social environment in unwelcome ways for many, who perceived government policies and regulations protecting or promoting these trends as the infliction of elitist values on an unwilling population by the ruling class. In this manner, government policies created widespread resentment among those opposing these trends, and a rift that for many had begun to define the fault lines between a traditional "silent majority" of the people in opposition to the elite and their political representatives in Washington. Socially conservative religious groups, organized as the political organization Moral Majority in the 1980s, evolved into an increasingly partisan movement known as the Religious Right, a coalition of conservative Christian groups, largely evangelical, but also attracting some Catholics, Jews, and Mormons. They became one of the most important constituencies of Donald Trump, heavily influencing his choice of anti-abortion nominees for judicial appointments.

Perhaps the most corrosive impact of government policy on public trust, however, came with the financial crisis that began in 2007 and lasted until 2012 in the United States, the largest banking failure since the Great Depression. Its widespread impact came from the fact that excessively risky mortgage lending by banks drove up housing prices and created a housing bubble. Credit rating agencies had mis-priced risk, exposing banks to failing loans when housing prices plummeted. As the bubble burst, many homeowners faced foreclosure, while stock markets crashed and unemployment rose. Credit dried up, the crisis spread to world markets, and global trade fell by 15%. Consumer wealth plummeted, amplifying the financial straits of many families already contending with job and wage losses in the industrial Rust Belt. This erosion of economic security translated into an erosion of trust in government and in the financial practices of Wall Street elites. Several banks "too big to fail" received government bailouts, while many government financial regulations and policies became objects of populist scorn. Right-wing populists, led by the new Tea Party movement, decried the bailout of banks, while left-wing populists staged Occupy Wall Street protests against the banks and their political influence, which had earned them bailouts and friendly regulations.

Trump's Presidential Campaign

The social, cultural, and economic anxieties and grievances of many US voters accumulated during the early years of the twenty-first century. Populist sentiment in the United States, which Mead (2011) maintained was always lurking just below the surface, by 2016 was poised to emerge as a major political force in the wake of the financial crisis that began in 2007. Attitudes toward trade itself had worsened among the relatively small group of workers who had lost their jobs to import competition during the financial crisis. Yet an even more important source of public trade skepticism arose during the crisis due to growing ethnocentrism and the perceived economic dangers of future globalization trends (Mansfield, Mutz, and Brackbill 2016). At first it seemed that these views would receive little public representation in third-party initiatives, and would instead be mediated by the major parties in national elections. Donald Trump, having tested the waters of a third-party candidacy in 2000, realized that a strategy outside the traditional two-party system was doomed to failure and could capture little more than a protest vote. A more promising pathway appeared: populist elements had developed within both the Democratic and Republican Parties, and voting patterns had become more polarized in recent elections (Autor, Dorn, Hanson, and Mailesi 2017).

Changing Party Politics

In contrast to the recent third-party presidential candidacies of Wallace, Perot, Buchanan, and Nader, populist sentiment was finding a home within the major parties: the Tea Party, and later the Freedom Caucus in the Republican Party, and the more loosely organized progressives in the Democratic Party. The Republican Party, in particular, was vulnerable to capture by an insurgent candidate. It had run unsuccessful presidential campaigns in 2008 and 2012 with moderate candidates John McCain and Mitt Romney, respectively, who championed traditional Republican platform positions that included pro-trade multilateralism. As the recent history of third-party candidates had shown, the real prize for any populist candidate would be to capture the nomination of one of the major parties, as this would extend the candidate's appeal to a traditional party's base and legitimize the platform as "mainstream." For Trump, the logic of pursuing the Republican nomination proceeded from the populist playbook of exploiting and amplifying anger and division. In 2016, the outgoing Obama administration and the Democratic candidate who would succeed him in the presidential race, Hillary Clinton, could be portrayed as the source of damaging liberal elite policies, from environmental protection and abortion rights to immigration and trade liberalization. All of these establishment policies together would be portrayed in the populist playbook as a rigged system intended to undermine traditional American jobs, values, and culture. Trump, the populist candidate, would take it upon himself to upset the entire system, providing a one-stop-shopping vote for the silent majority of the people to vent a myriad of grievances and "make America great again." He would communicate directly with his supporters via Twitter, unmediated by the critical mainstream press, and take advantage of social media networks to reinforce and amplify his attacks on his opponents. On the Democratic side, progressive Bernie Sanders launched a populist insurgent primary campaign within the Democratic Party, promoting universal healthcare, income redistribution, and financial reforms, among other issues. His left-wing populist positions contrasted with many of Trump's right-wing policy proposals except for one: Trump's and Sanders's populist trade proposals were both highly protectionist, if based on different ideologies.[18]

Trump's unexpected success depended in large part on his surprising ability to commandeer and remake the Republican Party in his own image, which Sanders also attempted in the Democratic Party but ultimately failed to achieve (see Gillies 2017). Both the Republican and Democratic Parties were suffering from a "representation deficit" among their traditional constituencies, providing an opportunity for a populist leader to enter the scene and exploit the rift between party leadership and voters. As noted in chapter 1, populism often begins with a failure of mainstream parties to provide representation to large numbers of their constituents. Trump's brand of cultural nationalism had the greatest resonance among conservative Republicans who were attracted to his unyielding stance on immigration, abortion, and gun rights. They provided a core voting base on which to build support for his disruption of traditional Republican—and subsequently national—politics. One of Trump's biggest differences with the Republican establishment was over trade policy, but his protectionism also drew on disaffected Democratic voter groups, especially blue-collar manufacturing workers who had suffered job losses due to imports. His ability to combine these economically and culturally disaffected groups in a common protest against government elites created the campaign juggernaut that caught his Republican primary opponents, and later his Democratic opponent, off-guard.

Trump falls into what has become the classic profile of a populist leader (see Viviani 2017). He fashioned himself as a self-made man whose success originated outside politics, but who denigrated traditional politics and entered the scene as a "political entrepreneur of disenchantment" (Viviani 2017, p. 287). He recreated a bond of representation with disaffected voters by amplifying both their rift with established party leaders and the crisis that prompted the people's discontent. He reinforced his anti-establishment bona fides by communicating directly with the people (by Twitter) in nondiplomatic, nonelitist, politically incorrect, and sometimes vulgar language. Trump's constant use of open political rallies, even after he was elected, acted as vehicles for divisive rhetoric and showcases for chanting by the crowd. The reported exhilaration of such events illustrated, perhaps more than any other campaign activity, the potency of populism, through the use of crowd psychology, to amplify and escalate participatory emotional responses.[19] Skonieczny (2018) analyzes Trump's trade narrative in his campaign speeches, emphasizing the role of emotional features in his populist appeal:

> Our workers' loyalty was repaid . . . with total betrayal. Our politicians have aggressively pursued a policy of globalization, moving our jobs, our wealth and our factories to Mexico and overseas. Globalization has made the financial elite, who donate to politicians, very wealthy. (Trump 2016)

Extending this concept to internet-based communication, Boucher and Thies (2019) document Trump's use of a polarized social network and its role as a self-reinforcing echo chamber to propagate his protectionist trade platform. As the defiant defender of the people's interests and as "one of them," he created an identity as their exclusive political representative. In this way the populist leader then became identified with the party itself, defining its platform and commanding a dedicated following. Thus the generally pro-trade Republican Party became Trump's protectionist Republican Party.

Trump's Anti-Trade Platform

Candidate Donald Trump's anti-trade platform incorporated economic nationalism and mercantilism. China was the most prominent villain among foreign countries, based on the large US trade deficit with that country, and in particular on Chinese import competition that displaced US manufacturing jobs. During the campaign Trump threatened 45% tariffs against China as part of its punishment for "raping" the United States (Haberman 2016; Diamond 2016). Screenings of Peter Navarro's propaganda film *Death by China* at Trump's campaign rallies in Rust Belt regions, for example, featured a metaphorical invasion of Chinese airplanes bombing US factories, along with a graphic depiction of a Chinese dagger thrust into the center of a map of the United States, creating a pool of blood. Archival footage of pro-trade US politicians, both Republican and Democrat, along with US multinational corporations that built production facilities in China, indicated who was at fault for the situation. These were the globalist elites. During the campaign, Trump went as far as suggesting that he would withdraw the United States from the WTO, whose rules would prevent him from imposing tariffs unilaterally (Mount 2016).

The other major culprit in the trade damage done to the United States was Mexico, part of the North American Free Trade Agreement (NAFTA) that also included the United States and Canada. NAFTA provided the framework for a number of supply-chain arrangements among the three partner countries, with Mexico exporting a large volume of finished automobiles and many other manufactured products to the United States. Trump heaped special scorn on NAFTA, declaring it "the worst trade deal ever" and a major cause of US manufacturing job losses that he would either renegotiate or eliminate upon becoming president (Gandel 2016). Current US trade policies, in his view, were not only bad for the economy but had also made the United States a laughing stock, a doormat for other countries to trample on with their flood of exports, and a humiliation for US workers, now deprived of their livelihoods and their dignity. He often combined his anti-NAFTA, anti-Mexico rhetoric at his campaign events with his signature "build the wall" rallying cry, promising protection from an invasion of terrorists, drug dealers, and rapists from Mexico and other Latin American countries who were destroying the American way of life. It is important to understand the populist appeal of Trump's view of trade and its link to immigration: he would "make America great again" by fending off the malign and hostile effects of *both* foreign trade and immigration.

Trump harbored protectionist views long before he became president. Unlike many other issues on which he has changed positions, he has consistently advocated protectionist measures since he first exhibited ambitions as a presidential candidate in the 1980s. He was particularly critical of Japanese auto imports during this period, which he saw as a failure of US trade officials to impose more severe trade restrictions. Influenced by Chrysler CEO Lee Iacocca, who lobbied for and received protectionist quotas on Japanese imports, Trump continued to argue for more tariffs on Japanese goods after these quotas were lifted in 1984. He turned his ire on China's trade economy after China joined the WTO in 2001, reportedly disgruntled that he could source many fixtures for his properties only from China, and yet had difficulty securing trademarks for his Trump-branded products in China (Schlesinger 2018). Steven Bannon, an anti-globalist, also strongly influenced Trump's approach to trade policy and his campaign strategy (Johnson 2018). In Bannon's view, America's economy lay in ruins, and the current trading system was part of an institutional structure that prevented the president from pursuing pro-American, mercantilist trade policies. Multilateral rules and negotiations, constraints on discriminatory practices, and the principle of "peaceful" third-party trade dispute settlement were anathema to his and Trump's concept of "America First."

Trade played a significant role in the 2016 election outcome. Trump's campaign appealed directly to manufacturing workers displaced by trade (see Autor, Dorn, Hanson, and Majlesi 2017; Alden 2017) and to anti-immigrant voters, with whom criticism of imports resonated (see Hays et al. 2019). Using county-level election and demographic data, Autor, Dorn, Hanson, and Majlesi (2017) examined statistical results from several closely contested battleground states and compiled a counterfactual analysis of how lower growth in Chinese import penetration would have altered the vote for Donald Trump. The three states with the closest margins favoring Trump—Michigan, Wisconsin, and Pennsylvania—provided his margin of victory in the Electoral College. According to their analysis, a 25% smaller growth rate in Chinese imports in Michigan and Wisconsin would have flipped the vote to Trump's opponent, Hillary Clinton. A 50% lower growth rate of Chinese imports would have flipped Pennsylvania as well, which would then have resulted in Clinton's victory.[20] For that matter, replaying China's import penetration with a lower growth rate could also lead to the conclusion that Trump would never have become a presidential candidate at all in 2016 (Schwartz and Bui 2016; Davis and Hilsenrath 2016).

In such a close election, counterfactual scenario-building, assuming incremental effects of an isolated factor in a vast sea of otherwise unchanged assumptions, is highly speculative. One could alternatively isolate any of a number of other potentially determining factors that would have changed the outcome.[21] Most voters did *not* in fact lose their jobs or suffer wage losses due to trade, and it is clear that there was equally passionate concern among other voter segments on single issues such as abortion and gun rights that did not directly involve trade. Many observers have concluded that trade had little to do with Trump's victory, citing the importance of cultural resentment among white voters, for example (see Oberhauser, Krier, and Kusow 2019). Yet the centrality of trade in Trump's populist narrative suggests that the "package" he presented to his supporters was successful in uniting diverse sources of anger and focusing their anger on a culpable elite. Trade was the linchpin, with its vivid images of destruction of jobs, lives, and communities. The same politicians who brought you damaging trade agreements, job losses, and devastated communities, according to Trump's message, also brought you liberal immigration policies, with yet more job losses, drug crime, and cultural encroachment . . . and more job-destroying global agreements on the environment. And yet more abortions and assaults on traditional values. The trade issue played a leading role in the larger narrative of nefarious foreign influences and government policy mistakes. Empirical research on the link between trade and Trump's victory suggests that the trade shock beginning in 2001 triggered a broader political shift among white voters toward politicians promising to defend their cultural and economic group identity (see Autor, Dorn, Hanson, and Majlesi 2017, pp. 5–6). Even voters who were not directly affected by trade itself saw the connection with other sources of their discontent, and they readily, and often exuberantly, bought into the populist package.

Summary

Trump's inauguration address summarized his view of the condition of the United States as a country, based on the message he had delivered to his supporters during the campaign. On economic issues, his populist message focused on the "carnage" inflicted by elite globalists on the people: American workers and families. Trump vowed to end the carnage with a straightforward plan of protection:

> For too long, a small group in our nation's Capital has reaped the rewards of government while the people have borne the cost . . . Politicians prospered—but the jobs left, and the factories closed. The establishment protected itself, but . . . for too many of our citizens, a different reality exists . . . rusted-out factories scattered like tombstones across the landscape of our nation.
>
> This American carnage stops right here and stops right now . . . One by one, the factories shuttered and left our shores, with not even a thought about the millions upon millions of American workers left behind. The wealth of our middle class has been ripped from their homes and then redistributed across the entire world.

From this moment on, it's going to be America First . . . Every decision on trade, on taxes, on immigration, on foreign affairs, will be made to benefit American workers and American families. We must protect our borders from the ravages of other countries making our products, stealing our companies, and destroying our jobs. Protection will lead to great prosperity and strength. (Trump 2017)

Based on a review of US history, the emergence of a nation-wide, populist, anti-establishment campaign tends to require the confluence of four factors, three of which apply generally to populism around the globe, and a fourth that applies specifically to two-party systems:

1. A significant and unifying crisis or threat perceived by a significant portion of the electorate;
2. Dissatisfaction and frustration among this group with the existing channels of political representation;
3. A charismatic leader who can focus the group's anger, identify the elitists in power who are at fault and present a compelling and straightforward narrative for redressing the injustice; and
4. Endorsement as a candidate by one of the two major political parties.

In the United States, electoral success since the Jacksonian era had always eluded populist candidates at the national level, with William Jennings Bryan coming closest in 1896. In 2016, Donald Trump fulfilled the fourth important requirement, riding the Republican Party to victory with a platform based on a cultural and anti-globalization backlash. Anxiety over global trade played a central role in the economic plank of his populist narrative, appealing directly to those who linked their job loss to imports or outsourcing, and indirectly to those who saw a link between trade and terrorism, global climate treaties, regional economic decline, immigration, and unwelcome social change. He identified the economic villains (the globalists) who committed a misdeed that must be undone (openness to trade and global economic cooperation). He presented himself as a strong leader, the one uniquely qualified to pursue justice for the people. Finally, he proposed a simple program for restoring the greatness of the past: restrictions on trade, on outbound foreign investment, and on immigration, and an overthrow of international institutions of cooperation. As Trump assumed office many wondered whether his radical trade policy was merely campaign rhetoric that he would soften in response to the role of the US president to lead the global trading system. As a committed protectionist, however, he would set out to turn his anti-establishment rhetoric into action.

5

Trump's Assault on the Global Trading System

Populism is about rejecting the establishment, and Donald Trump indeed announced early in his campaign that he would overturn the trade policy establishment. In addition, his top trade official, Robert Lighthizer, knew how to do it. Together, Trump and Lighthizer set out to rewrite US trade agreements, defy global trading rules and norms, and upset the WTO framework of reciprocal market access, trade negotiations, and dispute settlement. Trump's first trade policy step as president in January 2017 was relatively modest, announcing on his first day in office the US withdrawal from the Trans-Pacific Partnership negotiations. Later in 2017 he announced his intention to either renegotiate or cancel the NAFTA, a much more important and complicated political issue. His trade policy initiatives continued with traditional US trade law actions to impose anti-subsidy tariffs on Canadian lumber and provide safeguard protection to the US washing machine and solar panel industries, although these measures were part of a larger agenda. Trump's trade policy insurgency escalated significantly in March 2018 with his announcement that the United States would impose universal "national security" tariffs against nearly all imports of steel and aluminum. Part of the final plan for those trade restrictions included voluntary export restraint (VER) agreements, illegal under WTO rules. He also initiated another investigation regarding possible national security tariffs on automobiles, which, if enacted, would have been even more momentous. Turning his attention directly to China, he began imposing unilateral discriminatory tariffs against China over its alleged violation of US intellectual property and technology development, which quickly escalated into a US-China trade war. Other assaults on trade institutions during his first three years in office included an ongoing blockage of new appointments to the WTO's appellate body, crippling its dispute resolution mechanism, and his threatened use of discriminatory tariffs against Mexico over nontrade issues. The basic upshot of Trump's trade battles is that his policies not only restricted trade and thereby imposed protectionist costs on consumers and producers in the United States and foreign countries, but also damaged the institutional foundations of the global trading system itself. This chapter will

Populism and Trade. Kent Jones, Oxford University Press. © Oxford University Press 2021.
DOI: 10.1093/oso/9780190086350.003.0005.

show how US trade law itself came to favor executive branch discretion to the point where a protectionist president can wield largely unchecked power over trade policy. At stake is a global system whose rules may no longer be considered binding. This chapter will also review the specific WTO provisions and practices that Trump sought to violate directly, to alter fundamentally, or to subvert. The discussion then turns to the results of his policy initiatives during his term in office, and to what extent they have achieved his political and economic goals. The chapter concludes with a summary of the specific elements of the institutional impact of his trade policies.

The First Assault: Trade Law Tariffs and Voluntary Export Restraints

President Trump began his term in office with an official withdrawal from the Trans-Pacific Partnership, as expected, and in his first year otherwise limited his trade policy actions to trade law cases he had inherited from the previous administration. It was in his second year that his trade policy initiatives began to challenge WTO multilateral trade rules, including national security tariffs, unilateral measures against China, and the use of VERs. These actions set the tone for his disruptive approach to global trade institutions during his presidency.

Traditional Protection and Signs of Unilateralism

During his first year in office, Trump's trade policy was relatively quiet in terms of presidential decisions. He had expressed his disdain for the Trans-Pacific Partnership (TPP) during the campaign, and his decision on his first day of office, January 21, 2017, to withdraw from the negotiations had been widely expected. His rejection of the TPP reflected both his avowed rejection of any major Obama policy initiative and his fundamental refusal to consider any new multilateral trade agreement. Yet the agreement had never received the necessary Democratic support to pass in the second Obama administration, and his opponent, former Obama Secretary of State Hillary Clinton, had also opposed it during the campaign. The irony of Trump's position was that the agreement as it stood in 2017 included 11 Asia-Pacific countries that excluded China.[1] US participation in the earlier TPP negotiations had already established strong US influence on the rules, which could have placed pressure on China to moderate its own state-trading practices if it ever did joint the

agreement.[2] The remaining TPP countries, for their part, persisted in negotiations without the United States, and a revised version, the Comprehensive
and Progressive Agreement for Trans-Pacific Partnership (CPTPP), had
entered into force in January 2019. Trump's refusal to participate in it left the
United States outside a regional trade agreement that gave preferential market
access among member countries that left many US exports at a disadvantage.
Trump later found it necessary to negotiate a bilateral agreement on US-Japan
bilateral market access in September 2019, which still left several trade sectors
uncovered, especially automobiles (Schott 2019). Trump also began his promised renegotiation of NAFTA in mid-2017, the "worst trade agreement ever"
according to his campaign rhetoric (Trump and Clinton 2016). Negotiations
for a new agreement would continue for more than two years, an issue which
will be discussed at greater length later in this chapter.

In the first year of his presidency the Trump administration took a special
interest in three trade law cases. The first was his decision to impose countervailing duty tariffs on softwood lumber from Canada, a case that was part of a
long-running dispute between the two countries over the nature of Canadian
subsidies to the lumber industry. Rather than negotiate a new bilateral agreement over government regulation of Canadian lumber production, Trump
decided to escalate the dispute by directing the Commerce Department,
under his appointee Wilbur Ross, to impose anti-subsidy tariffs unilaterally,
perhaps a shot across the bow at Canada for upcoming NAFTA negotiations.
This had been a long-standing issue, leading to several similar tariff decisions
in the past. The subsidy investigation and decision-making process, pre-
dating the Trump inauguration, followed WTO rules, and while contentious,
the case remained within the traditional policymaking framework. During
his first year in office many US firms, encouraged by Trump's protectionist
rhetoric, filed anti-dumping and countervailing duty cases. However, Trump's
Commerce Department also took the unusual step of *self-initiating* anti-
dumping and countervailing duty cases against imports of aluminum, rather
than wait for private firms to file cases. These government actions would lead
to broader protectionist measures in the following year.[3]

The Trump administration took an even stronger interest in cases filed under
GATT Article 19 (the safeguards clause) against solar panels, mainly from China,
and against washing machines produced mainly by South Korean manufacturers
Samsung and LG. The final disposition of safeguards cases was largely subject to
the president's decision, once the US International Trade Commission identified
serious injury (or a threat of injury) to US firms from imports. Since the end of
the Uruguay Round, which set out new rules for the safeguards clause, the US
president rarely approved tariffs in such cases (as required by the statute) and

those that were approved by the United States and other countries were in most cases successfully challenged and overturned in the WTO dispute settlement system (Ahn et al. 2018). These results stemmed from the nature of the safeguards clause, which allowed a WTO member country, under strict conditions, to limit the imports of specific products from *all* countries based on their "unforeseen disruption" of the domestic market in the importing country, *without having violated unfair trade laws*. The potential abuse of WTO-approved universal trade restrictions against *fairly traded* goods has resulted in a narrow interpretation of the safeguards clause in WTO dispute settlement cases. If safeguards protection were easy to justify by the rules, WTO countries would be inclined to use this provision more often to protect politically sensitive domestic markets from imports. Trump's application of this provision therefore signaled a more aggressive use of safeguard remedies to import disruptions—he may even have been inviting a legal WTO challenge that he could then defy. Sure enough, the US announcement of the safeguards cases led almost immediately to a WTO dispute, setting up an early confrontation over WTO rules (WTO 2018c). Yet this confrontation was merely a foretaste of Trump's open attack on the long-standing interpretation of WTO rules that followed.

National Security Tariffs: Newly Interpreted as a Protectionist Tool

On March 28, 2018, in defiance of long-standing GATT and WTO practice, Trump announced that he was unilaterally invoking the National Security Clause (Section 232) of US trade law to apply universal tariffs of 10% on imported aluminum and 25% on imported steel. This provision of US trade law, based on the WTO's GATT Article 21, allows the president alone to take action to "adjust the imports of an article and its derivatives" if those imports "threaten to impair the national security." The original intention of the WTO rule was to allow such tariffs only in wartime and cases of national security emergencies. The new US interpretation flew in the face of all previous applications of this measure. The protectionist effect came by adding "unemployment in the industry" as a key argument for it, a factor previously rejected in all such cases. The US Commerce Department Report acknowledges that employment in the industry had not previously served as a criterion for justifying national security tariffs, but rejects this interpretation in a telling note:

> To the extent that the 2001 Report or other prior Department reports under Section 232 can be read to conclude that imports from reliable sources cannot impair the

national security when the Secretary finds those imports are causing substantial unemployment, decrease in revenues of government, loss of skills or investment, or other serious effects resulting from the displacement of any domestic products by excessive imports, the Secretary expressly rejects such a reading. (US Department of Commerce 2018, p. 17, n. 21)

Until this announcement, US trade law Section 232 had rarely been used, and had always been interpreted in light of the parallel provision in GATT Article 21, which limited the scope of such actions to trade in fissionable materials, traffic in arms, and measures "taken in time of war or other emergency in international relations." Trade relations in general under the GATT-WTO system require members not to exceed the maximum tariff levels that each country has negotiated as part of a WTO multilateral agreement. Waiving this requirement, as GATT Article 21 allows, would then also presume that the countries targeted with such tariff restrictions are at war with, or pose an immediate threat to, the country invoking this provision. In the case of aluminum and steel, however, the main US trading partners were Canada, Brazil, the European Union, Japan, and the Republic of Korea, most of which were US military allies, and none of which posed a threat to US military security. They were surprised, for example, that Trump had included them as aluminum and steel "enemies" under the national security tariffs, whose impact would proportionately reduce their deliveries to the United States much more than Chinese deliveries, which were already subject to prior US anti-dumping and countervailing duty restrictions on Chinese steel (Bown 2018). The national security clause had never been used as a trade restriction against any specific product except for oil, targeted either specifically against oil imports from Iran and Libya, or generally against oil imports from OPEC countries. In those cases, the United States had imposed tariffs at a time when its dependence on oil imports had raised national security concerns about the reliability of energy supplies from hostile countries.

President Trump, however, regarded the national security issue as one of having insufficient domestic aluminum and steel production capacity and employment, declaring: "If you don't have steel, you don't have a country" (Carter 2018). Absent from this calculation, however, was the self-inflicted damage imposed on US aluminum and steel *consuming* industries, whose costs would rise due to the tariffs, and whose workforce would in many cases decline as a result. Actual national security preparedness was not a valid consideration: less than 3% of steel and aluminum supply in the United States goes toward military ordnance (Jacobsen 2018). Imports of these products were, in the president's view, a national security threat, simply by virtue of the fact that they compete with or replace US production. Thus Canada, the main source of US aluminum imports through supply-chain arrangements involving cross-border investments between the two countries, was deemed a threat to US national security. The US firm Alcoa imports much of its raw aluminum stock from its Canadian subsidiary, where lower energy costs allow more efficient aluminum smelting. Steel from Canada, the European Union, Japan, South Korea, and many other countries had developed similar supplier arrangements with US customers, based on specialized varieties of steel, many of which are not produced in the United States. Downstream US steel-using firms thereby faced input shortages in their own steel production and fabrication. Several US firms dependent on steel inputs complained openly that the steel tariffs had raised their costs and were causing layoffs. In January 2020 Trump then announced that he would extend Section 232 tariffs to "derivative" products containing steel or aluminum (White House 2020), thus creating "cascading" tariffs for products disadvantaged by the initial tariffs. The problem for producers of steel and aluminum derivatives, of course, was the set of initial tariffs, and now the proliferation of tariffs down the supply chain would compound the cost of protection, disadvantaging a new set of consumers, both individuals and firms (Bown 2020a). One US importer filed a legal complaint against the new tariffs, claiming they were illegal under the Section 232 statute.[4]

Beyond its creative new interpretation of what constituted national security, the United States asserted that its decision under GATT Article 21 was "self-judging and non-reviewable." In other words, the United States claimed its absolute right to define national security criteria on its own, and that no country could legitimately challenge such criteria in a WTO dispute case.[5] This broad assertion of national trade policy sovereignty, immune from any external review, was emblematic of Trump's economic nationalism and of his populist challenge to WTO rules. What President Trump was doing was using the national security clause in order to pursue a protectionist policy favoring certain domestic industries. Yet this was more than just an instance of protectionism; it was a subversion of the WTO itself. In using GATT Article 21, he could claim that there was no restraint on the level of tariffs he could impose, or the countries whose shipments he could target, and he could also claim that other countries were not allowed to retaliate against it. He broke all precedent by stretching the definition of national security to include, arbitrarily, employment and output of industries that had little connection with national security, in products supplied by military allies of the United States. Article 21 had been a "use-in-case-of-emergency-only" provision, but the US precedent threatened to wreck the entire WTO system of trade relations.

The national security tariff weakened the WTO in other ways. Trump granted temporary exemptions from several countries at first, based officially on "strategic security relationships," including not only military allies like Australia, Canada, Japan, South Korea, and the European Union, but also Brazil and Argentina, two countries without a US military alliance.[6] Australia was initially the only country to receive a full exemption, and this arrangement was later extended to Canada and Mexico in exchange for concessions in the ongoing NAFTA negotiations. These exemptions, however, represented a violation of the most-favored nation (MFN) provision of the GATT. The United States had no logical argument in exempting these countries from tariffs based on the relative security of output and employment in its domestic industries, compared with other suppliers of steel and aluminum. Trump would later use his Section 232 powers to increase the steel and aluminum tariffs against exporting countries he unilaterally declared to have manipulated their currencies, which became the subject for further legal challenges. Trump doubled steel tariffs to 50% against Turkey in August 2018 after the Turkish lira fell, leading to a legal challenge by a US steel importing company, arguing that the president had no right under the Section 232 statute to raise tariffs for this reason. The US Court of International Trade eventually annulled the tariff doubling (Sikes 2019; Charnovitz and Hufbauer 2020). In December 2019, Trump declared that Argentina and Brazil also manipulated their currencies to lower their value, unilaterally reinstating the Section 232 tariffs for which these two countries had negotiated VER agreement in exchange for an exemption from the tariffs (Zumbrun et al. 2019). An official declaration of currency manipulation is subject to a determination of the US Treasury, based on overt foreign central bank purchases of US dollars on currency markets. Neither Brazil nor Argentina had done this.

In addition, the protectionist effect of Trump's actions was compounded when Canada, the European Union, Mexico, and China retaliated against the national security tariff with tariffs of their own against selected US goods, in most cases calculated to target products produced in states and districts with pro-Trump voters, especially with regard to agriculture goods for export. In defiance of the Trump/Lighthizer claim that retaliation was not allowed, the European Union declared that since the action was illegitimate under WTO rules to begin with, it would respond as though the United States had used the WTO safeguards clause. This provision requires "compensation" for trading partners harmed by the action (safeguards agreement, Article 8), including the freedom to impose retaliatory tariffs in order to rebalance the bilateral levels of market access. Trump responded to the retaliation with the threat of new Section 232 tariffs on automobiles and automotive parts, the single largest category of traded manufactured goods in the world economy. He would later brandish the threat of national security auto tariffs in the NAFTA and other trade negotiations. This measure would have increased the tariff damage considerably, since the United States purchases some $360 billion in automotive products annually from foreign sources, about 15% of all US import value. Further counterretaliation could then potentially target $160 billion in US automotive exports. Other goods, services, and investments could eventually enter the escalating fray, to replenish the ammunition needed to keep the so-called national security trade war retaliation going. When it comes to trade war tactics, escalation quickly throws WTO rules out the window and the confrontation becomes a battle of wills among the combatants. Lee (2019) points out that both the initial national security tariffs action by the United States and the retaliation by US trading partners were in violation of WTO rules. While the EU retaliation was understandable, WTO legal doctrine requires that each action be judged according to the criteria allowed in the rule. While using safeguards provisions to justify the need for compensatory tariffs was tempting, they could not provide the legal basis for retaliation in this case, which would have required a triggering safeguards situation (i.e., unforeseen fairly traded imports that threaten a domestic industry) to prompt a safeguards response. The European Union and other countries were sorely tempted to cite US practice and declare that they, too, can define their national security in such a way as to view US tariffs as a national security threat to *them,* and thereby invoke Article 21 in order to retaliate. And yet they did not do so, knowing that the Trump/Lighthizer response would certainly be: bring it on, now that we've dragged you out of the WTO rules and into the jungle— we'll see who prevails. This is the global trade policy environment that Trump wanted: the elimination of multilateral rules and a reversion to trade practices based on raw political and economic power alone. In this regard, the other major WTO members refrained from taking the bait and abandoning the multilateral system.

Voluntary Export Restraint: Anti-Competitive Quotas

The president also resurrected the use of VERs in negotiating steel and aluminum trade restrictions, in direct violation of WTO rules under the safeguards agreement. VERs are quota arrangements that the importing country negotiates with the exporting country, in this case as an alternative to the US tariffs. They have always been in violation of the GATT principle restricting the use of quantitative trade restrictions. However, GATT rules formally restricted only import quotas. Such "voluntary" trade restrictions are attractive to exporters who would otherwise face unilateral import tariffs from major trading partners, and for many years VERs allowed countries to skirt the rules. Under VERs no tariffs are collected by the importing country, and the exporters get to capture the scarcity value of the trade restriction, while consumers in the importing country pay higher prices and cannot benefit from any national tariff revenue. From 1955 to 1994, VERs were often negotiated on behalf of politically sensitive industries facing protectionist pressures, such as automobiles, steel, consumer electronics, machine tools, textiles, and clothing (Jones 1994, ch. 4). The largest VER arrangement was the multicountry multifiber agreement, a complicated network of detailed, bilateral country-by-country quotas covering a wide variety of textile and clothing products from 1974 to 2005. The transfer of control of trade to the exporting firms often creates an incentive for them to organize export cartels and raise their profits even higher, to the detriment of consumers in the importing country. Finally, VERs often create the incentive for exporters to escalate the value of their total shipments by allocating quota shares toward higher-value varieties of the restricted product. This new allocation then reduces the supply of less expensive grades of the product, raising prices for these products by an even higher percentage than the overall increase in prices and harming low-income consumers disproportionately. VERs thus conveniently motivate both domestic import-competing firms and foreign producers of the product to support the trade restriction, encouraging a "cooperative" protectionist conspiracy. It is no wonder that VERs can be negotiated quickly. Because such agreements so clearly promote trade restrictions, anti-competitive practices, and potentially large consumer welfare losses, GATT countries agreed to forbid their use under new safeguards provisions of the Uruguay Round agreement of 1994 (Jones 1994, p. 174).

New VER agreements applied to steel shipments to the United States from Korea, Brazil, and Argentina, aluminum shipments from Argentina, and potentially to auto exports from Mexico and Canada under the subsequently negotiated USMCA treaty (Esserman, Emerson, and Wang 2018; USTR 2019).[7] After the ban on VERs had been breached, further VERs became possible, especially if Trump imposed more trade restrictions on differentiated, high-value goods, which he threatened to do as a result of the Section 232 national security tariff report on automobiles. This scenario had already played out in the infamous US-Japan auto VER of 1980–1984, which imposed thousands of dollars of economic welfare cost on each US car buyer, especially low-income purchasers of compact cars, transferring revenue from increased prices to both US and Japanese auto companies. More generally,

VERs are well suited to populist, transaction-driven trade agreements, as they can quickly be negotiated by a major importing country to satisfy mercantilist goals of limiting imports in politically sensitive industries. A variant of newly resurrected VERs could also prove to be attractive as a possible way to manage overall trade balances, limiting total goods or manufactures trade, for example. In a similar vein, Trump also negotiated a quantitative "voluntary import expansion" of US agricultural goods with China in the January 2020 Phase One agreement, another trade-distorting measure that would violate WTO nondiscrimination rule by reserving parts of China's market exclusively for US products, to be described in the next section.

The US-China Trade War

President Trump's trade war with China became the centerpiece of his entire administration, a choice of pursuing unilateral confrontation with a major economic rival over negotiated, WTO-based dispute settlement. It defied the purpose of the multilateral rules-based trading system, which had been established in response to the global trade war that occurred in the 1930s. It began with a legitimate dispute by the US and other counties over the trade impact of China's state-owned enterprises and Chinese firms' appropriation of foreign intellectual property, but it never set out to resolve that issue. Tit-for-tat escalation and a "Phase One" managed trade "truce" in the war inflicted further damage on both countries, the world economy, and the world trading system.

Section 301: Unlimited US Retaliation

Trump continued his attack on WTO institutions on a different front by targeting China, the country with which the United States had the largest trade deficit, with tariffs. In March he unilaterally imposed 25% tariffs against $50 billion of imports from China across a wide range of goods. This action was ostensibly based on a US Section 301 complaint regarding Chinese technology investment partner demands that foreign investors share their intellectual property with them, in turn opening up the possibility that company secrets could be stolen. Normally, WTO rules would require such disputes to go to a formal dispute settlement arbitration. However, Chinese subsidy policies had evolved since its WTO accession in such a way they could often evade WTO rule "detection." The US delegation to the WTO maintained that at least part of its complaint was not specifically covered by WTO rules, giving the United States room to assert its own unilateral Section 301 action. This provision of US trade law empowered the US president "to obtain the removal of any act, policy, or practice of a foreign government that . . . is unjustified, unreasonable, or discriminatory." This open-ended provision of US trade law had been subject since 1998 to the constraint of a sort of WTO "gentleman's agreement" (WTO 1998) that the United States would not use it to evade WTO dispute settlement provisions. Trump nevertheless seized the opportunity to ignore the "gentlemen's agreement" and raise tariffs at his discretion against *any* Chinese imports that could fit his own variant of the Section 301 definition. In addition, the grievances that Trump demanded the Chinese address appeared to go beyond the intellectual property issue to include reducing the Chinese trade surplus with the United States, cutting production capacity in aluminum and steel, increasing the value of the Chinese currency in order to make Chinese goods less competitive, and forbidding China from pursuing policies to pursue technological superiority.

The underlying structure of Chinese state-trading practices often lacks transparency, making it difficult to monitor specific government actions systematically through a WTO dispute. It may be necessary to find new or untested methods to address them in the global trading system. But the dispute settlement issue is whether the eruption of a US-China trade war likely to solve the problem. Some trade law experts believe that WTO countries can bring WTO dispute cases against China for many of its recent government interventions in the market, including opaque measures that camouflage subsidies for state-owned enterprises, contribute to the theft of trade secrets, and force technology transfers by foreign investors (Bacchus et al. 2018, app. 2). According to this view, the United States gave up too easily on the WTO, or perhaps was eager to jettison the constraints and length of WTO rules-based review of its complaints.[8] A close reading of government transparency obligations for WTO members, the WTO intellectual property and subsidies agreements, and the China Accession Protocol, indicates that these issues may be actionable under existing provisions (Bacchus et al. 2018, app. 2).[9] In addition, even the absence of a specific rule violation allows WTO members to bring dispute cases against a country if its policies have "nullified or impaired" the complainant's trade benefits that derive from the responding country's WTO membership. While it is true that establishing proof of China's violations would be challenging, former appellate body (AB) jurist Hillman (2018) proposed a "big, bold WTO case" advanced jointly by the United States and a large group of WTO member countries. The formal dispute would tie China's specific accession commitments and WTO obligations with any

Chinese government actions that nullify and impair the trade benefits of other members, even if not specifically enumerated in WTO rules.[10] It is also noteworthy that the United States and other countries have been successful in the past winning dispute cases against Chinese violations of WTO rules, and China's record of compliance has been good.[11] It is therefore not impossible, as the United States has claimed, that WTO dispute settlement is incapable of resolving the China problem.

And so the United States abandoned WTO-based challenges in favor of a trade war. The unilateral US Section 301 action sparked a tit-for-tat escalation of tariff rates and coverage between the two countries that continued into 2020 (Bown and Kolb 2019 provide a timeline). Beginning in July 2018 several rounds of tariff escalation occurred, progressively increasing the volume of trade covered for each country, as well as the tariff levels imposed. The United States began with tariffs on Chinese capital goods and industrial input products, later expanding the scope of products to cover consumer goods, eventually including toys, footwear, and clothing. China's first set of tariffs targeted US agricultural products, expanding later to capital goods and automotive products. By September 2019 the average US tariff on all Chinese imports had risen from a starting WTO rate of 3.8% to 21.0%. China had raised tariffs on US imports from 8.0% to 21.0%, but had also lowered tariffs against other countries by 1.3%, increasing the margin of disadvantage for competing US exports. Planned tariff increases on remaining bilateral trade between the two countries would have raised the average tariff to about 26% for both countries against each other's imports, but the Phase One deal rolled tariff rates back to about 20% for US tariffs and 19% for Chinese tariffs in March 2020 (Bown 2019).

The US complaint about the lack of explicit WTO rules on certain Chinese trade practices has merit, but its response has undermined the entire GATT-WTO system, with no attempt to use WTO dispute settlement to achieve a meaningful resolution of systemic issues. The very purpose of the WTO, based on US leadership since 1947, had been to establish multilateral, mutually accepted rules that would promote stability and prosperity for all its members based on the gains from international trade. In the face of a challenge to deal with unanticipated disruptions from a new and growing trading power, the President Trump's reaction was to ignore the spirit and purpose of the institution, reject any multilateral channels of addressing the problem, and unilaterally assert his own aggressive economic nationalism. President Trump had threatened repeatedly to withdraw the United States from the organization since his inauguration (Woodward 2018), but he also seemed to have little in the way of a strategy to create new rules to discipline Chinese intervention in trade-related industries. His fury over China's trade practices has always been a mercantilist complaint about US trade deficits with China; he regards US payments for Chinese imports as foreign theft from the US economy. As long as Trump chose to focus on this issue, then Chinese reforms would not necessarily eliminate the US trade deficit with China, and even if they did, the overall US trade deficit would not improve as long as US net public and private investment exceeded savings. The trade war negotiations therefore centered on Chinese measures to purchase more US goods, open its financial markets to US banks, and manage its exchange rate to reduce its surplus with the United States. Trump favored achieving quantitative import commitments from China over the much more difficult task of forging new rules that would allow open trade to continue. Yet any improvement in the US trade deficit with China is likely to be offset by increased trade deficits with other countries, while the distortions of managed trade with China reduce the US gains from trade.

The Phase One Agreement: Further Damage to the Trading System

Meanwhile, it was not clear what Trump's end-game was. The original motive for the confrontation was China's "unreasonable" trade actions, based on US Section 301, but the negotiations revealed little in the way of systematically addressing these problems. Instead, the continued escalation of trade restrictions took on the character of a battle of wills, until Trump and Chinese Vice Premier Liu He agreed to a sort of truce, a Phase One agreement signed on January 15, 2020. It formalized some Chinese intellectual property commitments and market-opening measures for US financial service providers, most of which had already been implemented (Chorzempa 2020). The major feature of the agreement was a Chinese commitment to increase purchases of US exports during 2020 and 2021 by $200 billion over and above 2017 baseline levels (USTR 2020). The agreement thus appeared to be designed to address Trump's stated goal of reducing the US merchandise trade deficit, while mandating a generous increase in exports for beleaguered US farmers and for other US exporting firms:

> During the two-year period from January 1, 2020 through December 31, 2021, China shall ensure that purchases and imports into China from the United States of the manufactured goods, agricultural goods, energy products, and services

identified in Annex 6.1 exceed the corresponding 2017 baseline amount by no less
than $200 billion. (USTR 2020)

The agreement goes on to enumerate required minimum trade volume
amounts for calendar years 2020 and 2021, and required minimum Chinese
purchases of US exports of agricultural goods, energy products, and services
during these two years (USTR 2020). If these purchases were to take place
in a normal, market-based trading environment, they would presume the
existence of willing US sellers of $200 billion in exports of these goods and
services, in the prescribed categorical amounts, and willing Chinese import
buyers of this same amount and configuration of products. The problem is,
first of all, that the full prescribed and allocated amounts may not be available for US export, and Chinese import buyers may not want to purchase this
mix of US products. Furthermore, there may be other willing suppliers in
other countries besides the United States who would reasonably argue that the
agreement unfairly diverts exports, denying them market access to China. US
exporters may also prefer to sell their products to countries other than China.

The bilateral managed trade straightjacket is therefore economically non-
sensical, aside from being in clear violation of the WTO's most-favored nation
clause in GATT Article 1. It represents the sort of ignorance of country-to-
country trade transactions that a business executive would confuse with
company-to-company transactions. For example, a business may seek to
lock in an agreement with a downstream partner by concluding a contract
requiring the partner to purchase $200 million of its products over two years,
with specified amounts in certain categories. Such an agreement would be
subject to private commercial contractual enforcement. Yet what happens
when countries conclude such an agreement, which would presumably bind
the actions of perhaps hundreds or thousands of independent suppliers and
buyers who would otherwise be searching independently for the best deals in
a world market? Would a US supplier sell to China if a better price or deal were
available from a domestic or other foreign customer? The trade amounts in
the agreement are large, based on historical patterns, so US exports to China
may not be sufficient to fulfill the agreement. Would US trade officials have to
organize US export sales in order to fulfill the yearly quotas of sales to China?
This is the way communist countries managed centrally planned trade, or alternatively, the way export cartels would raise prices to all customers in the
United States, China and elsewhere. One might respond that the agreement
puts the burden on *China* to "ensure" imports from the United States of the
designated amounts; this provision would seem to require China to establish
centralized state-run purchasing cartels and pay whatever price is necessary

to make sure that China, and not other countries (or US consumers), buy the products. Ironically, this sort of implicit requirement would contradict the goal of correcting the sort of Chinese government behavior that ostensibly sparked the trade war in the first place: state practices through its control and oversight of companies that distorted trade. Instead of negotiating an agreement that would stem such practices, Trump insisted on guaranteeing a trade outcome diverting export business toward US farmers, manufacturers, and services suppliers, a political deal to pull Soviet-style trade levers in order to benefit favored constituencies.

In the context of US-China mandated bilateral trade requirements, the agreement's dispute settlement chapter offers the Trump administration's view of an alternative to WTO provisions, which remained in limbo in late 2020 as a result of the US blockage of appointments to the appellate body. Interestingly, the agreement mentions China's WTO obligations several times, including its reporting requirements for domestic industry support programs and agricultural trade restrictions, and its compliance with previous WTO dispute settlement judgments.[12] The agreement also confirms both parties' general WTO rights and obligations, including rights to initiate challenges under the WTO dispute understanding. The Trump administration, under US trade representative Robert Lighthizer, had therefore decided to hedge its approach to the WTO, reserving the option to respect WTO provisions if they served US trade interests while simultaneously bypassing or ignoring them when they did not. The agreement set up a bilateral dispute settlement protocol that kept the WTO out of the picture, except with regard to both parties' WTO rights and obligations that presumably were not in conflict with the US-China agreement (USTR 2020, ch. 7). However, there was no acknowledgment that the agreement itself might have violated both countries' WTO obligations regarding MFN treatment. The US-China agreement stipulated that any disputes stemming from its provisions would be subject to bilateral consultations, with the opposing parties alone left to interpret the meaning of many key provisions. In the absence of consensus on a resolution of the dispute, the complaining party, for example, could retaliate with measures "based on facts" and suspend agreement obligations or adopt "remedial measures" in a "proportionate way." If the other party considered that such actions were taken in good faith, it was not allowed to adopt a counterresponse. If the complained-against party considered the complaining party's action to be in bad faith, the remedy would be to withdraw from the agreement, presumably to resume the trade hostilities that the agreement had suspended (USTR 2020, ch. 7, art. 7.4.4b). One might have reasonably asked, in this context, at what point the response to a failure to meet the details of a managed trade agreement would stop reflecting good faith and start reflecting bad faith, what the facts were, and what a proportionate response was. There was of course no third-party appellate body in this agreement to lend any dispassionate legal reasoning to such matters. What the agreement did is leave the two largest trading countries in the world with a dangerously easy excuse to slip back into an unfettered trade war, which had paused with already high bilateral tariffs against each other. Furthermore, as a model of alternative, WTO-free international trade dispute settlement, what sort of outcome could be expected when a large country had a dispute with a small country?

Shutting Down the WTO Appellate Body

The WTO Appellate Body (AB), an instance of appeal to dispute settlement panel decisions, has increasingly sparked criticism among many WTO members because of its alleged tendency to go beyond the letter of WTO agreements in its decisions. For Donald Trump, the main problem with it was its ability to pass judgment on US compliance with WTO rules, which he rejected as a violation of US interests and sovereignty. His decision to cripple the AB also crippled the entire WTO dispute settlement system, enraging many WTO member trade officials, but also sparking proposals for reform.

The Dispute Over WTO Dispute Settlement

President Trump regarded WTO's dispute settlement system with special scorn. His public dissatisfaction centered on the fact that many judges overseeing dispute settlement cases involving the United States were non-US panelists and judges, often ruling against US trade enforcement interests, and therefore, in his view, unacceptable as arbiters of US trade policy disputes. He erroneously claimed that the United States loses most WTO cases that it faces, though in fact the United States has won 91% of dispute cases it files, and has a better than average success rate in defending its practices when challenged as a dispute respondent.[13] In addition, the United States, like all WTO members, benefits from the WTO dispute settlement framework, which results in out-of-court settlements between disputants in most of the cases. Trump's anger focused on the alleged lack of US representation on dispute panels and on adverse decisions by the AB, which acts as an appeals panel when one or both parties challenge the initial dispute panel decision. In protest against the WTO dispute settlement process, Trump ordered his WTO ambassador to veto approval of all new WTO AB court judges, a tactic made possible by the consensus system that requires the entire WTO membership to approve judge appointments. The approval of qualified judges had previously been a largely routine matter, but no longer. The resulting lack of judges significantly diminished the dispute settlement body's ability to review cases, and threatened to cripple the dispute settlement system altogether, as parties to any dispute would know in advance that they must submit to a panel decision without the opportunity to appeal.

It is important to note that the blocking of AB judge appointments had begun under the Obama administration in 2011, and continued with additional vetoes in 2014 and 2016 (Elsig, Pollack, and Shaffer 2017). The legal issues behind US discontent included procedural measures allegedly violating WTO dispute settlement rules and alleged overreach by AB decisions beyond their mandate. Specifically, the AB allegedly failed to respect national rules on technical issues in disputes involving US anti-dumping law that deny the validity of "zeroing," which allows US officials to calculate higher anti-dumping margins (see Payosova et al., 2018). Other countries were dissatisfied with the dispute settlement system as well because of its failure to address Chinese state interventions in the country's trade practices, an issue which led the United States to use of its own unilateral Section 301 rule, as described earlier. In general, the dispute settlement system was in need of updating in order to cover those unanticipated practices not specifically covered by current WTO rules. In the absence of clear guidelines from the text of WTO agreements in reviewing specific cases, dispute panels and the AB were sometimes left to interpret the rules more creatively, leading to charges of overreach beyond the intentions in the original text of WTO provisions (Payosova et al., 2018). In a consensus-based organization like the WTO, the rights and obligations of member countries need to be anchored securely in the legal texts in order to avoid conflicts over interpretation. The earlier GATT dispute settlement system, which predated the WTO, was in contrast more diplomatic in nature, relying on negotiations among contesting parties in order to reach a resolution. That system was successful when there was a smaller number of participating countries, with trade officials that had confidence that such diplomatic practices, rather than legal procedures, could legitimately protect their interests. The older GATT system eventually became less acceptable as trade cases became more complicated, which motivated Uruguay Round trade negotiators to propose dispute settlement reforms for the new WTO, launched in 1995. These reforms imposed a highly legalized process to replace the more informal GATT dispute settlement system. This significant change in the adjudication of disputes created the need for a more flexible process of renewing the rules, which is difficult when most decisions require consensus of the entire membership.

Reactions to the US Appointments Veto and Possible Solutions

Now the issue is one of achieving a more basic consensus on how, in principle, to solve the dispute settlement crisis. The earlier US blockages did not cripple the AB completely, and despite its continuing objections to AB practices, the Obama administration quietly allowed the reappointment of two vacant seats in the lame-duck period after the 2016 election, bringing the AB back to its normal complement of seven members for the time being (Elsig, Pollack, and Shaffer 2017). Subsequently, the Trump administration blocked any further appointments to the AB, which by December 2019 depleted it of a working complement of judges, threatening to paralyze the entire dispute settlement system. Petersmann (2019) regarded these US actions as patently illegal under WTO law, and claimed that Trump administration trade officials showed no interest in ending the crisis. He recommended that the other WTO members replace the consensus rule that gives the United States its veto power with emergency action under WTO Article 9, which would allow a majority of voting members to fill the AB positions (Petersmann 2019). This gambit, however, could lead to a complete US withdrawal from the WTO, not only based on Trump's repeated indication that he would welcome an excuse to do so, but also because many other US trade officials not associated with the Trump administration are also upset with the AB.[14] Other, less confrontational resolutions appear to be possible. Payosova, Hufbauer, and Schott (2018) propose a more diplomatic approach that involves completing updates in the dispute settlement rulebook, filling the necessary gaps in stated WTO rights and obligations, and instituting deliberative processes for resolving matters of legal uncertainty. They note that legalistic workarounds without US participation are politically dangerous, and would lead to an even greater systemic crisis if the United States withdrew from the organization. It was clear, however, that the Trump administration opposed the entire WTO dispute settlement process in principle, except in cases where the panel decision favored the United States. Trump declared, falsely, that the United States started winning WTO dispute settlement cases only after he became president, and he was willing to embrace the legitimacy of the 2020 WTO panel decision against the European Union on Airbus subsidies, for example. At the same time, Robert Lighthizer's strategy of working within the strict letter of WTO provisions on national security to extend US trade policy autonomy suggests that he would favor a return to the earlier GATT system of diplomacy to settle trade disputes. The underlying presumption of Lighthizer's solution is that the United States would then be in a position to bargain from a position of strength in most disputes, although Trump's record of trade war "diplomacy" with China offers little hope that such solutions would stabilize global trade relations.[15] The Trump administration was therefore never ready to bargain to end the dispute settlement crisis in a manner that would benefit the WTO and the interests of the global trading system in general. US repudiation of the primacy of WTO dispute settlement provisions overturned one of the key reasons the GATT-WTO system was established in 1947: to put an end to the unchecked escalation of self-destructive tariff wars that had contributed to the global economic crisis of the 1930s. Dispute settlement rules had put a lid on contentious trade issues, and the United States has benefitted from the system more than any other WTO member—until Trump's insistence on abandoning it.[16]

There has nonetheless been some evolution in Trump's view toward the existing trading system, under Robert Lighthizer's management. Compared to his initial outright condemnation of the WTO, Trump and his administration appeared subsequently to have pursued a more pragmatic relationship with the organization, without indicating a willingness to abandon their abuse of the rules. An interesting development regarding WTO rules occurred when Lighthizer negotiated an agreement with EU and Japanese trade officials in early 2020 to introduce new rules on trade-related subsidies, targeting the Chinese government's nontransparent support to its state-owned enterprises. The new rule would be enforced only as a WTO Annex 4 (plurilateral) agreement among individual countries willing to support the specific rule, and would apply to China only if it also joined the agreement (Brunsden 2020). This issue, one of the major points of contention between China and many of its trading partners, did not appear in the US-China Phase One agreement, suggesting that China balked at including any such provision in the bilateral deal. It is unlikely that a WTO plurilateral agreement will solve this problem on its own, but it is possible that Lighthizer's intention is to use it to pressure China into concessions on the issue in the future. The best solution would be an open challenge to China by these countries in a WTO dispute case, but that will not be possible unless the United States agrees to work with the European Union and Japan to resolve their differences on dispute settlement issues and allow a reinstatement of the appellate body. In the meantime the plurilateral agreement may give bargaining leverage to the European Union to bring the United States, Japan, and China to the bargaining table to resolve the underlying issues, introduce new subsidy rules through Chinese commitments that could be challenged in a WTO case, and restore the dispute settlement forum. European Union trade officials have indicated their desire to rejuvenate multilateral cooperation, and it will take a major diplomatic effort of this sort to put trade dispute resolution back in the WTO where it belongs (Brunsden 2020). The European Union led an effort by WTO countries, agreed in January 2020, to form a parallel appeals body for dispute cases, which would allow a review of WTO panel decisions for those countries in the agreement (Blenkinsop and Baker 2020). Participating countries, aside from the 27 EU member countries, included China, Australia, Brazil, Chile, Colombia, Costa Rica, Guatemala, South Korea, Mexico, New Zealand, Panama, Singapore, Switzerland, and Uruguay.

Unilateralism, Discrimination, and a New Type of Trade Relations

Other aspects of US trade policy under President Trump reflected a pattern of unilateralism, mercantilism, and his desire to subject all policy decisions to his personal, even micromanaged, control. His proposed (but never approved) Reciprocal Trade Act defied basic WTO principles, revealing his ultimate goal of direct presidential control of trade policy. His threat of unilateral discriminatory tariffs to force Mexico to change its immigration policy also, bore his personal stamp, extending the role of trade policy as a weapon in nontrade issues. In the case of the NAFTA renegotiation, despite the bluster of his campaign rhetoric, he found that there were limits to his ability to dictate legislative and negotiating outcomes in the face of political constraints.

The Proposed Reciprocal Trade Act

In late 2018 the Trump administration proposed trade legislation, the Reciprocal Trade Act (RTA), which would give the president additional powers to change tariffs unilaterally. While the proposed legislation received little support, even among Republicans, it provides insight into Trump's intentions of formally replacing multilateral trade institutions with unilateral measures and bilateral agreements, based on his notion of fair and reciprocal trade. Early in his administration, Trump promoted his idea of new, US bilateral trade agreements among Asian countries at the November 2017 Asia-Pacific Economic Cooperation (APEC) conference in Da Nang, Viet Nam

(Chandran 2017). The idea evidently frightened off most of the participants, as Trump's offer was for "fair and reciprocal trade" on US terms, which Trump insisted required trade balance between the partners. As of late 2020, no country had volunteered to enter such an agreement with the United States. Trade balances are the result of a country's own savings–investment gap, which is largely beyond the control of its trading partners, and Trump has shown his proclivity for imposing tariffs unilaterally as punishment for what he views as unfair trade surpluses. It is therefore not surprising that Trump found no takers on his offer. Perhaps disappointed in the refusal of countries to volunteer for such partnerships, the White House circulated a preliminary draft of proposed legislation in July 2018 designed to give the president the power to force all US trading partners, one by one, to submit to such bilateral relationships.[17] Trump appeared to expect the protectionist wing of the Democratic Party to embrace the bill, but by then Democratic opposition to Trump's presidency had hardened (Swan 2018).

Trump's version of the term "reciprocity" refers to the power of the president to raise any US tariff, item by item and country by country, that is less than its trading partner's tariff. Trump's own description of the bill is that it would allow the president to match tariff levels on particular products with individual countries when the foreign country's tariff is higher than the corresponding US tariff on the same good. This would force the foreign country to lower its tariff to the US level, or else face a new US tariff that matches the foreign country's higher level. Thus, Trump offers the example of India's whiskey tariff (150%), as opposed to the US whiskey tariff (0%). Under the RTA, India would need either to lower its whiskey tariff to 0%, or else face a US whiskey tariff (applicable to India alone) of 150% (White House 2019). Since it is unlikely that India would never succeed in selling its own whiskey to the United States in large quantities, it would probably accept the higher US tariff, and so this example is of little practical significance. There are in fact many cases in which foreign countries have high tariffs on their comparative disadvantage products compared to the United States, or for which the high tariffs are for social, public health, or revenue reasons. They have little incentive to change them.

However, there are practical concerns with implementing such a policy, even if it would theoretically force many, if not all, countries with higher tariffs on a product to lower them to the current, WTO-negotiated MFN US tariff level (known as schedule 1), especially for products where there is intra-industry trade with the United States. The RTA gives discretionary power to the president, so that he could choose to use this strategy only on products where the foreign tariff is higher, leaving the relatively higher US tariffs in place. While tariff levels currently differ between the United States and other countries on any given product, the overall average tariff levels are roughly the same for major US trading partners, such as the European Union, Canada, and Japan. Tariff "peaks" (spikes in tariff levels for certain products) and special protection exist for all countries in politically sensitive domestic markets (US sugar protection and the Jones Act, protecting intercoastal maritime transport, are two examples). It is unlikely that Trump's notion of reciprocity would lead to unilateral *reductions* in the level of protection enjoyed in these US markets, and in fact would be likely to raise the overall average US tariff as it matched any higher foreign tariffs. A second problem is the confusing use of the term "fair trade." As presented in the proposed RTA, this provision would seem to require balanced imports and exports at a minimum (a US trade surplus would evidently be acceptable). Trump therefore felt confident in declaring that the RTA would reduce or eliminate the US trade deficit. Yet as explained in chapter 3, it is clear from both economic theory and observation that changes in foreign and domestic tariffs do not tend to change a country's overall trade balance. The US trade balance worsened in 2018, for example, despite Trump's significant increase in tariffs on goods from China and on steel and aluminum, as well as other products. If the RTA were to be unsuccessful in reducing the US trade deficit, it is likely that Trump would double down on US tariff increases, whether or not the RTA allows such increases. It is also unclear what tariff benchmarks Trump would use to negotiate. If Trump were to withdraw from the WTO and revert to the higher US schedule 2 tariffs, for example, the baseline average US tariff level would jump from an unweighted average of 3.3% to 32.3% (Bown and Irwin 2018). Finally, the RTA, having abandoned the WTO most-favored nation (MFN) nondiscrimination principle, would transform US tariff schedules into an enormous— and probably very costly—matrix of potentially two million different bilateral tariffs, requiring extra labeling and customs monitoring of identical imports from different countries. In order to implement the RTA, the United States would have to negotiate with and keep track of all its trading partners on each and every traded good.

In short, the RTA illustrates a version of US trade policy as it might be without WTO rules and constraints (Bown and Irwin 2018). Its most prominent features would be the abandonment of WTO's MFN clause and its tariff-binding principle, which prohibits a WTO member from raising any given tariff above its negotiated maximum. In addition, reciprocity in Trump's view does not carry the same meaning as it does in the WTO, where trade negotiations typically proceed on the basis of reciprocally balanced "first difference" *tariff cuts* by most participants, with the goal of general global trade liberalization. In this approach tariff cuts are not expected to lead immediately to equal final tariffs for most products, and the tariff cuts themselves are not expected to be equal for a given product. Countries typically bargain over their general overall reduction in tariffs over time by an agreed-upon percentage formula, which in many cases is designed to cause the countries' overall tariff levels to converge after several years.[18] It is therefore possible to achieve universally low global tariffs across many sectors through WTO negotiations. The principle of WTO reciprocity in trade negotiations is to balance the relative increases in import market access allowed by each country and export market access gained by each country that the lower tariffs will produce. Product-by-product tariff levels may differ across countries, but the overall trade liberalization effect of the negotiations seeks to spread the gains among the participating countries. Countries will bargain hard for market access that is most important to them, in exchange for increased market access desired in the negotiations by other countries, often subject to the importing countries' political constraints. The logic of this approach rests on the concept of the gains from trade, from both imports and exports. The Trump administration has rejected this notion out of hand.

One other important political aspect of the RTA is that it would extend even greater trade policy power to the US president, giving him absolute discretion in the determination of tariffs. It is not clear what government agencies, currently subject to Congressional approval, would approve other negotiated aspects of trade policy, including international health and safety standards, international subsidy disciplines, and global intellectual property protection, since the presumption of the RTA is that the United States would effectively withdraw from the WTO. Trump could be expected to propose direct presidential control of these and other aspects of trade policy as well. Many Republican senators and congressmen, boxed in by political pressures to support Trump's protectionist impulses, seemed to draw the line at expanding his ability to seize even more trade policymaking authority from Congress.

NAFTA and the Limits of Populist Leverage

Given Trump's exuberant populist condemnation of the treaty during the campaign, NAFTA was an issue that many expected him to take a particularly hard line on as he entered the presidency. He had declared that he would either renegotiate it to his satisfaction or else eliminate it completely (Luhby 2016). In his detailed list of NAFTA negotiating points released in July 2017, however, it became clear that Trump had agreed to retain many elements of the original agreement (USTR 2017). The NAFTA, concluded in 1994, was ready for an update anyway, and the Trump plan included several issues put forward by the business community, including electronic commerce, transparency, updated regulatory measures, and compatibility with WTO standards in many areas. It even borrowed some ideas from the Trans-Pacific Partnership that Trump had so vehemently rejected, such as regulations regarding state-owned enterprise and currency manipulation, even though these issues did not apply especially to trade between the United States, Canada, and Mexico. The draft suggested that the US trade representative Robert Lighthizer had taken a pragmatic, incremental view toward the negotiations. It is likely that Trump's political advisors had informed him that many US states, especially in the Southwest and along the Midwestern and Northeast border with Canada, depended on NAFTA supply-chain and local market trade arrangements in their regional economies. The populist battle cry against NAFTA from the Trump administration became much more muted when it came to proposing realistic and politically acceptable changes to the agreement.

The first series of negotiations that began in 2017 ended in August 2018, and the three countries signed a renamed United States-Mexico-Canada Agreement (USMCA) on November 30, 2018. Some changes in the new agreement were not controversial, including updates on labor and environmental protection and the state-owned enterprise and digital trade provisions. It seemed that the main negotiating goal from Trump's perspective was to introduce protectionist measures for the US auto industry in order to declare a populist victory. These new measures increased the total North American content requirement from 62.5% to 75%, including a new North American steel content requirement of 70%. In addition, 40% of each auto's content would need to be made with labor paid $16 or more per hour, a rule designed to maintain more labor content in US auto production.[19] New content requirements and regulations would be enforced through the application to noncompliant autos and parts of the default 2.5% US import tariff.[20] Schott (2018) argues that the attractiveness to many auto producers of abandoning the new content requirements and paying the relatively modest 2.5% tariff increased the likelihood of 25% national security auto tariffs that Trump had threatened in 2018, in order to close this loophole. Canada and Mexico anticipated this contingency, and negotiated side letters exempting them from future auto tariffs in exchange for VER agreements on their auto shipments to the United States as long as they complied with the new content regulations. The other high-profile issue in the negotiations was Canadian restrictions on dairy imports, which Canada agreed to liberalize, allowing more imports from the United States. On balance, however, the new agreement was slightly more protectionist than its predecessor, implying moderately diminished trade, investment, efficiency, and net economic welfare for all three countries.

Yet Canada and Mexico, for their part, successfully bargained during the NAFTA negotiations for an end to the Trump steel and aluminum national security tariffs, in exchange for ending their own retaliatory tariffs against the United States. Canada also successfully resisted US pressure to end the NAFTA chapter 19 dispute settlement clause on trade law actions (involving such issues as Canadian softwood lumber countervailing duties, as mentioned earlier in this chapter 4), which Trump had targeted for elimination as an attack on US sovereignty.[21] Canada and Mexico also fought back a US demand for a five-year "sunset clause" on any new agreement, which would have allowed any partner to withdraw after five years. Such a "Sword of Damocles" provision would have severely diminished the attractiveness for long-term investment in cross-border business in the three countries. The final compromise was a 16-year sunset clause, with a possible extension after the first six years of the agreement. In summary, the USMCA negotiation reflected the problems Trump encountered in attempting to turn a complicated "establishment" commercial treaty into a populist symbol of his new trade policy. After 25 years of cross-border trade and investment relationships, a major unwinding or elimination of NAFTA would have resulted in widespread economic disruption for many parts of all three countries, generating a widespread political backlash that would have included Trump supporters. His negotiating strategy therefore had to lower its expectations and end by heralding the smaller changes as populist victories. The United States finally ratified the USMCA in early 2020, after the Democratic Party, which had regained control of the House of Representatives in 2018, raised objections to the agreement regarding labor rights, environmental protection and its enforcement, and patent protection for certain pharmaceutical products. Since Trump had lost political leverage in Congress, which had to approve any new trade agreement, his ability to threaten an end to NAFTA was diminished. Democrats succeeded in amending the labor rights provisions, winning support of US labor unions for the new agreement, and Trump acceded to the revised version of the USMCA.

Tariffs Threats as a Political Bargaining Chip

Throughout the spring of 2019 Trump demanded that Mexico impose new enforcement measures to prevent illegal migrants from crossing its border into the United States. On May 30, dissatisfied with Mexico's progress in reducing immigrant flows, he threatened to impose tariffs on all Mexican imports to the United States, starting at 5% on June 10 and rising by 5% each month thereafter, to a permanent level of 25%, until Mexico complied with his demand. Trump claimed that authority for this unilateral action came through the International Emergency Economic Powers Act of 1977, although the law had never authorized such action in the past, and White House lawyers privately expected the order to be subject to lengthy litigation (Savage 2019). Trump withdrew the threat the following week, after Mexico signed an agreement to implement specific steps to reduce illegal immigration, and the issue disappeared from public view as suddenly as it arose. Yet considerable damage had already been done, as Trump showed that he was willing to use threatened tariff restrictions in order to force US trading partners to submit to US policy demands, even on unrelated issues.

Summary

Table 5.1 highlights the president's specific trade policies with the largest impact on the WTO system. As noted in the institutional impact column, much of the damage to the trading system comes from exploiting the vague language of WTO rules, allowing the United States, for example, to exercise unprecedented discretion in its definition of national security. The United States justified its Section 232 (GATT Article 21) tariffs on steel and aluminum, for example, by introducing a new argument that declining employment levels in those industries represented a national security threat. The United States argued, in addition, that WTO members could not challenge a country's application of the national security exception, with the implication that a country can self-judge its own definition of national security for protectionist purposes. The Section 232 tariffs also resurrected the use of WTO-prohibited VER agreements as a protectionist tool, whose pernicious effects provide incentives for both importing and exporting countries to conclude costly and possibly anticompetitive trade restrictions. The only way to end VERs, so the Uruguay Round participants thought, was to have a consensus agreement foreswearing their use. Now that this pact has been broken, it may became difficult to put the VER genie back in the bottle.

The unilateral use of US section 301 retaliation against Chinese government trade practices presents another case of US exploitation of gray areas in the WTO rules. Chinese subsidies to state-run enterprises in particular had become difficult to document, since the benefits were hidden in nontransparent market interventions. As a result they proved difficult to prosecute under

Table 5.1 Erosion of Trade Institutions Under the Trump Administration

Date	US /GATT-WTO Trade Provisions	Application	Institutional Impact
April 2018	Section 232 (US Trade Expansion Act of 1962)/ GATT Article 21 (National Security)	Universal Steel (25%) and Aluminum (10%) Tariffs Also threatened: tariffs on auto trade	Ambiguous wording allowed US to introduce new criteria for potentially unlimited national security-based trade restrictions.
March 2018 (ongoing escalation)	US Section 301 (Trade Act of 1974) GATT art. 1.1 (MFN), II.1(a) and (b) (tariff binding); DSU art. 23 (primacy of WTO dispute settlement); DSU case DS 152	Unilateral retaliation against China trade practices; tit-for-tat retaliation and tariff escalation, continuing through late 2019	Lack of WTO rules coverage of Chinese practices triggered US refusal to honor previous gentleman's agreement restraining its use of Section 301; lack of DSU solution opens door to unilateral and unrestrained tariff retaliation (trade war). Could broader nullification argument have allowed a WTO solution?
2017–2020	WTO DSU (Annex 2), Art. 17.2. Appellate Body (AB) Appointments	US blocks AB judge appointments	US action progressively limits ability of AB to function and incentive for countries to file WTO disputes; AB quorum dissolves Dec. 11, 2019.
April 2018	WTO Agreement on Safeguards, Art. 11(b)	Voluntary Export Restraint (steel from Rep. Korea, Brazil, Argentina)	US negotiations with Korea, Argentina, and Brazil on steel quotas defy WTO ban on voluntary restraint agreements.
May 2019	US International Emergency Economic Powers Act (IEEPA) of 1977 [applicability disputed]	Threat of unilateral discriminatory tariffs against Mexico because of its immigration policy	WTO: Nullification and impairment of negotiated trade benefits; NAFTA/ USMCA violation; Pandora's box of unlimited protectionism for any reason.
January 2020	GATT Article I, WTO DSU	US-China Phase One Agreement: discriminatory Quantitative Import Requirements	Interim agreement requiring China to increase imports from US by $200 b over baseline amounts for 2020–2021, contravening MFN. Bilateral dispute settlement provision compounds trade war risk, impact on third countries.

WTO rules, which required overt proof of the source of the benefits in order to identify a violation. Faced with this difficulty, Trump and Lighthizer, declared that the harmful practice justified a reversion to the unilateral Section 301 solution, allowing the United States to take punitive action on its own. But what punitive action! The entire GATT-WTO system had been designed to prevent trade wars with unrestrained tariff escalations, and this is exactly what Trump initiated. Perhaps the biggest damage to the WTO in this instance, however, was the unwillingness of the United States to pursue any solution but a patently aggressive departure from the WTO principle of the peaceful resolutions of trade disputes.

A similar strategy of imposing an aggressive approach when alternatives could provide a peaceful solution was the US veto of all AB judge appointments to the point of crippling the entire dispute settlement system. Lighthizer's disdain for the WTO dispute settlement system is well known (Schlesinger 2019), and there is widespread acknowledgment that the original WTO rules are insufficient to resolve dispute cases without creative interventions by the AB. The choice in this case was whether to seek to change the system by tearing down the entire WTO Dispute Settlement Understanding and returning to Lighthizer's preferred GATT-era political process, favoring large countries, or to grasp the difficult nettle in a negotiation of new rules, interpretations, and policy space to provide a compromise solution. In the meantime, the major WTO pillar of dispute settlement was unable to function, and dispute settlement was in danger of reverting to the "law of the jungle," according to former US trade representative Carla Hills (Schlesinger 2019).

Finally, Trump inflicted additional damage to the trading system through use of unilateral tariff threats to force changes in Mexico's immigration policy, undermining the integrity of core WTO nondiscrimination and tariff binding principles, as well as US obligations under the USMCA. The fact that Trump did not carry through on these threats did not diminish the damage done to the system. Trump, the self-proclaimed "tariff man," asserted the right to raise them or threaten unilateral tariff increases in defiance of any international or bilateral agreement restraining him. Political constraints prevented him from applying this strategy in the case of the highly protectionist proposal of RTA tariff legislation, or his constant but ultimately empty threats of eliminating the NAFTA completely if Canada and Mexico did not submit to all his demands. The lesson for US trade policy, and for the benefit of the global trading system in general, is that legal, legislative, and political checks and balances need to be restored to US policymaking authority in order to maintain a stable, predictable, and principled environment for international commerce and commercial relations.

6
Brexit and the Crisis of European Integration

Introduction: The Roots of European Populism

European populism has been shaped by distinctive historical and social conditions, a small geographical space and diverse patterns of democratization. Conflict developed within countries based on religion and the legacy of feudal and aristocratic traditions. After centuries of European wars, efforts to reconcile national differences through economic integration culminated in the founding of the European Union, which ironically led to populist movements based on the perceived conflict between the people and the new elite.

Many Cultures and National Traditions in a Crowded Geography

European populism began to appear at approximately the same time as it did in the United States, but with a background of different historical traditions. The continent became a hotbed of populism as soon as democratic institutions developed to give voice to national identity (Eichengreen 2018, ch. 2). European politics continues to exemplify the competing human tendencies to barter and trade and to fear foreign incursion described in chapter 2. Crammed into a relatively small geographical space, Europe's 44 countries have experienced centuries of both cross-border commerce and cross-border conflict, accompanied by the cultural and economic benefits of interaction with neighbors, just as they have feared being overrun by foreign religions, cultures, populations, and irredentist neighbors. European countries live cheek-by-jowl with culturally and linguistically diverse neighbors, and diverse subgroups often live as minorities within countries' borders, often sharing cultural ties with adjacent countries. The close proximity of diverse nationalities and groups has led to the development of strong national identities, key to the formation of cultural populist movements. This chapter will show how populist parties won an increasing share of votes in national elections in the first part of the

Populism and Trade. Kent Jones, Oxford University Press. © Oxford University Press 2021.
DOI: 10.1093/oso/9780190086350.003.0006.

twenty-first century, at the expense of both center-right and center-left parties that had dominated European politics from 1945 to 2000. A combination of triggering events—the Eurozone and immigration crises—and a democratic deficit in European Union governance, led to the dramatic political shift. As a result, support for European economic and especially political integration has declined, with uncertain consequences for trade and trade policy in Europe.

A comprehensive review of the diversity of populist roots and traditions found across Europe goes beyond the scope of this study. Stanley (2017) and Taggart (2017) provide overviews of Central/East European and West European populism, respectively. The Swedish think tank Timbro monitors current trends in European populism and gathers detailed data on national and European Parliament election results.[1] The twenty-first century surge in right-wing populism in much of Europe has roots in nationalisms based on blood-identity and contested territory that had erupted in the early twentieth century, and lurked not far below the surface even after World War II. In Western Europe right-wing populism surged, while left-wing populism, which had been a stronger political force in the late twentieth century, declined in relative importance.[2] In the former communist states of Eastern Europe democracy began only in the early 1990s, after years of Soviet domination, and the resulting institutions often had shallow roots. This area of Europe—Hungary, Poland, the Czech Republic, and Slovakia—is where strong nationalist leaders were most successful in breaking through to install populist regimes, including Victor Orbán, Jarosław Kaczyński, Andrej Babiš, and Robert Fico. In contrast, southern European countries such as Spain, Portugal, and Greece emerged in the late twentieth century from authoritarian military dictatorships, which fostered left-wing populist parties, although right-wing populism also took root there. Italy, with its long postwar record of unstable and short-lived coalition governments, proved to be fertile ground for both right- and left-wing populist parties. Populism in the United Kingdom grew out of the country's identity as an island nation apart from Europe, increasingly resentful of EU decision-making in Brussels. Despite the diversity of the origins of populism in many of the EU member countries, events and trends converged to foster a broad-based challenge to the European Union's project to advance economic, regulatory, and political integration.

The Historical Context of Conflict Between the Elite and the People

More than most other parts of the world, Europe had an historical tradition of confrontation between the elite and the people, based on the development of democratic institutions alongside feudal and aristocratic legacies and growing nationalist movements. The era of nationalism began with the French Revolution in the late eighteenth century, and spread to many other European countries in the first half of the nineteenth century. Combined with the new democratic ethos of the Enlightenment, nationalism emphasized cultural attributes of national populations, while frictions created by existing social divides and aristocratic control persisted. Direct aristocratic government control finally ended in the wake of the World War I, leading to a tumultuous and ultimately catastrophic transitional period of populism and fascism that led to the World War II. The visionary efforts to create an integrated pan-European economy after World War II also had deep historical roots from the Middle Ages, based on merchant shipping, led by the Hanseatic League cities and finance centers in Venice, Antwerp, and other trading hubs supported by long-distance trade. The continent of Europe was remarkably integrated commercially as early as the fourteenth century, with large organized city markets and annual trade fairs connected by land routes and sea and river navigation that facilitated trade.

A politically unified Europe, on the other hand, is at best a distant historical memory, coming closest during the centuries of the Holy Roman Empire, when Catholicism ruled much (but certainly not all) of the continent and its feudal society. Even then unity was defined in part by a common external Islamic enemy, leading to a series of holy wars, the crusades, from the eleventh to the thirteenth centuries, to defend the ancient Holy Land. These became part of Europe's foundational religious narrative: the crusade against its Mohammedan "occupiers." This conflict of civilizations was to return later, as the Ottoman Empire staged a series of European invasions from the fourteenth to the end of the seventeenth centuries, highlighted by a European coalition's defeat of Kara Mustafa at the gates of Vienna in 1683, a key event of European history still emphasized in school classrooms.[3] The legacy of this conflict erupted in a different form more than three centuries later, as Islamic terrorist attacks on European soil and large numbers of refugees from Islamic countries helped spark the recent wave of anti-immigrant populism in many European countries.

Evolution of the European Union

European integration emerged in the period after World War II as a response to the previous 75 years of major wars in Europe, especially those featuring the two largest continental powers, Germany and France. Visionary leaders such as Jean Monnet led the efforts to forge closer economic ties between these two countries, in particular, as a way of increasing their interdependence, bringing their populations closer together, and reducing the motivation to wage war. The postwar period of the second half of the twentieth century established generally stronger democratic traditions in Western Europe, while the Cold War kept Eastern Europe under Soviet control until 1990. Yet efforts to create supranational institutions among West European countries, culminating in the European Union, cultivated technocratic, cosmopolitan traditions in popularly elected governments and in business that would later be viewed as part of a ruling pan-European elite, and the object of populist scorn. This became the modern version of older pan-European connections of religion and aristocratic bloodlines among the ruling classes. Elitist European traditions, in other words, continued and evolved from the Middle Ages to the present day. The European Common Market began as the 1957 Treaty of Rome among six countries, establishing the beginnings of a customs union, followed by growing dimensions of economic, regulatory, and legal integration. Membership grew as well, reaching 28 countries by 2013—the United Kingdom would then officially exit in 2020—but with more countries in line to accede. A cooperative monetary agreement was established in 1979 among a subset of the European Union, culminating in the launch of a monetary union with a single currency, the euro, in 1999. A major issue that lurked just beneath the surface of the growing integration among the EU members was democratic governance. Initially, the terms of the Treaty of Paris focused on establishing a customs union, but subsequently expanded to include legal and regulatory integration, with a decision-making structure concentrated in the European Commission, the executive branch of the European Union, and the European Council, representing the executive governments of EU states. The European Parliament, a democratically elected legislative body, was launched in 1979, but the European Commission retained the power of initiating legislation. Centralized control of most regulatory issues in Brussels, with qualified majority voting among high-level officials in the intergovernmental Council, left less direct democratic power in the European Parliament than most national parliaments would have, although the Parliament did have to approve the legislative proposals of the European Commission. Still, between the European Council and the European Commission, major policy initiatives and decisions took place in institutions that were removed from popular representation. The resulting democratic deficit played a key role in sparking EU populist movements in the early twenty-first century.

Brexit

Even though trade was not the major issue on the platform of the populist Brexit referendum, it became a major issue in the aftermath of the resulting UK departure from the European Union. The troubled history of its membership in the organization stood in contrast to the economic gains it achieved as part of the EU customs union and single market. These contradictory factors shaped the divisive Brexit campaign, and initially left the UK government without a plan for negotiating an orderly withdrawal from its EU trade arrangements. Questions over trade between Northern Ireland and the Republic of Ireland also complicated these negotiations. The Brexit referendum provides a cautionary tale of how populist movements can bypass deliberative democratic channels of decision making.

Trade as Collateral Damage from the Crisis

During the surge in populism from 2010 to 2020, the most prominent blow to the trading system next to Trump's protectionist assault on the WTO was Brexit, the electoral decision through a popular referendum for the United Kingdom to give up its membership in the European Union. Trade did not play the central role in Brexit that it did in Trump's 2016 election, and the Brexit platform was not overtly protectionist. Instead, the anger of Brexit supporters focused on the European Union's hegemony over its members' policies in general, which incidentally included trade policy, setting up trade as a major source of collateral damage. Many Brexiteers in fact professed strong preferences for open trade; their complaint was that EU headquarters in Brussels compromised British sovereignty by centralizing all trade policy negotiations and decisions. The Brexit slogan was "we want our sovereignty back," including the ability to maintain external trade relations independent of control from Brussels. In order to regain control over its trade policy—and also control over immigration policy and fishing rights in its territorial waters, more important Brexit campaign issues—the United Kingdom therefore had to give up the right to EU single market. At stake was full access of its goods and services exports to EU markets, extensive cross-border investments governed by EU rules, common EU regulatory standards for its production supply chains, and the free movement of its citizens in the EU. The UK insistence on regaining its sovereignty on economic issues thus clashed with the requirement that it give up the significant economic benefits of EU membership, with uncertain prospects of bargaining its way back into a favorable trade agreement with the European Union as an outsider.

The United Kingdom had always been a reluctant member of the European Union, having joined in 1973, 16 years after the Treaty of Rome. In the early discussions of a European Common Market after World War II, Winston Churchill had endorsed the idea, but declared that the United Kingdom would remain outside it, as it still carried the global banner of the British Empire and Commonwealth. Britain regarded its foreign and economic interests, in other words, as separate from those of the Europeans. As economic integration progressed in the newly launched European Common Market, the United Kingdom continued to remain outside it, deciding instead to maintain greater trade policy independence by joining the regional European Free Trade Association (EFTA) in 1960.[4] EFTA members agreed to mutual duty-free trade among themselves, but allowed each member to have independent trade policies regarding third countries, unlike the common external tariff and trade policy of the Common Market. Following World War II, however, the postcolonial British empire shrank dramatically, and postwar growth favored European countries in the Common Market, especially Germany, which was booming. The United Kingdom reconsidered its decision to remain aloof from European integration and eventually joined the Common Market in 1973 (Berend 2019, pp. 52–53).[5]

In the following years the United Kingdom benefitted economically from the progressive integration of European markets, through trade, finance, and investment. Campos et al. (2014) estimate that the United Kingdom's economic growth rate from 1973 to 2013 was 23% higher than it would otherwise have been as a result of EU membership. The economic gains have come through the expansion of UK markets into the European Union, the allocative efficiencies of specialization, the additional efficiencies (including productivity) due to competition and the harmonization of regulations (Giles 2017). The United Kingdom, however, valued its membership in the European Union primarily because of market access and economic integration, rather than as a project for European-wide political and legal governance. Some distinctive frictions between the United Kingdom and Brussels arose due to increasing intrusion of "ever closer union" on UK sovereignty. The United Kingdom opted out of the EU requirement of joining the single currency, and out of the Schengen Agreement, which eliminated border controls within the European Union for participating countries.[6] In 1984 Prime Minister Margaret Thatcher confronted the European Council over the size of the UK contribution to the budget, eventually negotiating a rebate, lowering its contribution. In general, the history of UK Euroskepticism—public and government opposition by a member country to EU rules and directives from Brussels—goes back to the time it joined. Among all EU countries, polling consistently showed that UK approval of the European Union among member state populations was among the lowest. UK residents also ranked lowest in identifying as Europeans, and regarded national sovereignty as more important than any other member country (European Commission 2011).[7]

Prelude to the Referendum

Euroskepticism continued throughout the years of UK membership in the European Union, but economic growth and the gains from market integration throughout the 1990s dampened calls for withdrawal. As was the case in the United States, the fair winds of prosperity tended to suppress populist sentiment. However, a subsequent combination of increased immigration, the global financial crisis, a worsening globalization adjustment crisis in industrial districts, and a remarkable political blunder by Tory Prime Minister David Cameron brought the United Kingdom's fraught relationship with Brussels to a head. The new European immigration problem of the twenty-first century, which was later to disrupt politics in all of Europe, began with the enlargement of the European Union in 2004, admitting several new East European countries as members.[8] The European Union's four freedoms included the free movement of people between the member countries, and many workers in Eastern Europe took advantage of the opportunity to seek jobs in the United Kingdom. From 1995 to 2015 the number of EU immigrants living in the United Kingdom tripled, from 900,000 to 3.3 million, with 29% of the total coming from Poland. The share of EU nationals in the UK population grew from 1.5% to 6.3% during this period (Wadsworth et al. 2016). The large influx of immigrants in some regions of the United Kingdom raised concerns among native-born UK residents about possible wage suppression, job losses, and draining of public services funding to support the new residents. Yet EU nationals migrating to the United Kingdom tended on average to be younger, better educated, and more likely to be working than UK workers, with no detrimental effects on wages and with positive fiscal contributions to tax revenues net of public services. Ironically, the aging British work force was in need of immigrant labor to maintain gross domestic product (GDP) growth and tax contributions for social spending. Negative perceptions of immigrants in some areas may have been linked with the recession and housing crisis induced by the global financial crisis, which occurred during this period (Berend 2019, pp. 7–9). Backlashes against trade and job losses in industrial Rust Belt areas also occurred at this time and contributed to the discontent (Faulconbridge 2018). The growing immigrant presence in many neighborhoods thus corresponded with broader economic and social change that was disrupting the settled cultural and demographic profile of native residents' communities.

These economic and social grievances festered until the run-up to the Brexit vote in June 2016. Dissatisfaction with the European Union had increased within the Conservative Party, and Prime Minister David Cameron's spectacular political blunder was to commit in 2013 to a nation-wide up-or-down referendum vote on remaining in the European Union, which would become part of his party's 2015 election platform. He believed at the time that such a vote would surely result in a victory for remaining in the European Union, silencing the Euroskeptics in his party, and he felt confident at the time that the more prudent approach of subjecting the issue to Parliamentary debate and vote was unnecessary. The referendum, however, played straight into the populist playbook: a direct popular vote on an issue that could be simplified, infused with emotion, and transformed into a one-size-fits-all expression of discontent over a wide array of issues. Brexit champions included Boris Johnson, a Euroskeptic Conservative Party member, and Nigel Farage, leader of the small but influential anti-EU party, UKIP. They provided the divisive and angry rhetoric— appeals to Britain's historical independence, glory, and honor—and often exaggerated claims of EU bureaucratic misdeeds. The "leave" side focused on the most explosive populist issues: EU immigration rules forced down Britain's throat, its denial of national sovereignty, and its exploitative and wasteful budget demands. Remain supporters tried to argue economics, ultimately to no avail. What of a leave-induced decline in the value of the British pound? The Brexit answer: it will be good for exports. What of the UK supply chain links to EU members? The Brexit answer: the European Union needs British factories and will not dare cut them off. How about the European Union's wide network of trade agreements that Britain will give up? The Brexit answer: the United Kingdom can do better negotiating trade agreements on its own. And finally, what of estimates by all major economic studies that Brexit will cause the UK economy to decline by 2% to 10%? Brexit answer #1: "people in this country have had enough of experts."[9] Brexit answer #2: we don't care; sacrificing a few percentage points of GDP is worth having our sovereignty back.

The Brexit Vote

The surprising results of the Brexit vote—52% leave, 48% remain—defied the predictions of most business and economics commentators, who had concluded that the heavy economic cost of leaving the European Union would surely result in a majority in favor of remain. However, British populism did not follow the logic of economic welfare analysis, as the traditional rational voting model would suggest. Becker et al. (2017) concluded that the voter demographic and profile information explains the results. Leave voters tended to be older, have lower education and lower income, greater dependence on manufacturing employment, and higher rates of unemployment. This profile corresponds to features of populist voters in other countries, especially in support of cultural/right-wing platforms. The authors apply their methodology to election results in the 2017 elections in France and found that right-wing populist leader Marine Le Pen's supporters had similar profiles. In their study, based on district results, the authors curiously find no connection with voter exposure to immigration or trade. They also conclude, however, that the demographic attributes of leave voters reflect their greater difficulty in adjusting to socioeconomic change. Colantone and Stanig (2018), in contrast, conclude that support for leave was in fact higher in districts harder hit by globalization, including trade disruption and immigration from EU accession countries. Their methodology used an instrumental variable approach to establish this causation, with individual voting decisions being determined by "sociotropic" considerations—that is, the voter's reaction to the overall economic situation in his or her district, rather than to their own personal situation, a "resonance" effect that also received empirical support in the 2016 US presidential election results.

Despite their apparently conflicting explanations, these two contrasting studies may identify different dimensions of the same populist impulses. For example, older and less educated voters may also be those who consider their district's overall economic fortunes when voting on changes to the status quo. These same voters may also regard trade-based deindustrialization and the large influx of EU immigrants (who dominated the immigrant surge in the years before the Brexit vote) as disruptive to the district's traditional identity, even if their own jobs were not directly threatened by these factors. Such an interpretation is consistent with what several studies concluded about populist support for Donald Trump in the US presidential election five months later, in which it was difficult to identify direct trade and immigration impacts on the voter as an individual in choosing Trump. The hypothesis about populist voting behavior is that trade and other economic factors in the voter's environment *mediate* concerns about cultural issues perceived to damage the community's identity and status. It is not so much that globalization has cost the voter his or her job, and therefore motivates a vote for the populist cause; it is the impact of globalization (and other factors) on the status of the voter's community, and perhaps on anticipated future economic disruptions for the voter, that motivates a populist voting preference.

Early Aftermath and Estimated Economic Cost

As of early 2020 the aftermath of Brexit has been, if anything, more traumatic than the earlier Brexit campaign itself. While the United Kingdom officially ended its membership in the EU in early 2020, the terms of the UK divorce from the EU single market were still unclear, as the UK Parliament could not agree on a unified negotiating plan. The extreme divisiveness of the Brexit issue in the United Kingdom points to one of the major costs of populism: its tendency to bring national legislative action to a screeching halt. The binary nature of the voting framework for Brexit—either remain or leave—meant that a leave vote left the government with no clear idea of *how* to leave, and what type of relationship the United Kingdom would have with the European Union as a result. Estimating the cost of Brexit has been correspondingly difficult, as noted shortly after the referendum by editors of the *Oxford Review of Economic Policy* (2017). Unlike discrete changes in tariffs, quotas, or single policy measures, Brexit represents a structural break that spans several different areas, including the replacement of an integrated economic system with the entire suite of trade restrictions, changes in the entire structure of investment and regulatory measures, migration, macroeconomic policies and impacts, financial services, agriculture, competition policy, and regional aid. Changes in climate change and industrial policy, market structure, research and development, and productivity need to be considered, along with incentives for future investments and policies. Compounding the problem from the perspective of 2020 was the fact that the final terms of Brexit were still unknown, despite Boris Johnson's Parliamentary victory in December 2019. The uncertainty of future policies therefore had real effects on its costs, especially in terms of the suppression of or delay in investment decisions. Possible scenarios ranged from an "ultra-soft" Brexit (free trade in goods and services, along with an investment-friendly agreement with the EU replicating all supply-chain advantages) to an "ultra-hard" Brexit (a full pull-out with no special trade and investment relations, and reversion to WTO tariffs).[10]

Even so, it was difficult to compose scenarios where the economic welfare cost of Brexit was insignificant. Many Brexiteers appear to have made rosy assumptions, severely discounting the costs of reconstructing UK trade relations, expecting large gains from the elimination of EU regulations, and counting on EU efforts to minimize the negative impacts on the United

Kingdom as the means for minimizing the European Union's Brexit costs. While it is clear that both the EU countries and the United Kingdom stand to lose from Brexit, in every realistic scenario the United Kingdom will lose more (Latore et al. 2019). In addition, several EU countries may insist that the terms of Brexit contain punitive elements, as a way of deterring other countries from following the same path. Furthermore, eliminating EU regulations will not significantly reduce UK production costs, despite widespread UK perceptions to the contrary (Latore et al. 2019). Regarding the reconstruction of EU third-country trade agreements, the United Kingdom faces two major problems. First, it is highly unlikely that the United Kingdom will, acting independently, be able to replicate the terms of most of the 41 existing EU external trade agreements, covering 72 countries. The EU had a total 2019 GDP of approximately €14 trillion and a population of 448 million (without the United Kingdom), while UK GDP was €2.5 trillion, with a population of 67 million. The UK economy is thus less than one-fifth the size of post-Brexit EU GDP, with less than one-sixth of EU population.[11] The EU has been able to negotiate more favorable trade deals for its members, based on its huge internal consumer market and the magnitude and attractiveness of its economy and investment opportunities. The United Kingdom sacrificed the advantages of this trade-bargaining leverage in exchange for Brexit. The second, related point is that the United Kingdom has not had a ministry dedicated to trade policy and trade negotiating since it joined the Common Market in 1973, when these functions were centralized in Brussels. It will have to build up this capacity in the coming years, which will delay the implementation of any new trade deals. In this regard, Brexit will carry a high negotiating transactions cost, with final trade results sure to be inferior to what they replace. As the United Kingdom's weaker bargaining position in retaining existing EU external trade agreements has become more apparent, the Conservative government's attention has switched to achieving new trade deals, especially with the United States. Prime Minister Boris Johnson has suggested that President Trump, a like-minded populist, would be open to such a trade deal. However, the prospects of a significant US-UK trade agreement were dubious. Despite the fact that large new post-Brexit trade expansion opportunities exist, the United States is likely to drive a hard bargain, as it tends to do in any bilateral trade negotiations, including any that take place in subsequent US administrations beginning in 2021. In addition, Boris Johnson's intention of negotiating continuing market access and standards harmonization with the European Union may compromise US trade opportunities with the United Kingdom, based in part on agricultural and food standard differences between the United States and the European Union (McGee 2019). Britain's task of jump-starting new bilateral or regional trade relations with third countries may also be made more difficult by a WTO system weakened by the lasting effects of Trump's policies.

It is therefore unlikely that new trade deals will be able to compensate Britain for lost trade due to Brexit. Heise and Boata (2019) estimate post-Brexit effects through 2018. Already, total UK merger and acquisition deals had declined by 60%, driven largely by a drop in cross-border deals. The prospect of supply-chain disruptions has increased UK business insolvencies. UK exports in Euro terms fell by 6% from 2016 to 2017, and UK consumers suffered losses in real purchasing power through higher import prices and a depreciation of the pound. As for the European Union, its exports to the United Kingdom had fallen by €60 billion in the 18 months since the Brexit vote, with Germany bearing the brunt of the decline. A hard Brexit, in particular, would compound these losses, and a reversion to WTO tariffs would result in an average of 5% tariffs applied by both sides, along with the cost and inconvenience of customs checks and processing. Latore et al. (2019) evaluate several different Brexit impact studies, based on 12 simulation models that estimate GDP changes due to Brexit as they would occur in future years ranging from 2020 to 2030. A soft Brexit scenario in these studies assumes a Norway-like arrangement, while a hard Brexit assume a full UK exit and reversion to WTO rules.[12] The various studies show reductions in British GDP ranging from -0.5% to -3.6% for soft Brexit and -1.15% to -7.5% for hard Brexit in most studies.[13] Studies estimating greater losses tend to include foreign direct investment effects of Brexit, a major consideration in the impact on supply chains. The EU countries would also lose, although by much less: from -0.07% to -0.24% for soft Brexit and -0.14% to -0.65% for hard Brexit. The studies attribute the lower impact of Brexit on the European Union to its relatively greater ability to re-source UK-based supply chains and export customers inside the European Union and among third countries. Latore and her coauthors conclude that the difficulty of pinning down more reliable Brexit impact estimates reflects the fact that the British government had no prior contingency plan for a for a leave scenario:

> What is clear is that the terms of the final agreement will be crucial to assess its economic damage. In this sense, the British referendum should have been preceded by a discussion of what economic UK–EU relationship would be adopted in the case of Brexit. Some politicians probably thought that the vote would not lead to Brexit, but it did, and now there is no good Brexit. (Latore et al. 2019, p. 15)

Northern Ireland and Scotland

There are two other notable trade impacts of Brexit. The most immediate issue was the question of free trade between the British region of Northern Ireland and the Irish Republic, which proved to be one of the most difficult issues to resolve in Brexit negotiations. The Good Friday agreement of 1998 had established freedom of trade between the two areas as part of comprehensive peace plan to end the troubles in Northern Ireland that had raged for decades.[14] Since both the Republic of Ireland and the United Kingdom were part of the European Union at the time, there was no conflict between the two countries' EU trade commitments and an opening of the Northern Ireland/Irish Republic border to free trade and dismantlement of military checkpoints. After the Brexit vote, both the European Union and the United Kingdom supported the continuation of the open border, but the European Union insisted that any open trade relationship between the United Kingdom and EU after Brexit would require an Irish "backstop" that would allow trade to pass freely between Northern Ireland and the Republic of Ireland as a continuation of the Good Friday Agreement that had ended sectarian hostilities in 1998. Such an arrangement implied the necessity of either a continued customs union arrangement between post-Brexit UK and the European Union, or between Northern Ireland and the European Union. Hard-line Brexiteers, on the other hand, demanded at a minimum an end to participation by the United Kingdom, including Northern Ireland, in the EU customs union. This arrangement would require some sort of customs controls between the United Kingdom and Irish Republic. In late 2019 Prime Minister Boris Johnson negotiated an Irish Protocol with the European Union that would regulate the passage of goods between Northern Ireland and the rest of the United Kingdom with green (free trade) and red (tariff) channels for trade, depending on their type and destination, to prevent smuggling between the United Kingdom and EU through Northern Ireland. Thus the United Kingdom as a whole would have its own customs area, external tariffs, and trade policy, maintaining a UK-EU free-trade (not customs union) agreement while still maintaining an open Northern Ireland/Irish Republic trading border (Foster 2019). The Democratic Unionist Party (DUP) of Northern Ireland, which continued to insist on full integration with the rest of the United Kingdom, opposed some elements of the plan, since it formalized a role for the European Union that it regards as a threat to Northern Ireland's links to the rest of the United Kingdom. Irish nationalists in Northern Ireland, for their part, opposed a diminution of trade links with the Irish Republic, which could be the result if the Irish Protocol involved cumbersome measures to regulate trade. The Irish

Protocol trade plan appeared in any event to be complicated to implement, requiring all parties to agree to administrative details yet to be announced. The uncertainty of how the arrangement will unfold, disturbing the status quo of more than 20 years, risked upsetting the fragile peace that had stabilized the region. In addition, Northern Ireland voted in the Brexit referendum with a 56% majority in favor of remain, preferring continued EU membership alongside Ireland. It is also noteworthy that for the first time, Irish Nationalists won more seats than Unionists in the December 2019 British Parliamentary elections, raising the possibility of renewed calls for Irish reunification. Dissatisfaction with British management of the Irish protocol could thus lead not only to administrative barriers to trade, but also to renewed sectarian conflict.

The other issue was Scotland's desire to remain in the European Union and the desire of many there as well for independence from Britain. Scotland had voted with an even larger majority than Northern Ireland in favor of remain (62%) in the Brexit referendum; earlier, in 2014, Scotland held a referendum on independence from the United Kingdom. A majority voted at that time to remain in the United Kingdom, partly because of the argument that an independent Scotland would have a difficult time negotiating its way back into the European Union. The Brexit vote changed that calculus, and in the December 2019 UK Parliamentary vote, the Scottish Nationalist Party (SNP) won most of Scotland's seats in that body. Scotland's First Minister Nicola Sturgeon announced immediately that Scotland would again seek to hold a referendum on independence. The British Parliament, now under the firm control of Boris Johnson, would have to approve a new independence referendum, however, and Johnson declared his opposition to it. The prospects for such a referendum were likely to depend on Johnson's handling of UK-EU market access negotiations and his ability to dampen Scottish fervor for independence. The Scottish Parliamentary elections, scheduled for 2021, would also probably reveal the degree of support for another referendum (Farquharson 2019).

Taking Stock of Brexit's Populist Impact

Late in December 2020, UK-EU negotiations finally led to a long-awaited agreement on Britain's exit from the trade-related aspects of its EU membership. The new arrangement called for the United Kingdom to exit from the EU customs union and single market, while retaining reciprocal duty-free and quota-free access to EU goods markets. The Good Friday accord was preserved, along with the earlier Irish protocol agreement. Sensitive issues regarding EU-UK divergences in environmental standards, labor law, and state aid would be monitored and subject to arbitration or legal challenges. Fishing rights in UK waters would be regulated and subject to further negotiation. UK auto exports to the EU would face tariffs based on non-EU production content limits, but would otherwise have preferential market access. Despite the free-trade arrangement, there would be new customs checks as well as certification and testing requirements on traded goods, with more restricted road haulage, introducing red tape into commercial and especially cross-border supply chain transaction cost. Professional travel and working relationships across borders would become subject to more restrictions and regulation. Financial services were not included in the deal, as they were made subject to separate negotiations in the future. All in all, UK businesses viewed the new agreement as superior to a "no deal," but anticipated significant adjustment costs and increased day-to-day costs of doing business with the EU. Final ratification of the agreement by both sides was expected in early 2021 (*Financial Times* 2020).

While not fulfilling the worst-case scenario, the new UK-EU relationship had the unusual character of a trade agreement that increased barriers rather than removed them. The principle benefit may be to prevent the flight of foreign direct investment from Britain, although the additional red tape cost alone will decrease its advantage compared to other countries. The door also appears to be open to future UK-EU agreements on harmonization and liberalization. In the meantime, the Brexit fiasco illustrates the damage that populism can do to trade relations, even when the main concern that motivated the referendum was not trade. The populist Brexit campaign and its aftermath exposed fault lines within the United Kingdom regarding Scottish and Northern Irish tensions over nationalism, which UK membership in the European Union had reduced. Britain's assertion of sovereignty through Brexit resurrected similar demands for sovereignty in these areas through Scottish national independence and Irish reunification. For Britain itself, its main interest in the European Union had always resided in access to its trade and investment opportunities, and it would have been far superior, even from a Euroskeptic perspective, to put British opposition to EU budgetary, legal, regulatory, and even immigration governance on a separate track. Margaret Thatcher, despite her confrontational relationship with the European Community, stopped short of British withdrawal from it over the 1984 budget controversy, negotiating a reduced UK contribution instead. By turning British concerns on specific aspects of EU policies and UK obligations into popular vote on the entire question of UK membership, unmediated by any broader and systematic political deliberation, the result was to throw out the gains-from-trade baby with the democratic deficit bathwater. Populist passions escalated the rhetoric into an apocalyptic confrontation over national sovereignty, with exaggerated claims of British victimhood. The result was divisive and toxic outrage, splitting the population into unyielding partisan camps. The preferred outcome for Britain in addressing its EU concerns would probably have been an arrangement along the lines of the Norway's association model with the European Union, which would have been easier to negotiate from within the European Union than outside it, when the British starting point in the negotiations as a self-exiled outsider became weaker. A more careful consideration of the various problems could have confronted the central immigration issue with an open Parliamentary discussion and public debate. This particular function of a democratic government could then have defused the overheated populist anger over the issue and led to a better immigration policy that would be best for the United Kingdom. Compromises between member states and Brussels over inner EU migration had occurred before, and would have been possible for the United Kingdom as well. In the meantime, a proper political debate would have corrected the largely uninformed campaign arguments over the EU budget costs and benefits.

Populism and Trade in the Rest of the European Union

The Brexit genie is out of the bottle, and the damage will remain unless and until the United Kingdom manages to negotiate renewed integration with the EU. In the meantime, it will make the United Kingdom a poorer country, and the larger question now is whether it will undermine existing European economic integration among the other member states significantly, or weaken support for multilateral trade and the WTO. Populism has proven to be contagious, and other EU member countries have monitored Brexit carefully. Throughout the European Union the same underlying social and economic problems have given rise to populist agitation, and the overall populist vote in member countries has been rising, reaching 22% across Europe in 2018 (see Figure 6.1). Among EU members in early 2020, there were six countries with populist governments in power: Bulgaria, the Czech Republic, Hungary, Italy, Poland, and Slovakia. In addition, nearly every EU member country had populist parties in left-wing, right-wing, or anti-establishment categories, as part of the more numerous parties in most member countries. This structure of formal political representation provides more direct information on their performance in electoral politics, as opposed the United States and the United

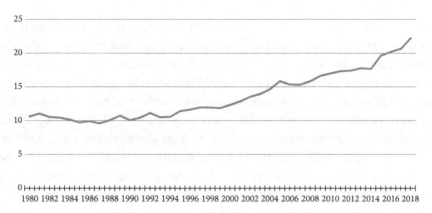

Figure 6.1 Average Share of Votes for European Populist Parties
Source: Economics and Political Science, https://cep.lse.ac.uk/pubs/download/brexit05.pdf.

Kingdom, where populist sentiment often tends to be hidden within factions of the major parties. In addition, the proliferation of populist parties in Europe reveals finer levels of differentiation among them regarding specific populist grievances against their home governments or against EU institutions.

The Role of the Eurozone and Immigration Crises

In the European Union, the impulse for populism in recent years sprang primarily from two sources: the 2008 global financial crisis, which also spawned the euro crisis, and the immigration crisis of 2015. The global financial crisis hit the entire European Union, but generated populist anger in different ways for different countries. Most countries suffered sharp losses in GDP, especially in southern and eastern regions of the European Union. The bursting of the credit-fueled real estate and consumption bubble was particularly severe in Ireland, Latvia, Estonia, Spain, and Greece, countries in which major banks also failed (Berend 2019, pp. 7–9). The financial crisis and its impact on the economies of the European Union sowed the seeds of discontent against many member countries' economic policies, which would later erode support for the center-right and center-left political parties that had dominated European politics since World War II. Yet the introduction of the euro, the new single currency for 19 EU member countries, amplified the problems of the financial crisis and contributed heavily to conflict among the Eurozone member countries. The part of the Eurozone that came closest to an optimal currency area was in its northern tier, where the more advanced industrial countries, especially Germany, the Netherlands, and Austria, were highly

competitive on global markets, had similar monetary traditions of low inflation, and pursued conservative fiscal policies. The euro, an amalgam of the
legacy currencies of its 19 members, provided a competitive boost for these
three countries' exports, as it lowered their real exchange rates compared to
what their value would have been under their individual national currencies.
Southern European members of the Eurozone, including Italy, France, Spain,
Portugal, and Greece, were less competitive on global markets and had his-
tories of higher inflation and more expansionary fiscal policies. For the
southern tier, the euro tended to raise their real exchange rates, lowering their
competitiveness. Lagging productivity, labor market inefficiencies, and a poor
record of tax collection also contributed to the southern region's vulnerability
to economic shocks. Based on the inability of Eurozone member countries
to use individual exchange rates to adjust to changing economic conditions,
Gasporotti and Kullas (2019) estimate per capita losses from 20 years of
Eurozone membership for the biggest losers of €73,500 (Italy), €56,000
(France), and €40,000 (Portugal). In the northern tier, Germany (+€23,100
per capita) and the Netherlands (+€21,000 per capita) were the winners.[15]
The inflexible Euro currency also created corresponding current account
imbalances among Eurozone countries.

Greece, however, suffered the most from the financial crisis, amplified by Eurozone effects and by the Greek government's mismanagement
of its economy. The ensuing sovereign debt crisis and collapse of the Greek
economy also threatened the Eurozone itself, requiring a massive bailout of
€262 billion, funded mostly by special assistance from European Central Bank
(ECB) and other EU government institutions. Most of the bailouts financed
Greek government debt that was owed to private banks, thus transferring private debt to public debt, financed by EU member country taxpayers (Frieden
and Walter 2017). Other EU countries suffering sovereign debt and national
banking crises also received bailouts, including Ireland (€45 billion), Spain
(€41 billion), Portugal (€50 billion), and Cyprus (€6 billion) (Gasparotti and
Kullas 2019, p. 1).

The Eurozone crisis sparked populist resentment in the (mostly) southern
debtor countries because of the austerity conditions, and in the northern
creditor countries because of the public bailouts used to finance the debt relief. The Eurozone system did not begin with any contingency plan for sovereign debt crises; the presumption was that governments would be prudent
in their fiscal and borrowing policies, and remain responsible for any debt
problems.[16] Creditor Eurozone countries, in particular Germany, insisted that
the debtor countries submit to corrective, austere economic policies as a condition for receiving the loans. The stage was set for populist movements in the

creditor countries, fueled by popular resentment against the publicly financed bailouts of the debtor countries, and in the debtor countries themselves, fueled by popular resentment against the austerity conditions. In Germany, populist resentment over the Eurozone bailouts led to the founding of the right-wing Alternative für Deutschland (AfD), which called for Germany to leave the Eurozone. Other right-wing populist parties were either very critical of the Euro, or called for its dissolution: the Dutch Partij voor de Vrijheid (PVV); the French Front National (FN), renamed the Rassemblement National (RN); the Austrian Freiheitliche Partei Österreichs (FPO); and the Finnish True Finns Party. Among debtor countries, Italy's right-wing Liga Nord and Forza Italia parties, its amalgam anti-establishment Five-Star party, and the left-wing Greek Communist and Popular Unity parties all took strong anti-Eurozone positions. Even the Greek left-wing Syriza and Spanish Podemos parties, while not calling for an end to the euro, joined all the other populist parties in debtor countries to condemn the harsh austerity policies associated with the single currency (Freiden and Walter 2017).

The other major influence on populism in Europe in recent years was the immigration shock of 2015–2016, when nearly three million immigrants flooded into Europe, mainly refugees from Africa and the Middle East. Most were fleeing wartime and economic deprivation caused by major conflicts in Syria, Northern Africa, and Afghanistan. The large impact of the immigration issue in Europe came not only from the suddenness and magnitude of the influx, but also because of contrasting views about it by the European Commission and large parts of the European Union population. The Commission had monitored the problem of slow population growth in many EU countries over the years, and the attendant threat of a rapidly aging and inadequate labor force to maintain economic growth, production, and tax contributions to EU and member country budgets in the future. It therefore regarded continued immigration as the only viable way to address the European demographic crisis and maintain a sustainable ratio of work force to total population (Berend 2019, pp. 12–13). Yet the very reasons for slow population growth, including birth rates well below the global average in many EU countries, raised fears among native European populations of demographic and cultural displacement by foreign refugees, many of whom were Muslim.[17] The perceived existential threat of status deprivation by outsiders provided a potent source of populist anger. German Chancellor Angela Merkel, born in East Germany and familiar with the incentives of refugees to flee their home countries, promoted a plan to accommodate all the new immigrants. The European Commission proposed a quota plan that would distribute the immigrants to all EU countries. Yet popular dissatisfaction with policies to accept the immigrants was palpable. While 20 EU member governments officially approved the plan, no country subjected the decision to a popular vote. In addition, the Czech Republic, Hungary, Poland, Romania, and Slovakia voted against Commission Plan, while the United Kingdom, Ireland, and Denmark used their Schengen Plan opt-out to exempt themselves from it (Berend 2019, p. 14). Public opinion was strongly negative on accepting the immigrants, especially since their arrival corresponded with an increase in high profile Jihadist (mainly Islamic State) terrorist attacks in Paris, Nice, Brussels, and Berlin, among other cities.[18] East European member countries reacted particularly harshly, with Hungary, under its populist President Orbán, building a border fence to keep immigrants from entering the country. However, most West European EU countries also introduced national border restrictions on immigrants that had entered EU territory, effectively ending the Schengen Agreement that had allowed free passage of all EU and non-EU citizens between participating EU countries. Countries of entry for the immigrants by sea included Spain, Greece, and Italy, and were often overwhelmed by the logistical problem of establishing accommodations and further passage for them to destinations in northern Europe. In Italy especially it became a major populist flashpoint, as Interior minister and right-wing Liga member Matteo Salvini blocked new immigrants from landing in Italian ports. Back in Germany, the backlash against Merkel's immigration initiative helped move the populist AfD party away from its original economic focus on anti-Eurozone protest toward a nativist, anti-immigrant, and anti-Merkel platform.

The Lack of Trust in EU Institutions and Trade Policy

The EU has a populism problem, driven not by a single candidate, but by a convergence of several forms of discontent in several countries. The focal point has been the European Union itself, and the mistrust of EU decision-making and institutions that grew in the wake of the sovereign debt and immigration crises. Populist party platforms in EU countries have increasingly taken positions in opposition to further European integration, and in some cases in favor of outright withdrawal from the European Union. In the wake of the Brexit vote, speculation abounded on the prospects of yet more populist-fueled withdrawals by France (Frexit), Sweden (Swexit or Swe-Done), Italy (Quitaly), and others. Dijkstra et al. (2018) tabulate polling results showing distrust of the European Union in 2018 at above 40% (in descending order) in Greece, Slovenia, the Czech

Republic, United Kingdom, Spain, Austria, France, Cyprus, Italy, Slovakia, and Croatia. Compared with 2004, distrust of the European Union had increased in all countries but Finland, Denmark, and Sweden, often by large amounts. In Greece, distrust grew from 18% to 67% (Dijkstra et al. 2018, p. 3). Voting from 2013 to 2018 favoring anti-EU populist parties from 2013 to 2018 was strongest in Greece, Italy, Hungary, and the United Kingdom, followed by the Netherlands, the Czech Republic, Denmark, France, Austria, and Slovakia (Dijkstra et al. 2018, p. 5). At the level of individual voters, there is some evidence, as there was in the United States, that adverse trade shocks mediate xenophobic views, fear of cultural displacement, and broader economic dissatisfaction into increased support for populist parties and candidates. Using data from nine West European countries, Hays et al. (2019) provide empirical evidence that import shocks significantly worsen voters' attitudes toward immigrants, thereby increasing support for right-wing populist parties. Runje (2018) argues that the globalization of the world's labor force shifted comparative advantage in labor-intensive goods to China and other Asian countries, causing populist parties in Europe (and elsewhere) to abandon EU free-trade principles. Loch and Norocel (2015) similarly maintain that European populist parties, which had previously focused on immigration and cultural issues to fuel anger against EU policies, adopted critiques of trade to their platforms, due to the impact of import competition on industrial workers wages and jobs. Dijstra et al. (2018 pp. 13–19) link the main sources of the anti-EU populist surge to long-standing economic and industrial decline in specific regions, voters with lower educational levels, and areas of lower employment opportunities. They conclude that trade and immigration issues are less important in determining populist voting patterns than the location of economic decline. However, as noted in earlier explanations of the Brexit vote and US elections, trade and immigration issues as perceived at the regional or national level, rather than at the individual level, may reinforce the more direct impulses for populist voting. One can add, based on the twin-crisis discussion earlier, that the sovereign debt crises in southern EU countries were accompanied by disruptive trade deficits and increasing unemployment in import-competing industries, giving support to populist parties, and possibly to more protectionist policies. Opposition to the immigration surge may also be connected in some voters' minds with the dangers of open trade, suggesting a causality in the reverse direction suggested by Hays et al. (2019). This connection appears also to have been evident in populist support for Donald Trump. In this regard populist Euroskeptic and anti-Eurozone sentiment seemed consistently to strengthen broader anti-globalization and protectionist sentiment in populist parties.

Prospects for Euro-Populist Protectionism

A more difficult question to address is whether populist opposition to EU governance and policies might transform into more protectionist trade policies. The channels for such protectionist sentiments could occur through populist victories in national elections, through populist influences on mainstream political leaders, and through the European Parliament. Volkens et al. (2019) have coded platform positions on protectionism and other issues of various political parties in Europe and elsewhere, based on the frequency of key words in their manifestos and campaign statements. Table 6.1 compiles and compares results for EU populist and nonpopulist party platforms for national elections from 2007 to 2019, with populist parties subdivided into right-wing, left-wing, and anti-establishment categories. In the European Union right-wing populism dominates, with 83 observations, compared to 35 for left-wing and 21 for anti-establishment populist parties. Nonpopulist party campaigns are represented in 589 observations for this period. On the indicator of protectionist rhetoric, EU populist party platforms exhibited more than twice the number of protectionist statements as EU nonpopulist parties on an unweighted basis (0.88% of platform statements vs. 0.31%). Right-wing protectionist parties accounted for most of this difference, with a protectionist rhetoric score of 1.29%, while left-wing and anti-establishment populist scores were 0.27% and 0.29%, respectively, lower than the score for nonpopulist parties.[19] Right-wing populists similarly exhibit the strongest anti-EU, anti-immigrant, and pro-nationalist rhetoric, compared both to other populists and to nonpopulists. Left-wing populists, while devoting less rhetoric to overt protectionism, nevertheless articulate policies favoring nationalization, Marxism, social justice, labor unions, price controls, and the welfare state at greater length than other populist and nonpopulist parties. These positions imply the possibility of protectionism in the form of discrimination against imports through industrial subsidization, regulation, the support of "national champion" industries, and tariffs to prevent social dumping. The anti-establishment populist parties, in contrast, devote more of their platforms to pro-capitalism, business incentives, and economic growth, on average, than all other parties. Their populist protest appears to be more focused on anti-corruption than on anti-globalization issues, implying a more favorable view toward trade.

Table 6.1 Content of European Party Platforms: Percentage of Text by Theme, Populist, and Nonpopulist Parties

Populist Type	Code	per110 anti-EU	per304 anticorrup	per401 Pro-capitlsm	per402 BusIncntv	per406 Protectionist	per410 EcnGrwth	per413 Ntlization
Left	Mean	0.86	1.50	0.14	1.31	0.27	0.96	1.93
Left	StdDev	1.17	1.78	0.36	2.69	0.47	1.31	1.85
Right	Mean	3.46	1.64	1.55	2.60	1.29	1.65	0.49
Right	StdDev	5.66	2.49	2.35	2.70	3.45	2.27	1.07
AntiEst	Mean	0.44	2.99	2.20	3.91	0.29	2.01	0.39
AntiEst	StdDev	0.93	3.03	4.88	3.72	0.54	3.55	0.66
AllPoplst	Mean	2.34	1.81	1.29	2.47	0.88	1.53	0.84
AllPoplst	Std Dev	4.61	2.46	2.70	2.97	2.72	2.33	1.41
NonPop	Mean	0.60	1.14	1.29	2.84	0.31	2.15	0.56
NonPop	Std Dev	1.68	2.17	2.65	2.93	0.92	3.06	1.41

Populist Type	Code	per504 ProWelfareSt	per601 ProNatlism	per701 ProUnion	per601_2 AntiImmgrt	per412 PriceCntrl	per415 Marxist	per503 SocJustice
Left	Mean	12.17	1.09	6.48	0.04	1.67	0.92	7.47
Left	StdDev	5.76	1.75	4.02	0.11	2.45	2.40	5.67
Right	Mean	8.32	7.10	2.97	3.02	0.59	0.24	3.33
Right	StdDev	5.19	6.34	3.63	4.82	1.08	2.05	3.26
AntiEst	Mean	8.52	1.93	1.93	0.13	0.55	N/A	3.71
AntiEst	StdDev	4.62	2.37	1.47	0.26	0.92	N/A	4.07
AllPoplst	Mean	9.32	4.79	3.70	1.88	0.86	0.37	4.44
AllPoplst	Std Dev	5.48	5.77	3.86	4.03	1.59	2.01	4.45
NonPop	Mean	9.59	2.08	3.47	0.51	0.69	0.46	5.70
NonPop	Std Dev	5.87	4.34	3.50	1.49	1.38	3.54	4.72

Information in Table 6.1 suggests that EU right-wing populists are in general more protectionist and anti-EU than other populists, reflecting a Trump-like economic nationalism, while left-wing populists also exhibit preferences for strong market intervention that could discriminate against trade. Even so, there are mitigating political influences at work when populist parties come closer to achieving political power in governing. While an aggressive nationalist trade policy or state-run economy may serve the purpose of energizing a populist constituency during a campaign, it may be less likely that these populist parties *in power* would implement highly protectionist policies, notwithstanding the major exception of the United States under Donald Trump. The EU's centralized trade policy, with its strong internal market integration, treaty commitment to WTO rules, and extensive global network of bilateral and regional trade agreements, would be difficult for any individual member country to overturn, even the large ones. Many populist parties—right, left, and anti-establishment—may therefore not want to dismantle the European Union or exit from it, because they would thereby be giving up participation in the largest trading bloc in the world, with its large collective bargaining leverage in any trade negotiation (Kandel and Gondaud 2019). This was a factor that many free-trade Brexiteers either overlooked or underestimated, and the post-Brexit turmoil over the United Kingdom's diminished ability to negotiate favorable terms in new trade agreements is likely to influence such thinking among EU populists in the future. Even protectionists would covet the opportunity to impose tariffs from such a position of bargaining strength. However, with no immediate prospect of implementing a new trade policy within the European Union as it exists now, some aspirational populist parties may therefore postpone strong protectionist positions until they can achieve more political power collectively, perhaps in EU-wide coalition with like-minded populists in other member countries in the European Council or the European Parliament.

The European Parliament is a venue where populists have the opportunity to caucus together and potentially develop similar strategies on specific issues. In EU-wide elections in May 2019 right-wing populist party members won 73 out of 751 seats, a coalition represented by the Identity and Democracy group. A smaller group of left-wing populists won 26 seats and joined the broader European United Green Left-Nordic Green Left group, which together held 41 seats (3% of the total). This scant populist representation of 13% of European Parliament voters was significantly less than the 22% populist representation in EU member national parliaments in 2018, and was widely viewed as a setback for the EU populist movement, which had hoped to build on the 2016 Brexit victory (Schultz 2019). Dennison and Pardijs (2016, p. 3) note that right and left-wing populist Members of the European Parliament in the eighth European Parliament term (2014–2019) tended in general to favor protectionism, but could not always find common ground on trade-related issues, the largest of which was the debate, before the 2016 election of Donald Trump, over the proposed Transpacific Trade and Investment Partnership (TTIP) with the United States. Interviews with 27 European Parliament populist party delegations revealed that most were generally against the TTIP, but several would favor it under certain circumstances.[20] TTIP was not, however, a touchstone populist issue, since there was broader EU opposition to it among center-right and center-left parties as well. It was also not clear at this point if EU populists, especially those on the right, would warm to a trade deal with the United States under Donald Trump, whose steel and aluminum tariffs against the European Union, along with subsequent threats of auto and other tariffs, were more likely to embarrass them rather than encourage them to revolt against EU trade policy. Trump's erstwhile advisor, Steve Bannon, had tried to rally EU populists before the 2019 European Parliament elections under the guise of a joint US-EU populist international movement, but his efforts were largely rejected by EU populist leaders, fearful of the appearance of US interference in their elections (Nossiter and Horowitz 2019).

Despite the lull in EU populism's electoral success in 2019, its influence in several member countries continued to be strong, with potential of pushing EU trade policy in a protectionist direction. The United Kingdom was one of the strongest pro-WTO influences in the European Union's collective trade policy, along with Germany and smaller members in the northern tier. The United Kingdom's departure may therefore diminish the European Union's pro-trade orientation, as the largest EU member countries have significant populist opposition parties. In Germany, the right-wing AfD party won 13% of the national parliamentary vote in 2017 and became the third-largest party in the country, and subsequently increased its representation in local legislatures, especially in the eastern part of the country. In France, the right-wing Rassemblement National and left-wing La France Insoumise together won 24% of the National Assembly vote in 2017, a potentially potent anti-trade combination if they maintain their mutual protectionist platform. In Italy, the coalition of right-wing populists and the anti-establishment Five-Star Movement garnered 70% of the Chamber of Deputies vote in 2019, continuing populist control of the government. While populist influence in the European Union in early 2020 appeared too weak to spark further exits of member countries, the populist influence on EU trade policy could more easily occur through piecemeal erosion of trade rules through European Council decisions. With the previously pro-trade UK out of the

European Union, a qualified majority for anti-trade measures could occur if EU populist-inspired protectionism continues to grow.[21] In order for EU countries to implement joint protectionist policies, both right- and left-wing populists would have to join forces both within countries and throughout the European Union, or else their influence on center parties would have to increase further. Van der Waal and DeKoster (2018) and Podobnik et al. (2019) note increasing alignment and cooperation among right- and left-wing populist parties in opposing globalization, based on the anti-globalization tendencies of their constituencies. While such left-right populist voting alliances have occurred within the Netherlands (Van der Waal and DeKoster 2018) and France (Kandel and Gondaud 2019; Vaudano and Dahyot 2019) on the TTIP issue mentioned earlier, a true EU-wide protectionist coalition to alter its trade policy orientation remains untested.

External triggers to spark EU opposition to multilateralism and WTO trade rules is still possible, however. Donald Trump continued to feud with the European Union in early 2020 over its airbus subsidies and its trade surplus with the United States, threatening 25% national security tariffs against automobile imports, and suggesting a possible broader trade war. In the earlier steel and aluminum tariffs, the EU retaliatory tariffs sought to stay in line with WTO rules (although their justification was legally dubious, as explained in chapter 4), new salvos in a trade war might push EU public opinion toward open-ended tit-for-tat retaliation, as occurred in the US-China trade war. In response to increasing economic nationalism by China and the United States, Germany introduced its own plan for future industrial policy in February 2019, including targets for manufacturing share of GDP, closing off EU value chains from Chinese imports, and promoting German national champions and other German firms with increasing state support, even if it reduces competition (Zettelmeyer 2019). These proposals emulate many Chinese policies supporting its state-run enterprises that EU countries themselves, not to mention the United States and many other countries, have so heavily criticized. They also undermine long-standing German and EU goals of internal competition, trade liberalization, and productivity growth.

Summary

The impact of Brexit and EU populism in general on the European Union itself may be indirect, but could become significant if populist influences in other EU countries, the United States, or the rest of the world increases. Despite the fact that the other EU member countries have also elected

populist governments, and many EU members also have significant populist movements, their governments have maintained establishment policies
regarding the European Union and WTO—so far. Most populist sentiment
in Europe came to focus on opposition to immigration from outside the
European Union, although intra-EU immigration from eastern and southern
member countries remained an issue. Yet it is not clear that European populism would reject the WTO, trade integration, and trade liberalization in
general, given EU member countries' smaller size and individual bargaining
power outside the European Union. Efforts by anti-WTO Trump advisor
Steve Bannon to establish an international populist association of European
countries with the United States were not successful in 2017–2019. Still, the
anti-globalization and pro-Russian links with European populists continue
to raise concerns about the future of the European Union, and of its commitment to WTO-sponsored trade liberalization. Regional liberalization continued with the Canada-EU Comprehensive Economic and Trade Agreement
(CETA), which entered into force in 2017, but the proposed US-EU
Transatlantic Trade and Investment Partnership (TTIP) negotiations, which
predate the Trump administration, have stalled. Brexit will tend to weaken the
WTO by removing a pro-trade vote on the European Council, which must approve major EU trade policy and WTO-related decisions.

7

Populism and Trade Around the World

Do populist governments actually increase protectionism? Observations of recent populist regimes suggest possible links between authoritarian and nationalist tendencies of charismatic populist leaders and mercantilist trade policy, and between the populist appeal of antiglobalization movements and trade skepticism. Yet there is considerable room for skepticism regarding systematic links between populism and protectionism. Many small countries do not have enough market power to impose severe trade restrictions without risking isolation and self-inflicted economic damage, a strategy that may not appeal to the potential populist base. Furthermore, as noted in chapter 2, a given populist movement itself may not call for protectionist policies, and may in fact support trade liberalization if the populist base opposes the ruling elite's embrace of tariffs or other antitrade regulations. This may be especially true in the case of antiestablishment populism, sparked, for example, by the corrupt or inefficient trade policies of an elite that protects national monopolies from foreign competition. Protectionism is also a widespread phenomenon, not exclusive to populist governments, and might arise from a variety of political circumstances that grant import relief to domestic firms. Finally, the most prominent observation in favor of the populism-protectionism link is certainly the trade policy of Donald Trump, so the question arises as to whether protectionism in populist regimes may depend on specific characteristics of the populist leader.

The chapter begins with a regression study of the impact of populist regimes on measures of a country's trade restrictiveness, followed by a case-by-case global review of individual populist country trade policies. The goal is to see if any systematic patterns emerge either through the regression results, or through observations of individual countries in their distinctive circumstances.

Populism and Trade Openness: An Empirical Study

The regression study sets out to establish a statistical relationship between a country's degree of protectionism in its trade policies and the attribute of "populism" in the government's political regime. The following sections discuss

Populism and Trade. Kent Jones, Oxford University Press. © Oxford University Press 2021.
DOI: 10.1093/oso/9780190086350.003.0007.

the data and hypothesis, the numerical results of the various regression runs, and an assessment of the results, including a consideration of their possible role in explaining US protectionism under President Donald Trump.

The Data

If a populist government tends to have higher tariffs or otherwise intervenes in its domestic economy to restrict trade or promote trade, then objective measures of this activity can indicate a change in the country's trade policy index score. Four such indicators of trade openness include the Trade Freedom index, the Fraser index, and the global trade alert (GTA) counts of liberalizing and discriminatory trade measures. The Trade Freedom index, for example, is a composite measure of the restrictiveness of tariffs and nontariff measures, with a maximum (free trade) index of 100.[1] The Fraser index is a more granular measure that combines information on tariffs, regulatory barriers, the presence (if applicable) of black market exchange rates, and regulations on capital flows, investment ownership and restrictions, and the freedom of foreigners to visit the country.[2] The GTA numbers, in contrast, are simple count data, measuring the number of trade liberalizing policy interventions implemented by the country in a given year and the number of trade-restricting interventions implemented in a given year.[3] The GTA data tally any changes in tariff and nontariff measures, including administrative murky protectionist measures that the Trade Freedom and Fraser indexes do not consider, and which may not be covered by explicit WTO rules.[4] The global data set consists of all democratic countries, defined in the "Polity 5" database compiled by the Center for Systemic Peace as a combination of the 100 countries with the highest democracy index scores from 1995 and from 2018, the beginning and ending years of the sample period.[5] Nearly all countries are members of the WTO. Within this sample there are 40 countries that experienced periods of populist government rule for at least one year during the period 1995–2018, representing 342 out of 2,296 total observations. The designation of populist governments is determined by a review of the academic literature, and each populist regime is coded either "left-wing," "right-wing" or "anti-establishment" based on the categorization scheme of Kyle and Gultchin (2018).[6] A chart summarizing the populist country and regime time period designations appears at the end of this chapter. The regression study tests the hypothesis that the different types of populism also differ in their impact on trade openness. It thereby seeks to test the degree of association between the dependent variable and an array of independent variables, rather than causality. The World Development Indicators database provides a number of economic control variables, including unemployment and economic growth rates, current account balance (% of GDP), the country's share in global trade, and foreign direct investment inflows and outflows. The World Bank Governance Indicators database provides indexes for six measures of government quality.[7]

Results of the Regressions

Table 7.1 reports representative regression results for all democratic countries, with fixed country and fixed year effects, variously using either the Trade Freedom or Fraser indexes of trade openness as the dependent variable. In early regressions attempting to link populism with the degree of trade openness, a general populism dummy variable, combining all three types across all regression variants, failed to yield any significant results. The regressions presented here replace the general populism dummy with three dummy variables representing left-wing (LW), right-wing (RW), and anti-establishment (AE) populism. While the differentiated populism dummy variables reveal some significant patterns for the various types of populist governments, the results vary sharply between the two indexes. Trade Freedom regressions fail to show any significant link between trade scores and various stripes of populism. Six out of seven Fraser regression variants show negative coefficients for LW populism, but a significant negative value in only one variant, indicating that a LW populist regime lowers the Fraser score by 0.27. Fraser results for RW populism are much stronger, with significantly *positive* coefficients (5% level) in four of seven variants, increasing the score by a range of 0.29 to 0.34. AE dummy coefficients are consistently positive in all seven Fraser regressions, with two at 10% or better significance, raising the score by 0.14 to 0.24. Clearly, populism does not always imply less trade openness, although the data suggest that protectionism is more likely in LW than in RW and AE populist governments. The data in fact suggest that variations in trade policy scores occur for many other reasons besides populism, and that it is necessary to find other ways to explain different levels of trade openness.

For example, Fraser index scores for the entire sample are significantly associated with higher index scores of several World Bank governance indicators, with coefficients for voice and accountability (+0.47) and government effectiveness (+0.38), both at 1% significance, as well as regulatory quality (+0.63), rule of law (+0.56), and control of corruption (+0.31) at 5% significance. The Trade Freedom index regressions include significant coefficients only for

Table 7.1 Determinants of Trade Policy Indexes. Dependent Variables: Trade Freedom Index, Fraser Index

	(1)	(2)	(3)	(4)	(5)	(6)	(7)	(8)	(9)	(10)	(11)	(12)	(13)	(14)
	TrFreedm	TrFreedm	TrFreedm	TrFreedm	TrFreedm	TrFreedm	TrFreedm	FrasrIndx	FrasrIndx	FrasrIndx	FrasrIndx	FrasrIndx	FrasrIndx	FrasrIndx
FuelExp	-0.103**	-0.087**	-0.090**	-0.082*	-0.082*	-0.084**	-0.081*	0.0004	0.0048	0.0037	0.0038	0.0033	0.0035	0.0038
	(-2.48)	(-2.10)	(-2.11)	(-1.89)	(-1.95)	(-2.01)	(-1.89)	(0.08)	(0.98)	(0.75)	(0.80)	(0.74)	(0.76)	(0.81)
LWPop	-2.007	0.198	0.408	-0.110	0.966	0.757	0.758	-0.267***	-0.178	-0.222	-0.138	-0.0857	-0.0178	0.234
	(-1.38)	(0.12)	(0.27)	(-0.09)	(0.61)	(0.43)	(0.35)	(-2.65)	(-1.07)	(-1.32)	(-0.91)	(-0.47)	(-0.08)	(0.70)
RWPop	2.358	0.650	1.261	2.566	4.189	2.073	1.572	-0.0539	0.336**	0.114	0.289**	0.303**	0.306**	0.181
	(1.06)	(0.28)	(0.73)	(0.77)	(1.00)	(0.75)	(0.60)	(-0.43)	(2.14)	(1.08)	(2.07)	(2.12)	(2.14)	(1.65)
AEPop	0.694	-2.035	0.626	-3.066	-2.136	-0.414	-0.359	0.141*	0.244**	0.0208	0.0338	0.165	0.140	0.0933
	(0.44)	(-1.26)	(0.41)	(-1.36)	(-0.65)	(-0.21)	(-0.16)	(1.89)	(2.32)	(0.25)	(0.26)	(1.11)	(1.20)	(0.65)
LWPop*FuelExp		-0.063	-0.068	-0.097**	-0.061	-0.046	-0.076*		-0.0024	-0.0050	-0.0014	0.0110	0.0101	0.0008
		(-1.31)	(-1.36)	(-2.36)	(-1.31)	(-0.97)	(-1.82)		(-0.36)	(-0.94)	(-0.22)	(1.62)	(1.08)	(0.09)
RWPop*FuelExp		0.149	0.107	0.0823	0.0398	0.0920	0.0986		-0.0493***	-0.0494***	-0.0527***	-0.0536***	-0.0539***	-0.0532***
		(1.00)	(0.83)	(0.64)	(0.31)	(0.69)	(0.77)		(-5.66)	(-5.18)	(-4.92)	(-4.43)	(-5.56)	(-5.07)
AEPop*FuelExp		0.0764	0.0585	0.182	0.0672	0.109	0.117		-0.00331	0.00582	0.00291	-0.00501	-0.00463	0.000557
		(0.96)	(0.50)	(1.64)	(0.47)	(0.93)	(0.91)		(-0.41)	(0.74)	(0.33)	(-0.50)	(-0.52)	(0.06)
V&A		1.261							0.470***					
		(0.95)							(3.17)					
LWPop*V&A		1.953							0.202					
		(0.75)							(0.40)					
RWPop*V&A		1.819							-0.378*					
		(0.71)							(-1.98)					
AEPop*V&A		5.957**							-0.263***					
		(2.39)							(-2.97)					

(Continued)

Table 7.1 Continued

	(1)	(2)	(3)	(4)	(5)	(6)	(7)	(8)	(9)	(10)	(11)	(12)	(13)	(14)
	TrFreedm	TrFreedm	TrFreedm	TrFreedm	TrFreedm	TrFreedm	TrFreedm	FrasrIndx	FrasrIndx	FrasrIndx	FrasrIndx	FrasrIndx	FrasrIndx	FrasrIndx
PolStab			0.778							-0.0152				
			(0.82)							(-0.20)				
LWPop*PolStab			0.528							-0.295				
			(0.17)							(-1.54)				
RWPop*PolStab			-0.508							-0.0347				
			(-0.35)							(-0.32)				
AEPop*PolStab			3.784*							-0.0221				
			(1.85)							(-0.41)				
GovEffect				1.338							0.378**			
				(0.81)							(2.10)			
LWPop*GovEffect				-4.136**							0.139			
				(-2.31)							(0.52)			
RWPop*GovEffect				-2.315							-0.322*			
				(-0.76)							(-1.98)			
AEPop*GovEffect				7.653***							0.0526			
				(3.65)							(0.55)			
RegQual					4.090***							0.633***		
					(2.77)							(3.66)		
LWPop*RegQual					-0.509							0.840**		
					(-0.22)							(2.25)		
RWPop*RegQual					-4.371							-0.282*		
					(-1.08)							(-1.70)		
AEPop*RegQual					3.809							-0.134		
					(1.10)							(-0.88)		

	(1)	(2)	(3)	(4)	(5)	(6)	(7)	(8)	(9)	(10)	(11)	(12)	(13)	(14)
RuleLaw						2.359 (1.27)							0.559** (2.52)	
LWPop*RuleLaw						1.032 (0.41)							0.740 (1.45)	
RWPop*RuleLaw						-1.186 (-0.46)							-0.339 (-1.55)	
AEPop*RuleLaw						5.517*** (2.75)							-0.0981 (-1.25)	
CtrlCrrupt							1.963* (1.69)							0.331** (2.00)
LWPop*CtrlCrrupt							0.547 (0.14)							1.045 (1.24)
RWPop*CtrlCrrupt							-0.809 (-0.27)							-0.198 (-1.08)
AEPop*CtrlCrrupt							5.564** (2.27)							-0.00335 (-0.03)
TradeGDP	0.0294 (1.34)	0.0379* (1.82)	0.0403* (1.87)	0.0371* (1.77)	0.0358* (1.70)	0.0375* (1.82)	0.0355* (1.69)	0.000855 (0.41)	0.00177 (0.88)	0.00120 (0.58)	0.00127 (0.62)	0.00153 (0.84)	0.00138 (0.67)	0.00105 (0.54)
ShWrldTrade	0.382 (0.54)	-0.0356 (-0.05)	-0.0576 (-0.09)	-0.112 (-0.18)	-0.0488 (-0.08)	-0.0909 (-0.14)		0.237*** (4.05)	0.269*** (4.68)	0.280*** (4.96)	0.266*** (4.95)	0.282*** (4.68)	0.299*** (5.24)	0.271*** (4.64)
EU	4.820** (2.61)	3.995* (1.96)	3.986** (2.00)	4.310** (2.12)	4.492** (2.22)	4.089** (2.04)	4.402** (2.15)	4.439** (2.59)	4.358** (2.17)	4.333** (2.20)	4.346** (2.08)	4.358** (2.19)	4.281* (1.68)	4.341** (2.05)
GdpCap	-7.1e-04* (-1.85)	-4.1e-04 (-1.05)	-4.4e-04 (-1.12)	-5.0e-04 (-1.33)	-6.0e-04 (-1.58)	-5.4e-04 (-1.41)	-4.8e-04 (-1.23)	-1.2e-05 (-0.49)	1.3e-06 (0.05)	-2.4e-06 (-0.10)	-1.4e-05 (-0.60)	-2.5e-05 (-1.06)	-1.9e-05 (-0.75)	-2.3e-06 (-0.10)
GdpCap^2	1.4e-09 (0.56)	-6.1e-10 (-0.24)	-3.3e-10 (-0.13)	2.0e-10 (0.08)	6.7e-10 (0.27)	3.7e-10 (0.14)	-3.1e-11 (-0.01)	-4.2e-10** (-2.28)	-4.7e-10*** (-2.71)	-4.5e-10** (-2.56)	-3.3e-10** (-2.05)	-3.6e-10** (-2.01)	-3.6e-10** (-2.04)	-4.5e-10*** (-2.67)

(Continued)

Table 7.1 Continued

	(1)	(2)	(3)	(4)	(5)	(6)	(7)	(8)	(9)	(10)	(11)	(12)	(13)	(14)
	TrFreedm	TrFreedm	TrFreedm	TrFreedm	TrFreedm	TrFreedm	TrFreedm	FrasrIndx	FrasrIndx	FrasrIndx	FrasrIndx	FrasrIndx	FrasrIndx	FrasrIndx
Growth	-0.0294	-0.0054	-0.0113	-0.0009	-0.0010	0.0033	-0.0047	0.0146**	0.0137**	0.0142**	0.0139**	0.0141**	0.0157**	0.0134**
	(-0.58)	(-0.07)	(-0.15)	(-0.01)	(-0.01)	(0.04)	(-0.06)	(2.12)	(2.09)	(1.99)	(2.03)	(2.06)	(2.22)	(2.08)
CA/Gdp	-0.0362	-0.0292	-0.0380	-0.0414	-0.0176	-0.0316	-0.0289	-0.00795**	-0.00467	-0.00575	-0.00655*	-0.00445	-0.00636*	-0.00606*
	(-0.86)	(-0.72)	(-0.99)	(-1.06)	(-0.46)	(-0.80)	(-0.73)	(-2.30)	(-1.32)	(-1.66)	(-1.80)	(-1.23)	(-1.83)	(-1.71)
Unempl	-0.303**	-0.281**	-0.268**	-0.283**	-0.271**	-0.287**	-0.281**	0.00694	0.00682	0.00410	0.00743	0.00607	0.00576	0.00788
	(-2.45)	(-2.49)	(-2.45)	(-2.51)	(-2.54)	(-2.57)	(-2.52)	(0.46)	(0.51)	(0.30)	(0.54)	(0.53)	(0.45)	(0.57)
N	2073	1759	1759	1758	1759	1759	1759	1491	1396	1396	1396	1396	1396	1396
R-sq	0.50	0.50	0.50	0.50	0.50	0.50	0.50	0.17	0.20	0.17	0.19	0.26	0.22	0.20

t statistics in parentheses

* p<0.10 ** p<0.05 *** p<0.01

Note: Yearly dummy variables not reported.

Sources: Heritage Foundation (Trade Freedom Index), Fraser Institute (Fraser Index), World Bank (World Development Indicators, Worldwide Government Indicators).

Table 7.2 Determinants of GTA Intervention Counts. Dependent Variables: GTA Liberalization, GTA Discriminatory

	(15)	(16)	(17)	(18)	(19)	(20)	(21)	(22)	(23)	(24)	(25)	(26)	(27)	(28)
	GTAlib	GTAlib	GTAlib	GTAlib	GTAlib	GTAlib	GTAlib	GTAdiscr	GTAdiscr	GTAdiscr	GTAdiscr	GTAdiscr	GTAdiscr	GTAdiscr
FuelExp	-0.0560	-0.0863**	-0.0832**	-0.0692*	-0.0772**	-0.0620	-0.0809*	-0.143*	-0.174**	-0.166**	-0.176**	-0.144*	-0.156*	-0.163*
	(-1.31)	(-2.06)	(-1.99)	(-1.74)	(-2.00)	(-1.63)	(-1.93)	(-1.68)	(-2.17)	(-2.08)	(-2.16)	(-1.81)	(-1.85)	(-1.94)
LWPop	-5.263	-8.217**	-9.133*	-8.677**	-7.271**	-8.612**	-9.463*	0.585	-2.555	-2.782	-3.888	-4.949**	-5.324	-4.848
	(-1.44)	(-2.11)	(-1.75)	(-2.06)	(-2.17)	(-2.38)	(-1.71)	(0.17)	(-0.67)	(-0.63)	(-1.01)	(-2.06)	(-1.42)	(-0.85)
RWPop	-1.119	-1.928	-0.816	-5.163**	-3.757*	-2.381	-2.047	-8.625	-1.792	-11.71	7.326	5.398	0.0363	-5.084
	(-0.51)	(-1.09)	(-0.34)	(-2.10)	(-1.97)	(-1.35)	(-0.97)	(-0.83)	(-0.35)	(-1.35)	(0.80)	(0.70)	(0.01)	(-0.84)
AEPop	5.989*	6.550	2.666	8.312	21.55***	7.936*	7.682**	4.077**	0.812	-2.921	3.062	8.801	0.426	-0.459
	(1.93)	(1.08)	(0.64)	(1.38)	(3.26)	(1.67)	(2.03)	(2.00)	(0.57)	(-0.89)	(0.62)	(1.17)	(0.11)	(-0.13)
LWPop*FuelExp		0.204**	0.134	0.152*	0.181	0.174	0.166		0.177	0.175	0.117	0.162**	0.128	0.160
		(2.02)	(1.50)	(1.70)	(1.52)	(1.51)	(1.58)		(1.37)	(1.36)	(1.03)	(2.13)	(1.51)	(1.29)
RWPop*FuelExp		0.0130	0.0418	0.0960	0.0343	-0.0481	0.0464		0.602	0.154	-0.0786	0.0570	0.392	0.0511
		(0.06)	(0.29)	(0.59)	(0.29)	(-0.28)	(0.32)		(0.76)	(0.17)	(-0.09)	(0.06)	(0.62)	(0.07)
AEPop*FuelExp		0.163	0.198	-0.00974	-0.551	-0.230	-0.241		0.490***	0.476**	0.290	0.0877	0.339	0.400
		(0.55)	(0.74)	(-0.04)	(-1.38)	(-0.74)	(-1.02)		(3.09)	(2.05)	(0.97)	(0.23)	(0.76)	(1.12)
V&A		-0.645							0.0666					
		(-0.30)							(0.02)					
LWPop*V&A		-7.202*							1.280					
		(-1.66)							(0.17)					
RWPop*V&A		1.433							-24.03					
		(0.36)							(-1.26)					
AEPop*V&A		-5.255							-4.751					
		(-0.79)							(-1.63)					

(Continued)

Table 7.2 *Continued*

	(15)	(16)	(17)	(18)	(19)	(20)	(21)	(22)	(23)	(24)	(25)	(26)	(27)	(28)
	GTAlib	GTAlib	GTAlib	GTAlib	GTAlib	GTAlib	GTAlib	GTAdiscr	GTAdiscr	GTAdiscr	GTAdiscr	GTAdiscr	GTAdiscr	GTAdiscr
PolStab			-0.644							0.842				
			(-0.49)							(0.44)				
LWPop*PolStab			-4.547							-1.398				
			(-1.27)							(-0.31)				
RWPop*PolStab			2.429							-9.474				
			(1.21)							(-1.36)				
AEPop*PolStab			-7.404							-9.740*				
			(-1.45)							(-1.97)				
GovEffect				4.464**							-0.309			
				(2.00)							(-0.09)			
LWPop*GovEffect				-6.202							-12.18***			
				(-1.47)							(-2.73)			
RWPop*GovEffect				9.277*							-40.11			
				(1.96)							(-1.47)			
AEPop*GovEffect				-9.130							-8.702			
				(-1.03)							(-1.28)			
RegQual					-0.231							-0.938		
					(-0.11)							(-0.26)		
LWPop*RegQual					4.757							-9.631**		
					(0.79)							(-2.28)		
RWPop*RegQual					5.693							-32.58		
					(1.56)							(-1.54)		
AEPop*RegQual					-23.56***							-14.01		
					(-3.14)							(-1.38)		

	(1)	(2)	(3)	(4)	(5)	(6)	(7)	(8)	(9)	(10)	(11)	(12)	(13)	(14)
RuleLaw						4.484*							2.119	
						(1.69)							(0.53)	
LWPop*RuleLaw						−3.109							−10.20**	
						(−0.60)							(−2.22)	
RWPop*RuleLaw						7.030*							−40.68	
						(1.70)							(−1.64)	
AEPop*RuleLaw						−21.62***							−9.753	
						(−2.83)							(−0.66)	
CtrlCrrupt							0.687							−0.0622
							(0.30)							(−0.02)
LWPop*CtrlCrrupt							−3.343							−6.570
							(−0.40)							(−0.73)
RWPop*CtrlCrrupt							6.266							−37.12
							(1.37)							(−1.47)
AEPop*CtrlCrrupt							−18.22**							−6.065
							(−2.41)							(−0.69)
TradeGDP	0.0641**	0.0567*	0.0563*	0.0534*	0.0607**	0.0635*	0.0588*	0.0502	0.0436	0.0473	0.0395	0.0382	0.0429	0.0394
	(2.03)	(1.84)	(1.81)	(1.74)	(2.00)	(2.08)	(1.89)	(1.12)	(1.00)	(1.07)	(0.86)	(0.88)	(0.93)	(0.87)
ShWrldTrade	−2.157	−1.929	−1.808	−1.723	−1.846	−1.520	−1.880	−23.42***	−24.11**	−23.88**	−23.86**	−23.03**	−24.00**	−23.83**
	(−0.34)	(−0.29)	(−0.27)	(−0.26)	(−0.28)	(−0.23)	(−0.29)	(−2.80)	(−2.50)	(−2.50)	(−2.44)	(−2.35)	(−2.44)	(−2.38)
EU	2.639***	2.576***	2.720***	2.803***	2.914***	2.168**	2.513**	7.563***	7.955***	7.706***	7.614***	8.121***	7.776***	8.122***
	(3.07)	(2.91)	(3.14)	(3.27)	(3.31)	(2.18)	(2.45)	(4.94)	(5.09)	(5.04)	(5.07)	(5.99)	(5.36)	(5.54)
GdpCap	−8.8e−04	−9.3e−04	−8.0e−04	−9.4e−04	−6.2e−04	−7.4e−04	−8.0e−04	−4.0e−04	−0.000982	−0.000693	−0.00108	−0.000825	−0.00126	−0.000812
	(−0.96)	(−1.01)	(−0.89)	(−1.02)	(−0.70)	(−0.82)	(−0.89)	(−0.34)	(−0.74)	(−0.57)	(−0.80)	(−0.66)	(−0.93)	(−0.61)
GdpCap^2	4.10e−09	4.40e−09	3.52e−09	4.78e−09	2.38e−09	3.41e−09	3.55e−09	1.29e−09	5.70e−09	3.43e−09	6.30e−09	5.26e−09	8.25e−09	4.99e−09
	(0.51)	(0.54)	(0.44)	(0.59)	(0.31)	(0.43)	(0.45)	(0.13)	(0.53)	(0.34)	(0.57)	(0.50)	(0.74)	(0.45)

(Continued)

Table 7.2 Continued

	(15)	(16)	(17)	(18)	(19)	(20)	(21)	(22)	(23)	(24)	(25)	(26)	(27)	(28)
	GTAlib	GTAlib	GTAlib	GTAlib	GTAlib	GTAlib	GTAlib	GTAdiscr	GTAdiscr	GTAdiscr	GTAdiscr	GTAdiscr	GTAdiscr	GTAdiscr
Growth	−0.0902	−0.0650	−0.0737	−0.0655	−0.102	−0.0958	−0.0803	−0.0368	−0.0315	−0.0262	−0.0392	−0.0247	−0.0330	−0.0463
	(−0.89)	(−0.63)	(−0.73)	(−0.63)	(−0.96)	(−0.91)	(−0.76)	(−0.22)	(−0.19)	(−0.16)	(−0.24)	(−0.16)	(−0.21)	(−0.29)
CA/Gdp	0.101	0.0890	0.0965	0.0695	0.0996	0.0820	0.0926	−0.000416	0.0111	0.0220	0.0283	0.0112	0.0331	0.0230
	(1.40)	(1.22)	(1.34)	(0.96)	(1.44)	(1.15)	(1.29)	(−0.00)	(0.12)	(0.23)	(0.28)	(0.11)	(0.33)	(0.23)
Unempl	0.528**	0.543**	0.529**	0.623***	0.536**	0.601***	0.565***	0.553*	0.371	0.407	0.239	0.360	0.219	0.331
	(2.40)	(2.46)	(2.41)	(3.07)	(2.52)	(2.86)	(2.77)	(1.73)	(1.13)	(1.23)	(0.72)	(1.14)	(0.66)	(1.05)
N	1007	996	996	996	996	996	996	985	974	974	974	974	974	974
R-sq	0.32	0.32	0.33	0.33	0.33	0.33	0.33	0.18	0.19	0.19	0.21	0.21	0.21	0.21

t statistics in parentheses

* p<0.10 ** p<0.05 *** p<0.01

Note: Yearly dummy variables not reported

Sources: Global Trade Alert (GTA indexes), World Bank (World Development Indicators, Worldwide Government Indicators)

regulatory quality (+4.1) at 1% significance and control of corruption (+2.0) at 10% significance for the entire sample. Thus greater trade openness is associated with efficient government institutions in all democracies, with the strongest evidence in the Fraser index data. Additional variables tested interaction effects between the governance indicators and dummy variables for LW, RW, and AE populist regimes, with varying results for Trade Freedom and Fraser scores.[8] Based on the general association of governance indicators with openness described earlier, the initial hypothesis is that such interaction with any populist regime's dummy variable will be positive. That is, within a sample of populist governments, a higher governance indicator score will be associated with more openness, and a lower score with less openness. This hypothesis receives support in some Trade Freedom regressions, with positive coefficients for AE populism interaction with government effectiveness (+7.7%) and rule of law (+5.5) at 1% significance; voice and accountability (+6.0) and control of corruption (+5.6), both at 5% significance, and political stability (+3.8) at 10% significance. These coefficients are larger than those for the respective indicators for the entire sample of countries, and are consistent with the typical orientation of such regimes in fighting the corrupt practices of their predecessors in office. However, other results show mixed and sometimes contrary results. The Fraser regression in fact contradicts the Trade Freedom results for voice and accountability in AE populist regimes, in posting a *negative* coefficient (-0.3, at 1% level), and goes on to post a negative coefficient for RW populism as well (-0.3, at 10% level). These results are also in sharp contrast to the strongly significant positive coefficient for voice and accountability for the entire sample. Government effectiveness interaction coefficients are unexpectedly negative for both LW (-4.1, at 5% level, Trade Freedom) and RW (-0.3, at 10% level, Fraser) populist regimes' trade scores. In the Fraser regressions, regulatory quality interaction has a positive coefficient with LW (+0.8, at 5% level) and a negative coefficient with RW (-0.3, at 10% level) populist regimes. If the contrarian results are not spurious, they may reflect differences in the information content of the two indexes, and their sensitivities to differences in governance scores. Assuming comparable ratings of tariff and nontariff barriers shared by both indexes, the Fraser index may show differences or changes in foreign direct investment, capital flow, and travel restriction policies that are not included in the Trade Freedom index. In addition, higher government and regulatory quality, while generally showing a direct relationship with trade openness for the entire sample, may reflect strong government bureaucracies even in cases where they result in more trade restricting policies. If this is the case, stronger government effectiveness among ideological populist regimes would thus seem to work against trade openness, in contrast to anti-establishment regimes, whose anti-corruption measures may also involve trade policy.

Another important explanatory variable in the regressions is fuel as a percentage of total exports. Overall, democratic countries more dependent on fuel exports tend to exhibit a significant decrease in the Trade Freedom index, reducing it by about 0.1 in all seven regressions at 5%-10% significance, indicating perhaps a lower importance of trade openness for energy exporters, whose market access abroad for those products is not dependent on their general openness to trade. For the Fraser index, however, this variable appears not to matter. When interacted with populism dummies, only one regression showed that a higher fuel export percentage among LW populist regimes is linked with a lower Fraser index score (-0.3, at 1% level), but there is no evidence of a significant relationship for the Trade Freedom index. In sharp contrast, four of seven regressions show that RW populist, fuel exporting regimes have lower Fraser index scores (about +0.3, all at 5% level), whereby the Trade Freedom results show no such relationship. Other economic control variables show varying results for the entire dataset, not always consistent between the Trade Freedom and Fraser index results. For all democratic countries, economic growth contributes significantly to higher trade policy scores for the Fraser, but not the Trade Freedom, index. Increasing unemployment rates are associated with lower Trade Freedom scores, implying a stronger protectionist tendency with joblessness, but not with the Fraser score. Similarly, a higher ratio of trade as a percentage of GDP is associated with a higher Trade Freedom score, implying that the stakes of open trade are higher for such countries, but this effect does not show up in the Fraser score. A country's share of world trade shows a significantly positive effect in the Fraser, but not the Trade Freedom index. The square of a country's per capita GDP is associated with a decrease in the Fraser index, indicating a dampening negative effect as GDP per capita increases, but not with the Trade Freedom index (GDP per capita itself is insignificant in all regression runs). A country's current account as a percentage of GDP shows some weak linkage with a lower Fraser, but not Trade Freedom, score. Again, the different composition of the two trade policy indexes may serve to explain these contrasting results, as previously explained. The differences in the indexes' contents indicate that any general examination of trade policy openness is likely to be sensitive to the measures used, and a separate examination of populist country data alone exhibited a similar split in the impact of certain economic control variables.[9] It is also important to note that EU countries, including several mostly smaller populist member countries at various times from 1995 to 2018, have a uniformly significant and high boost in their baseline trade policy index scores, by about 4 to 4.8 for the Trade Freedom and about 0.3 to 0.4 for the Fraser index. As noted in chapter 5, all EU member countries are subject to a common trade policy, so populist governments within the European Union have little influence on the collective trade policy.

Table 7.2 shows results for the GTA liberalizing (pro-trade) and discriminatory (anti-trade) count measures by country. Since these statistics show the number of state interventions to either impose or remove measures across a broad range of trade administration, they include traditional policy measures that are captured in the Trade Freedom and Fraser indexes, but also many more obscure bureaucratic measures that are not. So-called murky protectionism includes government domestic industrial bailouts and other types of subsidies, contingent protection measures such as anti-dumping and anti-subsidy duties, government procurement measures designed to favor domestic suppliers, and red-tape burdens on foreign importer suppliers or domestic exporters. The results of these regressions tend to support the hypotheses associated with trade openness explored in the Trade Freedom and Fraser index regressions, with some exceptions. Based on the entire database of democratic countries, those with a higher percentage of fuel exports tend to exhibit fewer liberalizing measures, by .07–.08 for each additional percent of fuel exports, as suggested by their lower export market exposure to trade restrictions and the results of the Trade Freedom regressions. However, this group of countries also appears to impose fewer discriminatory measures, by 0.14–0.18. Coefficients for both liberalizing and discriminatory measures are consistently significant at the 5%-10% level. It is possible that these countries are simply less active in trade policy management in general, given their focus and dependency on fuel exports. Among the governance indicators, higher government effectiveness and rule of law index scores showed significantly positive relationships with the number of trade liberalizing measures at 5% significance. No other governance indicators showed a significant relationship among all democratic countries with greater liberalization or fewer discriminatory measures. The ratio of a country's trade as percentage of GDP showed the expected positive sign for liberalizing measures, but no significant relationship for discriminatory measures. A country's increasing share of world trade also had the expected negative sign for discriminatory measures, but no corresponding positive relationship with liberalizing measures. The expectation regarding world trade share is generally that an increasing share of world trade will typically motivate greater openness, except for fuel exporting countries. Only the very largest trading entities, such as the United States and the EU countries acting together, might have the policy leverage to increase their protectionist interventions because of their size and role in global trade.[10] A higher unemployment rate in a country appears, curiously, to be associated with a larger number of liberalizing measures, significant at the 5% level or better in all seven regressions, with no corresponding significant increase in discriminatory measures. These results seem to contradict the significantly negative coefficients for unemployment in the Trade Freedom regressions. While the usual political expectation is that higher unemployment will breed fewer liberalizing and more discriminatory measures, these results together suggest that countries may combine traditional and contingent trade restrictions with trade-friendly administrative measures and countercyclical macroeconomic and transfer policies to combat unemployment, a subject for further research. Finally, as noted in the discussion of Trade Freedom and Fraser regression results, it is also important to remember that European Union membership makes a difference, increasing EU member country liberalizing measures by 2.2 to 2.9 and discriminatory measures by 7.6 to 8.1, with all coefficients at 1% significance. Thus the largest trading block in the world is active in implementing both liberalizing and discriminatory measures.

As in the case of the Trade Freedom and Fraser regressions, sorting the effects of populism on the number of liberalizing and discriminatory measures requires differentiating among the various types of populist regimes. A dummy variable identifying LW populist governments had consistently negative and significant coefficients ranging from -7 to -9 for trade liberalizing measures, at 5%-10% significance, and the RW dummy also had consistently negative, but statistically weaker coefficients of -4 to -5. AE populist regimes, in contrast, showed significantly positive coefficients of 6 to 22 at the 10% level or better in four of the seven regressions. Thus, there is evidence in these results that ideological populist governments tend to take the fewest trade liberalizing measures, with weaker evidence in this direction for right-wing regimes, and some supporting evidence that anti-establishment regimes, focusing on fighting corruption and improving efficiency, enact a greater number of trade liberalizing measures. However, there is no consistent trend in any of the populist categories regarding the number of discriminatory measures they implement. Interaction terms between the three types of populism and other explanatory variables exhibited mixed results regarding the trade openness hypotheses. For example, the LW/fuel exporter interaction results have unexpectedly positive coefficients for trade liberalizing measures, although they are insignificant in four of six regression runs, in contrast to the significantly negative coefficients in the entire country sample. The evidence is not strong enough to conclude that LW populist fuel exporting countries systematically favor trade-liberalizing measures, perhaps because of the small sample size of such countries, but this result also suggests that Venezuela's famously fuel export-dependent and otherwise anti-trade economy may be an exceptional case. Neither the RW nor AE regime interaction terms with fuel exporting showed any significant pattern for liberalizing measures. The AE/fuel export interaction term showed significantly positive coefficients in two of six regressions for trade-discriminating measures, while comparable RW and LW interaction terms with fuel exporting showed no consistently significant trend, although all but one of the coefficients for the three types were positive.

Populism interaction terms with the governance indicators showed some pro-trade and effects with regard to liberalizing and discriminatory measures, based on the hypothesis that larger governance indicators will generally be associated with more open trade. The AE/political stability interaction term, for example, shows a negative and significant (at 10% level) coefficient of -9.7 for discriminatory measures, a pro-trade result. Similarly, the LW/government effectiveness, LW/regulatory quality, and LW/rule of law interaction terms showed significantly negative coefficients of -12, -10, and 10, respectively, for discriminatory measures, at 1%, 5%, and 5% significance. Another pro-trade result is the RW/government effectiveness interaction coefficient for trade liberalizing measures, which is significantly positive (9.3) at 5% significance. However, a number of AE interaction terms with governance indicators showed unexpectedly anti-trade effects, with significantly negative coefficients for liberalizing measures linked with regulatory quality (-24, at the 1% level), rule of law (-22, at the 1% level), and control of corruption (-18, at the 5% level). Thus, higher levels of governance quality, as measured in the World Bank indicators, seem at times to be associated with more liberalizing and fewer discriminatory measures in the populist country's record, and at times the opposite.

Assessing the Regression Results

As suggested in the discussion on the three types of populism and trade, it appears that undifferentiated populism is too broad a category to establish consistent statistical links to the degree of trade openness. Yet there also seems to be significant variance in trade policy within LW, RW, and AE populist regimes. One confounding factor in this regard is that the EU dummy variable shows that populist member countries are locked into a common, generally open, trade regime. This factor alone makes it difficult to distinguish the trade policy orientation of eight EU populist regimes during the sample period from those of both other populist regimes and nonpopulist regimes: Bulgaria, the Czech Republic, Greece, Hungary, Italy, Poland, Romania, and Slovakia. Nonetheless, the Fraser regression results do provide at least partial support for the hypothesis that left-wing populist tends more toward protectionism, based perhaps on its stronger ideological opposition to capitalist globalization. Most LW populism observations come from Latin America, where there is a long tradition of import substitution, which may also play a role. Evidence regarding RW populism breaks both ways, with Fraser index results supporting openness and GTA liberalizing measures suggesting (with weaker results) protectionism. The most statistically significant and robust result in the entire set of regressions was to identify right-wing fuel-exporting populist governments with weaker Fraser index scores. Yet overall the inconsistent evidence on RW populism and trade is perplexing, especially in view of its presumed preference for economic nationalism, and in particular President Trump's embrace of tariffs. However, Trump's protectionist campaign did not begin in earnest until 2018, and US data for that year were not included in this study (Fraser index numbers ran only to 2017). This single instance of populist protectionism was highly consequential, but would not have altered the regression results in this model significantly. A follow-up study on the impact of the Trump tariffs would have to take into account the spread of protectionism through retaliation and the China trade war. Thus Trump's RW populist protectionism, through its erosion of trade institutions, also provoked nonpopulist countries to impose tariffs in response. Similarly, the number of GTA discriminatory measures spiked in 2017 and 2018, suggesting a sort of populist contagion in those measures, even among nonpopulist regimes, while the number of liberalizing measures declined during those years (Evenett and Fritz 2019, pp. 15–16). Another factor, as noted in chapter 2, is that small open economies tend to be constrained in their trade policy. Israel's right-wing populist governments have typically had high trade policy index numbers, whereby the cultural element of its social policies does not interfere with an open trade and investment economy. In addition, several populist regimes in the European Union have been of the right-wing variety, and have therefore been constrained institutionally by EU centralized trade policy. There may also be more ideological reluctance among some right-wing populist regimes to rock the boat on trade, especially if pro-business forces influence trade policy in those countries. Immigration and other issues may take precedence on their policy agendas, which, as noted in chapters 2 and 6, may differ from their campaign platforms. Again, Trump is the singular exception to this observation. The results do show that AE populism tends more toward trade openness in general, with limited support in the Fraser index, and stronger support in the GTA liberalizing regressions. The inference appears to be that this variety of populism tends to carry out pro-trade policies, possibly in reaction to the alleged corruption, cronyism, and inefficiency of the preceding government. There were fewer observations in this category than for the other two, drawing largely on neoliberal populist regimes in Latin America and pro-business regimes in Eastern Europe, all of which replaced more protectionist predecessors.

Finally, the lack of consistency in the results may reflect the nature of the measures of trade openness. As noted earlier differences in the content of Fraser and Trade Freedom indexes could have resulted in diverging sensitivities to some of the explanatory variables. Furthermore, GTA liberalizing and discriminatory measure data, while supporting some of the differences in trade policy among different types of populist regimes, also show inconclusive results regarding discriminatory measures. GTA results for the entire sample in terms of the governance indicators and their interaction with populist dummies also tend to be less significant than for the Trade Freedom and Fraser regressions. These problems may be due to the smaller GTA dataset, which began only in 2008, restricting the number of observations compared to the other regressions. In addition, GTA measures include murky government intervention at the administrative level. Many of these government interventions are not covered by WTO rules, thus allowing members, both populist and nonpopulist, some room for both extra-WTO mischief and extra-WTO liberalization, not captured completely in trade policy indexes. Many countries across the globe intervened with administrative and other measures after the financial crisis began (which in fact motivated the establishment of GTA monitoring), and continuing in the years immediately following the crisis. Financial crisis-inspired interventions could therefore have occurred for several of the years represented in the database, in part because such actions did not directly violate WTO obligations. Populism may not have been a strongly differentiating factor in this phenomenon.

Populist Regimes in Power

Table 7.3 shows the 25 populist governments that were in power from 2017 to early 2020, based on a list by Kyle and Gultchin (2018), updated to include developments since 2018. The list excludes a number of countries that have some populist traits, but lack sufficient democratic institutions to generate legitimately democratic elections, or lack a populist head of state.[11] The influence of populism on these countries' trade policies varies. The following

Table 7.3 Populist Governments in Power, 2017–2020

Country	Leader or Party	Years in Office	Type of Populism	Fraser'17
Argentina	Alberto Fernandez	2019–		6.55
Belarus	Alexander Lukashenko	1994–	Anti-establishment	7.18
Bolivia	Evo Morales	2006–2019	Left-wing	7.03
Brazil	Jair Bolsonaro	2018–	Right-wing	7.00
Bulgaria	Boyko Borisov	2009–2013, 2014–2017, 2017–	Anti-establishment	8.12
Czech Republic	Andrej Babiš	2017–	Anti-establishment	8.23
Ecuador	Rafael Correa	2007–2017	Left-wing	6.52
Greece	Syriza	2015–2018	Left-wing	7.68
Hungary	Viktor Orbán	1998–2002, 2010–	Right-wing	7.95
India	Narendra Modi	2014–	Right-wing	6.08
Indonesia	Joko Widodo	2014–	Anti-establishment	6.95
Israel	Benjamin Netanyahu	1996–1999, 2009–	Right-wing	8.22
Italy	Five Star Movement/League coalition	2018–2019	Anti-establishment	8.25
Mexico	Andrés Manuel López Obrador	2018–	Left-wing	7.64
Nicaragua	Daniel Ortega	2007–	Left-wing	7.80
Philippines	Rodrigo Duterte	2016–	Right-wing	7.16
Poland	Law and Justice party	2005–2010, 2015–	Right-wing	7.91
Russia	Vladimir Putin	2000–	Right-wing	6.83
Serbia	Aleksandar Vucic	2014–2017, 2017–	Right-wing	7.60
Slovakia	Robert Fico	2006–2010, 2012–2018	Right-wing	8.30
South Africa	Jacob Zuma	2009–2018	Left-wing	6.87
Sri Lanka	Mahinda Rajapaksa	2005–2015, 2018–	Right-wing	5.89
Turkey	Recep Tayyip Erdogan	2003–	Right-wing	7.27
United Kingdom	Boris Johnson	2019-	Right-wing	8.43
United States	Donald Trump	2017–	Right-wing	7.65
Venezuela	Nicolás Maduro	2013–	Left-wing	3.28

Source: Kyle and Gultchin 2019, with updates by the author. Legend: Fraser'17 refers to the 2017 Fraser Index score for trade openness, ranging from 0 to 10 (most open).

sections examine populist countries and their trade regimes in Latin America; the Middle East and Asia; Russia and Belarus; the European Union, Serbia, and Turkey; and South Africa.

Latin America

In Latin America populism is in flux, as there have been several changes in government or in their circumstances in recent years. Most populist countries in this group had left-wing regimes, although their level of trade openness varied. The most protectionist, by any measure, was Venezuela, which began its populist regime under Hugo Chavez in 1999 and was succeeded after his death in 2013 by Nicolás Maduro. Since then, Venezuela has continued to descend into an increasingly harsh dictatorship, with a collapsing economy. Its oil-dependent economy suffered from reduced output capabilities due to a lack of investment and equipment maintenance. Along with generally low petroleum prices during this period, export revenues are weak and external debt has soared. Imports were tightly controlled by government import licensing and permit requirements, along with exchange controls that ration access to import funding. Because of these bureaucratic restrictions, along with galloping inflation, black market activity flourished. The International Trade Centre ranked Venezuela's market access in 117th place out of 132 countries. Its 2017 Fraser Index was 3.28, lowest of all the populist countries in the sample.

Venezuela's economic collapse has affected neighboring populist states. In 2004, at the beginning of a ten-year oil boom, Venezuelan President Chavez and Cuban President Fidel Castro founded the Bolivarian Alliance for the Peoples of Our America, known by its Spanish acronym ALBA, an organization of Caribbean area countries that sought to provide an alternative framework for regional trade outside the WTO. Aside from Venezuela it notably included three other left-wing populist states: Ecuador, Bolivia, and Nicaragua.[12] ALBA represented the tendency of populist countries to form regional or bilateral relationships with like-minded regimes in order to avoid isolation. Venezuelan oil-funded largesse was important in this regard, offering loans and trade credits that would have been difficult for weaker and often cash-strapped populist regimes to acquire. Cuba, a fully communist regime, benefitted from this arrangement for similar reasons (Jones 2018). ALBA countries also formed a common regional currency, the sucre, to facilitate trade within the group. During this period Ecuador, also an oil exporter with a dollarized economy, had difficulty remaining competitive on world markets. Correa's government attempted to address this problem by pursuing policies that increased state control of the economy and protectionism, including import substitution, which discouraged inbound foreign direct investment and suppressed productivity (WTO 2012). Ecuador's 2017 Fraser index of 6.52 was brought down largely by its use of nontariff and regulatory barriers. The end of the oil boom in 2015 diminished Ecuador's ability to finance its budget and trade deficits, and ALBA's effectiveness as a framework for regional trade, along with use of the sucre, also declined. Correa's term ended in 2017, and his successor, Lenin Moreno, although from the same populist party PAIS (Patria Altiva I Soberana), distanced himself from Correa's policies and from the alliance with Venezuela, withdrawing Ecuador from ALBA and the sucre currency arrangement in 2018. During 2020 the country was attempting to recover from the structural and debt problems inherited from its populist policies, which had prompted President Moreno to apply for International Monetary Fund (IMF) loans, necessitating an unpopular program of budgetary austerity.

Bolivia, under Evo Morales since 2006, also pursued inward-oriented economic policies, with ties to ALBA and trading mainly with South American countries and China. Its 2017 Fraser index of 7.03 was better than Ecuador's, reflecting more modest government control of the economy, but still was still hampered by its use of nontariff barriers, restrictions on foreign investment, and capital controls (WTO 2018). Venezuela provided financial support to Bolivia early in Morales's regime, and he continued to support Venezuela under Maduro throughout 2019, but the aid dried up as Venezuela's economy declined. The Morales regime lost favor after a series of scandals, including allegations of election rigging in late 2019, and he subsequently fled to Mexico. Yet Morales remained popular at home, especially among his indigenous base, and Bolivia's immediate political future remained uncertain in 2020. Nicaraguan trade policy under Daniel Ortega since 2007 presents a different picture, heavily influenced by its integration into the Central and North American economies. Its 2017 Fraser index is 7.80, highest of all populist governments in the Western Hemisphere, including the United States, whose score of 7.65 was based on information before Donald Trump took office. Nicaragua's relative trade openness comes from its membership in DR-CAFTA, the Central American Free Trade Agreement with the United States, and its harmonization of most tariff rates with its neighbors Costa Rica, El Salvador, Guatemala, and Honduras. Its score is brought down somewhat by its use of capital controls, investment ownership restrictions, and nontariff barriers. In general, however, its trade policy suggests that when presented with valuable trade opportunities in its region, a left-wing populist government will value trade openness over ideology. On political issues, in contrast, Ortega remains firmly allied with authoritarian regimes, keeping Nicaragua in ALBA, supporting the Maduro regime in Venezuela, and accepting military aid from Russia (Chaguaceda 2019).

Mexico's left-wing populist president, Andrés Manuel López Obrador, took office in December 2018. Although his performance two years into his administration cast doubt on his ability to eliminate many Mexican domestic economic problems, including poverty and unequal income distribution, it is unlikely that he will change Mexico's trade policy, which remains more open than most others in Latin America. Mexico has 14 free-trade agreements with 50 countries, including the EU countries, the European Free Trade Association (EFTA), the South American trade bloc *Mercado Común del Sur* (Mercosur), the Comprehensive and Progressive Agreement for Trans-Pacific Partnership (CPTPP), and most importantly, the US-Mexico-Canada Agreement (USMCA). The United States dominates Mexican trade, serving as the destination for about 80% of Mexican exports and the source of about half of Mexican imports. The importance of this trade relationship outweighs any ideological preferences of the Mexican government, and its pursuit of a large portfolio of trade agreements provides an important, if limited, set of additional and diversified trading partners. The resulting anchor of multiple integration agreements effectively locks in an open trade policy for Mexico. In this instance it is highly doubtful that populism—left, right, or anti-establishment—will influence trade policy. In the years of the Trump presidency, populism from the north of the border has been a greater threat to the Mexican economy.

Argentina, with its long-standing tradition of Peronist populism, elected Alberto Fernández as president, who took office in December 2019. The transition to a new populist regime ended the centrist government of Mauricio Macri, who had failed to stabilize Argentina's precarious economy. Fernández's vice president was former President Christina Fernández de Kirchner, whose own populist regime had implemented international economic policies that came to be known as *kirchnerism*—import substitution, opposition to multilateral trade agreements, and capital controls. Argentina's 2017 Fraser index of 6.55 was based on more open trade policies during the Macri period, but still showed weaknesses in terms of heavy capital controls and burdensome nontariff barriers and other trade regulations. Fraser index scores from the years of Christina Fernández de Kirchner's administration were much worse, averaging 3.73 during the final four years of her term, ending in 2015. The question arises as to whether the new regime will revert to earlier protectionist policies. An important mitigating factor is that the new Fernández government inherited the legacy of earlier economic mismanagement and debt accumulation, and as a result faced severe policy constraints from IMF conditions on the continuation of loans it will need in order to recover. Some observers expected more centrist policies in order to achieve IMF compliance and a reduction in its debt burden, but with weak economic growth (EIU 2019). Argentina's populist cycle, with intermittent periods of crisis and reform, appeared likely to continue.

Brazil's right-wing populist President Jair Bolsonaro took office in January 2019. He was the sole right-wing populist in power in Latin America in 2020, and in his first year in office appeared to be pursuing trade policy through serial bilateral transactions with like-minded populists, holding personal consultations and state visits with Donald Trump, Boris Johnson, Norendra Modi, and Benjamin Netanyahu. He had earlier expressed anti-globalization, anti-WTO, and anti-China sentiments along the lines of Trump's campaign platform. Yet his investment in a closer relationship with Trump generally proved to be problematical, especially as it placed Bolsonaro in the middle of the Trump's trade war with China, Brazil's largest trading partner. In addition, Trump impulsively reinstated steel and aluminum tariffs against Brazil in December 2019, convinced that a fall in the value of the Brazilian real was the result of malign currency manipulation by Brazil, despite his warm words for Bolsanaro earlier in the year at a White House visit. After an urgent phone call by Bolsonaro, Trump did remove the tariffs, but it was becoming clear that transactional populist trade relations with Trump would not involve loyalty from Trump's side. Bolsonaro gradually adopted a more pragmatic approach to trade and turned to the task of improving relations with China, which had diverted its import purchases from the United States to Brazil on soybeans and other goods because of retaliation against in the trade war. He also supported the conclusion of the regional free-trade agreement between Mercosur and the European Union, although the relationship between Argentina and Brazil within Mercosur remained tense (Schipani et al. 2019).[13] More importantly, in November 2019 Bolsonaro joined other BRICs nations (Brazil, Russia, India, and China) in condemning the rise in protectionism in the global economy (Jackson 2019), just as his government announced its intention to reduce the country's tariff levels (Noticias Financieras 2019). A divided Brazilian Parliament is likely to move Bolsonaro's policies on economic issues toward more centrist positions, which will tend to favor at least some trade liberalization if the Brazilian economy improves.

The Middle East and Asia

In the area spanning the Middle East and Asia, five countries have populist governments: Israel, India, Indonesia Sri Lanka, and the Philippines, with trade policies the range from open (Israel) to strongly protectionist (India). Israel (2017 Fraser index: 8.22) is an example of a small economy with a highly educated workforce, specializing in high-tech goods and services, that prospers in an open trading economy. Among its numerous free-trade agreements are those with the United States, the European Union, Mercosur, and EFTA, and in 2020 it was negotiating agreements with China, India, and the Republic of Korea, Vietnam, and others (WTO 2018b). Its right-wing populist focus is largely on the internal Palestinian issue, and its prosperity depends on access to world markets. Sri Lanka, another relatively small country with a right-wing populist government, is in contrast to Israel dependent largely on low-tech exports of clothing, tea, and other agricultural goods. The main burdens on its trade policy (2017 Fraser index: 5.83) included a large proportion of unbound tariff rates, allowing unexpected tariff hikes, nontariff trade regulations, restrictions on foreign direct investment, and capital controls. These items made Sri Lanka's trade policy unpredictable. The civil war, pitting the minority Tamil population against the majority Sinhalese, ended in 2009, but ethnic tensions remain, amplified by authoritarian measures imposed by the populist government and decreasing the attractiveness of the country for foreign investment. Aside from objective measures of trade policy, the Transparency International corruption index for Sri Lanka was 39 (100 indicates least corrupt), ranking 89th out of 180 countries in 2018.[14] There was also a large presence of state-owned enterprises in the economy, and in combination with corruption tended to create nontransparent trade restrictions. Public debt problems, associated in part with state-owned enterprises, revealed the need for structural reforms, which would improve Sri Lanka's trade policy performance, along with economic efficiency and growth.

India's right-wing Populist Narendra Modi was elected president in 2014, and one of his first acts in office was to torpedo the WTO Bali declaration, which had been agreed upon by his predecessor in office.[15] Modi later relented, agreeing to a compromise brokered by the US administration, but his action indicated that his political instincts were to overturn WTO negotiations first and negotiate a compromise later. His defiance of a WTO agreement provided a small foretaste of Donald Trump's more consequential defiance of WTO rules on national security tariffs four years later, but without any consideration of compromise. The signal of Trump's harsh treatment of existing trade arrangements was not lost on Modi. He had visited Trump at the White House in 2017, thinking, perhaps, like Brazil's Bolsonaro, that friendly relations with a fellow populist would pay off in a stable trade relationship. Yet in June 2019 Trump abruptly suspended the Generalized System of Preferences (GSP) program for India's imports to the United States, claiming that India was treating US imports unfairly with its high tariffs. In the course of negotiating this issue, along with other disputes, Modi visited the United States again in September 2019, but this time arranging for the added fillip of a rally with Trump in front of 50,000 Indian Americans, all presumably qualified to vote in the 2020 US presidential elections (Upadhyay 2019). Populism as a political tool thus moved to the stage in which Modi attempted to leverage his influence among four million Indian-Americans in his trade relationship with Trump.[16] Modi later hosted Trump in his state visit to India in early 2020, but efforts to resolve the GSP issue were unsuccessful. India's trade regime has a 2017 Fraser index score of 6.08, with relatively high tariffs and nontariff barriers, along with foreign investment restrictions and capital controls. There is no sign that its trade policy will become less restrictive under Modi's administration. In attempting to jump-start India's participation in global supply chains, as China did earlier, Modi pursued a policy of economic nationalism, imposing import duties of up to 25% on several cellphone and electronic components and appliances (Aiyar 2019). He also imposed new duties of up to 50% to protect the profits of domestic light manufacturers. Such populist policies tended to raise prices and misallocate domestic resources, destroying incentives for more efficient production and development. Because of its population size, more than its trade volume, India has become a major player in the WTO, and Modi's populist rejection of WTO disciplines bodes poorly for the WTO to regain its influence or achieve significant trade liberalization in the near future. His continued trade skepticism was expressed in late 2019, when he withdrew from trade negotiations with the Regional Comprehensive Economic Partnership (RCEP) countries, repelled by the requirement of lowering Indian tariffs significantly in order to join the agreement.[17]

Philippines, under its flamboyant president, Rodrigo Duterte, had a 2017 Fraser index of 7.16, with trade policy problems in foreign investment restrictions, capital controls, and regulatory trade barriers. More troubling for international trade was President Duterte's capricious and unpredictable governing style, along with the endemic corruption that the Philippines economy has long exhibited. Its Transparency International corruption score is 36 out of 100, ranking 99th among 180 countries listed. Increased foreign investment, in particular, could boost its burgeoning manufactures sector. Duterte's policy of extrajudicial executions of drug addicts and criminals, along with his detention of government officials, journalists, and others who oppose his policies, sparked human rights inquiries that threatened the Philippines' GSP status, putting its duty-free exports to several Organization for Economic Cooperation and Development (OECD) countries at risk. Duterte, like many populists, was attempting to manage his country's trade policy, along with its political relations, on a personal basis. He found favor with Donald Trump on his aggressive domestic drug war, reinforcing the Philippines' longstanding economic and security ties with the United States, but he has also sought closer economic ties with China's Xi Jinping, despite (or perhaps because of) China's aggressive assertion of sovereignty over most of the South China Sea. He was thus put in a position of balancing relations between the two large countries at odds with each other in the context of popular disapproval at home of Chinese incursions in Philippines territorial waters.

Populist President Joko Widodo of Indonesia, with the fourth-largest population in the world and the largest Islamic population, has been in office since 2014, winning his second five-year term in 2019. Indonesia's trade economy is based largely on commodities such as mineral oils, palm oil, and rubber, with some manufacturing in electrical machinery, vehicles, computers, and steel. Indonesia's 2017 Fraser index of 6.95 reflected the influence of regulatory trade barriers and foreign investment restrictions, particularly in agricultural and natural resource sectors (EIU 2019c). Patunru (2018) describes Widodo's trade policy as "populist-protectionist," although he defeated his more authoritarian political opponent in the last election by a small margin, who would probably have installed an even more nationalistic trade regime. Hence Kyle and Gultchin (2018) have categorized Widodo as an anti-establishment, rather than a culturally nativist right-wing, populist. There is a strong Islamic nationalist movement in Indonesia that plays a significant role in trade policy, based on its resentment toward the country's Chinese minority, and of Chinese foreign investment and migrant workers in the country (Warburton 2018). A more open Indonesian economy would benefit the relatively small manufactures sector by expanding the country's supply-chain links to the rest of Southeast Asia, but this would require more foreign investment, especially from China, as well as structural changes in agriculture, which currently locks in labor and other resources due to protection. The political constraints on trade openness were comparable in some ways to India's, with its large rural farming population. As long as political stability in Indonesia is fragile, it seems that economic and trade policy reforms will have to wait.

Russia and Belarus

The Russian Federation plays a unique role in global populism and trade. Having joined the WTO in 2011, after a lengthy and hopeful accession process, its membership has had little impact on either its own economy or on trade relations. Russian exports continued to consist mainly of oil, natural gas, and other natural resources that do not typically face import restrictions, and therefore do not benefit greatly from WTO-based trade rules and liberalization. The country's main potential benefit from WTO membership would have come from diversifying and developing its production in higher value-added goods and services, with the help of WTO market access rules. Instead, Russia's economic nationalism, supported by protectionism, high domestic market concentration, corruption, and lack of foreign investment, have weakened its economy's ability to take advantage of growth opportunities in the global economy. Its noncommodity products are largely uncompetitive on global markets (EIU 2019b). Its 2017 Fraser index is 6.83, with nontariff barriers, foreign investment ownership, and capital controls identified as major problems. Thus one major cost of Russian populist economic policies is that they have prevented the country from achieving the gains from trade that WTO membership would have made possible. Another cost of Russian populism came from its irredentist claim on (and seizure of) Ukrainian Crimea, followed by an invasion of eastern Ukraine, which led to crippling economic sanctions against Russia.

Russian protectionist policies have also led to several failures to comply with its WTO obligations, as outlined in its first WTO Trade Policy Report in 2016 (WTO 2016b; see also EIU 2019b). Beyond these concerns, the global cost of populism has increased due to the efforts of Russia to spread its influence. In a WTO dispute case in 2016, Russia responded to a complaint by Ukraine about Russia's imposition of unilateral tariffs, claiming that it had the right to impose unilateral national security tariffs after its invasion of Ukraine, which were not subject to any WTO review regarding their justification.[18] President Trump had taken office by the time the WTO panel reviewed the case, and supported Russia's arguments despite the official US position that Russia's invasion of Ukraine was illegal. The WTO panel in the end approved Russia's use of national security tariffs, skirting the issue of whether the invasion itself was legal under international law, but it did deny Russia's claim that national security tariffs were nonjusticiable and nonreviewable. The United States would take this issue to a new level of WTO defiance in its unilateral use of national security tariffs in the steel and aluminum tariffs of 2018. Russia had thus previewed the US populist argument for unilateral tariffs that would be outside any WTO review. Russia engaged in more direct promotion of populist disruptions in its efforts to interfere in the Brexit referendum in the United Kingdom in 2016 and presidential elections in the United States (2016) and France (2017) (Kim et al. 2018; Hamilton 2019). The Russian disinformation campaigns set out to sow discord in the target countries, promoting populist candidates. The ultimate goal was to undermine the countries' abilities to oppose Vladimir Putin's foreign policy agenda, including the weakening of NATO and the European Union, and US disengagement from Russia's sphere of influence in the Middle East (Gvosdev 2019). The Russian interference took the form of social media disinformation campaigns on pre-existing and divisive social and political issues, such as immigration, race, Islamic terrorism, gun control, and alleged scandals regarding political candidates. Trade issues appear not to have played a role in the disinformation campaigns, as other populist hot-button controversies were more likely to excite the desired outrage and political division. However, as noted in the accounts of the US 2016 presidential election (chapter 4) and the Brexit referendum (chapter 6), the trade issue was swept up in the populist agenda, based on its mutual reinforcement with the more emotional cultural and partisan sources of outrage against global elites. Undermining the WTO, in which the United States played the leading role and Russia remained essentially an outsider, was consistent with the Russian strategy of targeting the United States and supporting its openly protectionist candidate, Donald Trump. Undermining the European Union had the clear Russian goals of influencing the UK Brexit vote in favor of leave, and influencing elections in France in favor of left- and right-wing populist party presidential candidates, both of which were protectionist. Putin has also cultivated ties with European populist parties, many of which have become pro-Russian in their views on the sanctions issue.

The populist leader of Belarus, Alexandr Lukashenko, was the longest serving head-of-state in Europe in late 2020, having remained in power since 1994. The inclusion of Belarus on the list of populist governments as a democracy is certainly dubious, as observers have questioned the validity of its elections over the years, especially since 2010, when the United States and EU refused to recognize the validity of the elections and imposed sanctions on him and other Belarusian officials. In 2020, Lukashenko again claimed a landslide victory, quickly crushed subsequent protests against his rule, and forced his main political opponent to flee the country (Necheporenko and Troianovski 2020). Members of the diplomatic community now commonly refer to him as the last dictator in Europe (Lennon 2019). Nonetheless, the first election in 1994 appeared to be reasonably open, and for that reason Belarus has remained on the populist country list along with near-dictatorships Venezuela and Russia. Belarus, a land-locked neighbor of Russia, is one of only two countries (with Serbia) on the populist list that is not a member of the WTO, although it applied to join in 1993.[19] It exports mainly refined oil, basic industrial products, and agricultural goods, with about 40% of industry still controlled by state-owned enterprises. Lukashenko has been content for most of his in office to partner with Putin and trade mainly with Russia, which accounts for about half of Belarusian imports and exports. The two countries have a formal bilateral economic integration agreement, supplemented by a broader trade agreement, the Eurasian Economic Union, which now includes Kazakhstan, Kyrgyzstan, and Armenia (Lennon 2019, p. 324). Such partnerships between authoritarian populists have their limits, however, as seen with Trump's treatment of fellow populist heads of state. Putin abruptly cut off Belarussian meat and dairy imports in 2014, ostensibly for health safety reasons, and ended preferential treatment to Belarus on its oil pricing in 2018. Lennon (2019) reports that Lukashenko had refused to retaliate in solidarity with Russia against Western sanctions on Russia after the annexation of Crimea, and that Putin's trade restrictions and price hikes may have been intended to teach Lukashenko a loyalty lesson. Lukashenko, for his part, announced he was open to alternative partnerships. Over the years Belarus had also traded with Ukraine, China, and some EU countries, and he has trade agreements with Latvia, Lithuania, and Poland. He hoped to expand and supplement these ties, perhaps including the United States. Belarus' 2017 Fraser index of 6.78, while not indicative of openness, did show a reasonably transparent trade regime. Its Fraser index would have been closer to 8.00 if it had developed a more open foreign investment regime. However, the lack of WTO membership was a barrier to building any extensive trade relationship, and the Ukrainian conflict discouraged the European Union and China from pursuing entanglements in that region that would provoke Russia further. Donald Trump was also not inclined to cross Putin by cozying up to his recalcitrant neighbor. After the August 2020 elections, Putin himself may have been losing patience with the volatile Lukashenko's behavior, as Kremlin pressure led him to announce in November that he would step down once a vague process of constitutional reform took place (Lawler 2020). Belarus thus remains isolated and dependent on Russia for the foreseeable future, a cautionary tale for a populist government with only one large, populist friend.

The European Union, Serbia, and Turkey

As of early 2020, the European Union included a number of populist governments, including right-wing Hungary (7.97), Poland (7.89), and

Slovakia (8.30);[20] anti-establishment populist governments Bulgaria (8.11), the Czech Republic (8.22), and Italy (8.24), forming a broader nonpopulist coalition in 2019; and the left-wing populist government in Greece (7.68), ousted in 2019 elections (2017 Fraser index numbers shown in parentheses). Chapter 6 described the general state of populism in the European Union, and this discussion will focus on the consequences of populist rule for trade within each country. As noted earlier, all of these countries belong to a centralized EU trade regime, and so the tariff component of their Fraser index numbers will be identical. Of the six remaining components in the index, only three show any sizable variance among the eight countries in the sample: prevalence of nontariff barriers, openness of the foreign direct investment regime, and capital controls. A comparison of the composite Fraser index numbers shows that the anti-establishment populist governments rank highest: Slovakia, Italy, the Czech Republic, and Bulgaria, all scoring 8.1 or higher. Right-wing populists Hungary and Poland come next, scoring just below 8.0, while the left-wing Greek Syriza government ranks lowest, at 7.68. The index score for Greece, however, does not reflect populist policies as such, since it is the result of the low capital controls score imposed by the European Central Bank, IMF, and European Commission during the austerity program, in response to the Greek financial crisis (Stamouli 2017). One can therefore lay the blame for the deterioration in Greek trade openness in 2017 to a combination of original flaws in the structure of the Eurozone and economic mismanagement by the earlier Greek administration that precipitated the crisis. The populist backlash in Greece that resulted in the 2015 victory for Syriza did not, in the end, lead to left-wing populist policies because of the conditions imposed by the international financial bailout. As the crisis eased and austerity was phasing out in 2019, new elections brought the center-right New Democracy party to power, replacing Syriza. As for populist trade-related policies in right-wing Hungary and Poland, their Fraser scores were brought down by capital controls and less-open foreign direct investment (FDI) regimes. These are policy domains that remain partially in the hands of individual EU member countries, even among the three Eurozone countries in the group (Greece, Italy, and Slovakia).[21] The index ranking among the EU populist governments, though based on relatively small differences, supports the broader conclusion that anti-establishment populism tends to support more open trade policies, compared to EU right- and left-wing populist governments.

Despite the differences in some policy details of trade openness, the common, centralized trade policy in the European Union still dominates, and the free circulation of goods and services maintains this uniformity. But there is another dimension of possible intra-EU differences in trade performance and trade policy: immigration policy. It is not included directly in any of the trade policy indexes, but may play a role in trade policy to the extent that xenophobia is linked to attitudes on trade, as discussed in chapter 2. It is difficult to see this linkage in the trade policies of EU members, given its customs union and generally unified trade policy. However, the platform positions of EU right-wing populist parties show a correlation between anti-immigrant and protectionist rhetoric, as noted in chapter 6. If such populist countries do acquire the opportunity to define their own trade policy, protectionist impulses may predominate. Anti-immigrant sentiment and policy tend to be strongest among the populist governments of central Europe and Italy.[22] In response to the EU immigrant crisis of 2015, Poland, the Czech Republic, Hungary, and Slovakia jointly declared that they would not accept any proposal involving mandatory and permanent quotas dictated by Brussels (Maurice 2015). The Slovak populist government elected in 2020 had close ties to the French anti-immigrant Rassemblement National party, which was also highly protectionist. Hungary, under the increasingly authoritarian rule of Victor Orban, introduced the most severe restrictions on immigration from non-EU countries. Although Poland initially accepted refugees under the EU solidarity plan, the right-wing populist Truth and Justice Party subsequently won a majority of seats in the Polish legislature and reversed the decision. The Czech Republic also maintained highly restrictive immigration policies (Drbohlav and Janurová 2019). The replacement of Italy's right-wing populist Matteo Salvini as Interior Minister in 2019 softened the country's harsh treatment of immigrants, especially asylum seekers (Peitromarchi 2019). At stake in these countries—as well as in the rest of Europe—was not just anti-immigrant attitudes, although policies to promote assimilation and integration into the host societies will be necessary to alleviate this problem. Equally important was the fact that Europe's low birth rate risked shrinking its population, lowering its ability to finance future pension and welfare systems and to maintain production and international competitiveness with a younger workforce. A potential cost of anti-immigrant populism, in other words, was the ability to maintain or increase the population's standard of living in a global economy.

In early 2020 Serbia had a pro-EU populist government, led by Aleksandar Vucic, which applied to join the European Union in 2009. Since 2011 it has been an official candidate for accession, and was in the midst of this process in 2020. In conjunction with this application, Serbia also applied to join the WTO in 2005, which is a precondition for joining the EU (European Commission 2015). Serbia's WTO accession negotiations moved slowly in the ensuing years, as it had to implement legislation to make its trade regime compatible with WTO requirements, and it also had to conduct bilateral negotiations with all interested WTO members before its final accession agreement could be completed. The main impediments to its EU membership application, aside from the dilatory WTO bilateral negotiations, were Serbia's unresolved border and sovereignty issues with its former province, Kosovo, whose independence Serbia did not recognize, but which the European Union did recognize. A Serbian minority also lived within Kosovo's borders. Given the difficulty of these issues, final EU accession was not expected before 2025, implying a similar time frame for WTO accession.[23] Serbia's trade regime, as shown by its 2017 Fraser index of 7.62, had weaknesses regarding nontariff barriers, FDI regulations, and capital controls, but the interim EU assessment of its progress toward membership was good (European Commission 2015). The discipline of the dual EU/WTO legislative adjustments and accession reviews was likely to keep Serbia's trade regime in line with the rigors of the requirements of membership in both organizations. In the meantime, President Vucic faced the task of having to keep his nationalist Serbian base in check and negotiate a resolution to the Kosovo question in order to reach his goals of joining the European Union and the global trading system.

Turkey's right-wing populist President Recep Tayyip Erdoğan first took office in 2003. Under his leadership, the Justice and Development (AKP) Party became increasingly nationalist and authoritarian. Turkey is a large upper middle-income country with a diversified economy and a strong reliance on trade. It has integrated extensively with the European Union on trade matters, concluding a customs union agreement in 1996, and has replicated most EU free-trade agreements with the same partners, and officially became a candidate for full membership in the European Union in 1999 (WTO 2016). As of 2020, approximately 40% of Turkey's trade was with EU countries. Its 2017 Fraser index of 7.27 reflected the positive rating of Turkey's integration with the EU tariff regime, but also showed weaknesses based on capital controls, foreign investment restrictions, nontariff barriers, and a high dispersion of tariff rates, indicating government use of tariffs to carve out special protection for certain industries. Turkish trade policy thus contained elements of both openness and restrictiveness. In view of the economic value of its ties to the European Union, Erdoğan's populist government was unlikely to challenge the EU trade regime or the WTO trading system. At the same time, Turkey's efforts to become a full EU member reached a standstill, based on several factors. Erdoğan's authoritarian tendencies violated the requirement that EU members be democracies. His treatment of the country's Kurdish minority and refusal to acknowledge the 1915 Armenian genocide cast doubt on his commitment to human rights. Disputes with EU members Greece and Cyprus on territorial and political issues remained unresolved. Finally, popular opinion in EU countries tended not to support Turkish accession because of its predominantly Islamic population (in contrast to Christian Europe), as well as its size, which would make it the largest EU country and change the EU balance of power in EU representative bodies. It was not clear, in an age of heightened identity politics, that any other Turkish regime would have overcome these objections by 2020, but there is evidence that Erdoğan's populist authoritarianism increased EU negative attitudes toward Turkish membership (Lindgaard 2018). Turkish public opinion—once strongly in favor of Turkish membership—also cooled significantly, partly in reaction to these EU views, and to the neglect with which EU governments treated the accession process (Şenyuva 2018). Any additional benefits to Turkey and the European Union of increased integration will likely need to wait at least until the populist cycles on both sides run their course.

In the Turkish domestic economy, Erdoğan's populist government exhibited many typical problems of authoritarian governments, as when he appointed his son-in-law as finance minister, precipitating a currency run on the Turkish lira and policies that decreased the independence of the Central Bank (Turak 2019; Van Eck 2018). Crony capitalism and corruption reduced efficiency and discouraged foreign investment, and a number of needed economic reforms to improve market efficiency and the business and investment climate remained unaddressed (EIU 2019b). Political risks continued to hamper the economy, especially since the attempted military coup in 2016, which led to renewed crackdowns on opposition parties and political dissent, the purge of thousands from the military and civil service, and the summary closure of several universities, liquidation of their assets, and dismissal of their entire corps of faculty. The targeting of education officials, teachers, and professors was reportedly part of a plan to refocus public education on nationalist and Islamic principles (Kirby 2016). The crackdown on universities also precipitated a brain drain of academics. Unrest in Kurdish regions continued, with some terrorist attacks in major Turkish cities, and there were no efforts as of early 2020 for either the government or Kurdish separatists to negotiate an end to the violence (EIU 2019b). The sum of these developments on the Turkish economy were likely to be negative, particularly in terms of business incentives, domestic and foreign investment, technological advancement, research and development, and consumer confidence. In the absence of a strong challenger Erdoğan may remain in power for years, but his continued populist management of the economy may be very costly for Turkey's trade competitiveness and performance in the future.

South Africa

South Africa emerged from the white-minority apartheid government in the early 1990s, with the 1994 election of its first black president, Nelson Mandela, who served until 1999. He managed the country's peaceful transition to a multiracial democracy by the strength of his personality and stature both at home and abroad. Yet his party, the African National Congress (ANC), continued one-party rule through 2020, eventually leading to widespread corruption, cronyism, and economic mismanagement. Left-wing populist Jacob Zuma was president from 2009 until 2018, when he was forced by his own party to resign over a corruption scandal. His successor, Cyril Ramaphosa, promised clean government, economic reforms, and efficient management of the economy. Rich in natural resources and endowed with the most developed infrastructure and market institutions on the continent, South Africa began the post–apartheid era with hopes for economic growth. Freed of the global market isolation of the apartheid-era embargo, expectations were that a stable, democratic government and well-managed economy would eliminate unemployment, poverty, and income inequality. Populist grievances grew, however, as the government failed to overcome the problems of inefficient state-owned enterprises, lack of investment in infrastructure (especially electricity generation), restrictive labor regulations, skilled worker shortages, and political instability. Unemployment remained at 30% or higher for most of the post–apartheid years, and poverty was still rampant. The rate of violent crime was among the highest in the world, imposing not only human costs on society, but also high security costs for business. Housing and educational opportunities were still lacking, and the poor conditions in many large townships were still visible. Investment-starved power plants were subject to frequent electricity outages, another drag on business and a disincentive for investors in the economy (England 2015). Populist anger boiled up spontaneously, often among angry crowds focusing on foreigners from neighboring countries alleged to be stealing jobs, on white farmers with large landholdings, and on foreign companies allegedly extracting value from the economy without improving it. Eventually corrupt South African politicians became the target.

President Zuma jumped onto the populist bandwagon in an attempt to shore up his waning public support, despite the fact that his administration's policies were responsible for many of the problems. His initial land reform program was proceeding very slowly, and his decision to support landless farmers and a new plan of expropriation without compensation raised concerns that it would spark new racial violence and political instability, scaring off foreign investment (Zukowski 2017).[24] He also shifted blame for anti-foreign riots from violent crowds to local shop owners and foreign drug dealers (Businesstech 2017), and promised free university education for the all young South Africans without any plan for financing it (Grove 2017). In the meantime, foreign investors, concerned over electricity shortages, the security of property rights, and unpredictable foreign investment policies, began to exit the South African market (Businesstech 2018).

South Africa has extensive trade with global markets, exporting fuel, machinery, vehicles, and iron and steel to African markets, and gold, diamonds, fruits and nuts, wine, and industrial inputs, as well as machinery and vehicles, to European markets. Other major trading partners include China, the United States, and India. South Africa is also a large services exporter to African countries, particularly in travel, insurance, and telecommunications, and the source of much of the foreign direct investment in the rest of Africa (Tralac 2019). It is part of the South African Customs Union (along with Botswana, Namibia, Lesotho, and Eswatini), and several other African regional trade agreements. The prospects for South Africa's economic growth, based on its natural resources and legacy of industrial and market infrastructure, will depend on the ability of a new post-Mandela leadership to resist corruption and find political solutions to difficult economic and social problems. Under the populist Zuma regime, corruption increased while international competitiveness decreased.[25] Its 2017 Fraser Index of 6.87 reveals trade policy weaknesses regarding the protectionist dispersion of tariff levels (tariff peaks), regulatory trade barriers, and foreign investment restrictions. Zuma fell all too easily into populist grandstanding in the face of the nation's weak economic performance, and his successor, Ramaphosa, also took up the populist issue of land reform without compensation in the 2019 elections under similar conditions. The danger of allowing this and other divisive issues to produce political instability will further hamper economic growth, attractiveness for foreign investment, and international competitiveness. Another populist, Donald Trump, seized on the South African land reform issue as a possible reason to exclude the country from the US African Growth and Opportunity Act (AGOA) preference program. Progress on economic reforms, infrastructure, and employment may suppress the populist temptation and promote improvements in its trade and foreign investment performance.

Summary

This chapter has provided some statistical evidence that left-wing, right-wing, and antiestablishment populism are correlated with different degrees of trade openness under certain conditions and with different measurement indexes. Generally, left-wing populism is associated with weaker trade openness, while antiestablishment populism is associated with stronger trade openness. Results for right-wing populism are more ambiguous, with strongest link with protectionism among the subset of fuel-exporting right-wing populist governments. Yet even these results are not highly robust, and this chapter has shown the difficulty of establishing a systematic link between the varieties of populism and protectionism. Statistical evidence, as well as a case-by-case examination of current populist regimes, indicates that trade policies pursued by populist governments appear to be the result of many contextual and mediating factors. Regional influences and trade agreements, historical factors, and the country's export structure appear to exert significant influence on their trade policies. While there was some evidence that interaction variables of the three populism types with quality-of-governance indexes yielded interesting and at times statistically significant results, they were not always in the expected direction. Given the fact that trade openness varies across both populist and nonpopulist governments, most of the quality-of-governance indicators, tested independently, indicated a more consistently significant statistical impact on trade openness for the entire sample than did any of the populist dummies.

What is missing from the data and even from the case studies at this point is evidence of the populist impact of the Trump administration not only on US trade policy, which was too recent to be included in the indexing surveys, but also on the global trading system and trade policies of other countries, populist and nonpopulist. Clearly, Trump's personal affinity for tariffs played a role in his policies, but with the United States as the erstwhile champion of rules-based global trade, his abandonment of WTO rules sent a shockwave through the entire system. This factor, which amplified the welfare cost of his protectionist policies, will figure prominently in an assessment of the cost of populist protectionism in the following chapter.

Trade Freedom and Populism: Methodology

The final section of this chapter describes the methodology used in the regression study. Tables 7.4 and 7.5 report results from the following model:

$$TFI_{it} = \beta_0 + \beta_1 LPOP_{it} + \beta_2 RPOP_{it} + \beta_3 APOP_{it} + \beta_4 X_{it} + \alpha_i + \lambda_t + u_{it}$$

Table 7.4 Populist Governments in Trade Restrictiveness Regression

Country	Leader or Party	Years in Office	Type of Populism
Argentina	Carlos Menem	1989–1999	Anti-establishment
Argentina	Néstor Kirchner	2003–2007	Left-wing
Argentina	Cristina Fernández de Kirchner	2007–2015	Left-wing
Belarus	Alexander Lukashenko	1994–	Anti-establishment
Bolivia	Evo Morales	2006–	Left-wing
Brazil	Fernando Collor de Mello	1990–1992	Anti-establishment
Brazil	Jair Bolsonaro	2018–	Right-wing
Bulgaria	Boyko Borisov	2009–2013, 2014–2017, 2017–	Anti-establishment
Czech Republic	Miloš Zeman	1998–2002	Anti-establishment
Czech Republic	Andrej Babiš	2017–	Anti-establishment
Ecuador	Abdalá Bucaram	1996–1997	Left-wing
Ecuador	Lucio Gutiérrez	2003–2005	Left-wing
Ecuador	Rafael Correa	2007–2017	Left-wing
Georgia	Mikheil Saakashvili	2004–2007, 2008–2013	Anti-establishment
Greece	Syriza	2015–2018	Left-wing
Hungary	Viktor Orbán	1998–2002, 2010–	Right-wing
India	Narendra Modi	2014–	Right-wing
Indonesia	Joko Widodo	2014–	Anti-establishment
Israel	Benjamin Netanyahu	1996–1999, 2009–	Right-wing
Italy	Silvio Berlusconi	1994–1995, 2001–2006, 2008–2011, 2013	Anti-establishment
Italy	Five Star Movement/League coalition	2018–2019 (?)	Anti-establishment
Japan	Junichiro Koizumi	2001–2006	Anti-establishment
Macedonia	Nikola Gruevski	2006–2016	Right-wing
Mexico	Andrés Manuel López Obrador	2018–	Left-wing
Nicaragua	Daniel Ortega	2007–	Left-wing
Paraguay	Fernando Lugo	2008–2012	Left-wing
Peru	Alberto Fujimori	1990–2000	Anti-establishment
Philippines	Joseph Estrada	1998–2001	Anti-establishment
Philippines	Rodrigo Duterte	2016–	Right-wing
Poland	Lech Walesa	1990–1995	Anti-establishment
Poland	Law and Justice party	2005–2010, 2015–	Right-wing
Romania	Traian Basescu	2004–2014	Anti-establishment
Russia	Vladimir Putin	2000–	Right-wing
Serbia	Aleksandar Vucic	2014–2017, 2017–	Right-wing

Table 7.4 *Continued*

Country	Leader or Party	Years in Office	Type of Populism
Slovakia	Vladimír Meciar	1990–1998	Right-wing
Slovakia	Robert Fico	2006–2010, 2012–2018	Right-wing
South Africa	Jacob Zuma	2009–2018	Left-wing
Sri Lanka	Mahinda Rajapaksa	2005–2015, 2018–	Right-wing
Taiwan	Chen Shui-bian	2000–2008	Anti-establishment
Thailand	Thaksin Shinawatra	2001–2006	Left-wing
Thailand	Yingluck Shinawatra	2011–2014	Left-wing
Turkey	Recep Tayyip Erdogan	2003–	Right-wing
United States	Donald Trump	2017–	Right-wing
Venezuela	Rafael Caldera	1994–1999	Anti-establishment
Venezuela	Hugo Chávez	1999–2013	Left-wing
Venezuela	Nicolás Maduro	2013–	Left-wing
Zambia	Michael Sata	2011–2014	Left-wing

Source: Kyle and Gultchin (2018).

Where TFI_{it} is one of the four measures of trade freedom: the Trade Freedom index, the Fraser Institute's trade index, and Global Trade Alert's indicators of the number of trade-liberalizing and trade-restricting policies that countries implement each year.

X_{it} are characteristics of country i at year t including GDP per capita, GDP growth rate, unemployment rate, current account as a percentage of GDP, trade-to-GDP ratio, an indicator of the EU member, and world trade share. World trade share measures each country's annual proportion of world trade. The hypothesis is that countries with greater trade shares will be more likely to impose trade restrictions because of their trade-bargaining power: α_i are country-fixed effects and λ_t is the year fixed effect, that is, dummy variables for years. Robust standard errors (SE) are clustered at the country level.

In this model, we measure populism in four categories: left-wing ($LPOP_{it}$), right-wing ($RPOP_{it}$), anti-establishment ($APOP_{it}$), and no populism. β_1 to β_3 measure the effect of each type of populism compared to no populism.

Note that this model is evaluating the association between the listed factors and countries' trade openness. Although we control country characteristics, year and country-fixed effects, there could be other omitted time variant variables that are correlated with included variables, X_{it} and that are driving

Table 7.5 Regression Variables

Dependent Variables

TrFreedm	Trade Freedom Index (0–100)
FrasrIndx	Fraser Index (0–10)
GTAlib	Global Trade Alert: annual number of trade-liberalizing measures
GTAdiscr	Global Trade Alert: annual number of trade-restrictive measures

Independent Variables

FuelExp	Fuel exports as percentage of GDP
LWPop	Left-wing populist government (dummy)
RWPop	Right-wing populist government (dummy)
AEPop	Anti-establishment populist government (dummy)
LWPop*FuelExp	Interaction: Left-wing populist*fuel export%
RWPop*FuelExp	Interaction: right-wing populist*fuel export%
AEPop*FuelExp	Interaction: Anti-establishment populist*fuel export%
V&A	Voice & Accountability governance index
LWPop*V&A	Interaction:Left-wing populist*Voice&Accountability
RWPop*V&A	Interaction:Right-wing populist*Voice&Accountability
AEPop*V&A	Interaction:Anti-establishment populist*Voice&Accountability
PolStab	Political Stability governance index
LWPop*PolStab	Interaction:Left-wing populist*Political Stability
RWPop*PolStab	Interaction:Right-wing populist*Political Stability
AEPop*PolStab	Interaction:Anti-establishment populist*Political Stability
GovEffect	Government Effectiveness governance index
LWPop*GovEffect	Interaction:Left-wing populist*Government Effectiveness
RWPop*GovEffect	Interaction:Right-wing populist*Government Effectiveness
AEPop*GovEffect	Interaction:Anti-establishment populist*Government Effectiveness
RegQual	Regulatory Quality governance index
LWPop*RegQual	Interaction:Left-wing populist*Regulatory Quality
RWPop*RegQual	Interaction:Right-wing populist*Regulatory Quality
AEPop*RegQual	Interaction:Anti-establishment populist*Regulatory Quality
RuleLaw	Rule of Law governance index
LWPop*RuleLaw	Interaction:Left-wing populist*Rule of Law
RWPop*RuleLaw	Interaction:Right-wing populist*Rule of Law
AEPop*RuleLaw	Interaction:Anti-establishment populist*Rule of Law
CtrlCrrupt	Control of Corruption governance index
LWPop*CtrlCrrupt	Interaction:Left-wing populist*Control of Corruption
RWPop*CtrlCrrupt	Interaction:Right-wing populist*Control of Corruption
AEPop*CtrlCrrupt	Interaction:Anti-establishment populist*Control of Corruption
TradeGDP	Trade as percentage of GDP
ShWrldTrade	Share of World trade (decimal)

Table 7.5 *Continued*

EU	European Union member (dummy)
GdpCap	GDP per capita ($)
GdpCap^2	GDP per capita value squared ($)
Growth	Real economic growth (%)
CA/Gdp	Current Account balance as percentage of GDP
Unempl	Unemployment rate (%)

the value of the trade freedom index, TFI_{it}. There is also a possibility of reserved causality. Instead of populism affecting trade freedom, it is possible that the degree of trade freedom is influencing populism. In future research, it is worthwhile to look into possible solutions such as including the lagged value of the trade freedom index, TFI_{it-1} in the model, and the GMM estimator developed by Arellano and Bond (1991).

8

Assessing the Cost of Populism to Global Trade

What is the cost of populism to the global trading system? Before addressing this question, it is first necessary to acknowledge the populist movement itself as a signal that the current political system has failed to represent or respond to the grievances of a large portion of the population. A populist movement that achieves power through a democratic election thereby represents a sort of self-correction through legitimate political institutions, even if the consequences may be dangerous for democracy itself. When political parties that are in power, as well as those in representative opposition, remain aloof from widespread stresses and shocks battering the society, there will be fertile ground for a populist backlash—and vulnerability to demagogic populist leaders and dangerous policies. The underlying problems call for solutions that will make the country better off and defuse the situation, an issue that the final chapter will address. In most cases economic problems play a role in creating the environment for the populist revolt, since it is rare for populist movements to arise when economic growth is strong and prosperity is widely shared. Unfortunately, populist policies and politics often tend to offer solutions to the country's problems that will worsen the country's economy, especially in terms of protectionism, the focus of this book.

This chapter therefore begins with the traditional economic cost of protectionism, but it does not end there. These pages have explored the possibility that trade restrictions in a populist regime may prove to be a different sort of protectionism, as shown in the case of President Trump's assault on the WTO, which not only closed markets, but attacked trade institutions and caused the protectionism to spread. The erosion of institutions may also occur as collateral damage to populist campaigns focused on other issues, such as Brexit. Populist trade policy may ignore or manipulate existing rules and norms of conduct, creating chaos, disruption, and uncertainty in trade relations, which may in turn spark direct tit-for-tat tariff retaliation or an abandonment of the rules by trading partners. Thus the damage of populism to the domestic

Populism and Trade. Kent Jones, Oxford University Press. © Oxford University Press 2021.
DOI: 10.1093/oso/9780190086350.003.0008.

market spreads to foreign markets and may even amplify trade conflict into trade war. If bilateralism replaces multilateralism and discrimination replaces MFN treatment, trade diversion will tend to cause rebound protectionism to spread, further closing off international markets. Even within the political dynamics of domestic economies, populism can lead to more protectionism, as empirical research indicates that entrenched populist regimes tend to dismantle democratic institutions in order to secure their continued political power. As authoritarian rule intensifies, trade policy will tend to have fewer checks and balances and become increasingly subject to cronyism, corruption, and the desire of the populist leader to play favorites.

The following discussion sets out to identify the different types of cost that populist protectionism has inflicted on economic welfare in the United States and the global trading system. It is important to note, as shown by the results of the study so far, that populist governments are not always protectionist. Given the disruptions that populism can cause, there will be a need to address the root causes of the populist issues, and the final chapter will address that problem, with the view that economically less costly solutions are available as alternatives to protectionism. In this chapter the focus is on the sum of negative trade effects of populism, beginning with an assessment of the traditional economic welfare cost of populist protectionist policies, focusing on Donald Trump's agenda of trade restrictions and the withdrawal of the United Kingdom from Brexit. It then turns to the institutional damage these trade policy changes have imposed on global trading system. Finally, populist costs can cause other changes in domestic policies and institutions that are detrimental to the country's trade policy in the future, further diminishing the gains from trade.

Basic Economic Costs of Protection: Trump's Tariff Policies

The imposition of a tariff introduces market effects that reduce efficiency in the economy. This section begins with the basic welfare analysis of a tariff and the additional costs of reduced product variety, rent seeking, and X-inefficiency and then reviews empirical estimates of these costs regarding President Trump's tariffs in beginning in 2017. There follows a discussion of how the cost of these tariffs extended to other countries, and were amplified by their populist, rule-breaking nature, sparking foreign retaliation, and global investment uncertainty.

Welfare and Efficiency Costs

Protectionist measures—whether motivated by populism or not—include any government measures designed to restrict or distort trade in favor of a country's import-competing or exporting industries. The list includes tariffs, quotas, export restraint agreements, domestic production subsidies, export subsidies, administrative measures, and trade law enforcement intended primarily to favor domestic producers. Such policies either raise the price domestic producers receive, encourage additional sales at home or abroad, or reduce the availability of competing imports in the protected market. By distorting the market-driven outcome of competition in free and open markets, such measures tend to reduce economic efficiency and impose a net welfare cost on the home country and on the global economy. One economic argument against protectionist policies is therefore that they reduce the gains from trade and make countries less efficient and their people poorer. Import tariffs, for example, tend to reduce import competition, thereby increasing the domestic price of the product. Typically, domestic consumers suffer an economic loss defined by the amount to which they pay more for the protected good and consume less of it. This group may include private consumers of the product, or businesses that buy the good as an intermediate input in production. The tariff typically transfers a portion of the consumer loss to the domestic producers of the protected good, who increase their output and revenue per unit due to the trade restriction. This amount of the transfer will depend on how close a substitute the domestic product is for the import-competing good. Another portion of the consumer loss goes to the government in the form of tariff revenues. The rest of the economic cost of this aspect of the import restriction comes generally from its "deadweight loss": the reduction in the country's allocative efficiency due to the shift of productive resources away from efficient use in other parts of the economy and toward their less efficient use in the protected sector. But this is just the beginning of counting the cost of populist protection.

Another cost of import tariffs—one that is not so apparent—is that they systematically reduce exports as well. A tariff on imports is in many ways also a tax on exports. This effect does not include foreign retaliation provoked by the initial tariff, which has been an important element of the cost of populist protection and will be discussed later. Yet import tariffs themselves tend to suppress exports by increasing the relative price of the protected domestic good, drawing the country's resources away from export goods and other production and reducing the amount available for export. In addition, high US tariffs placed on a wide range and large volume of foreign goods tend to decrease the value of the foreign currency in terms of US dollars, as the subsequent reduction in foreign exports decreases the demand for foreign currency. The resulting appreciation of the tariff-imposing country's currency acts like a tax on exports, raising their price in terms of the foreign currency and lowering the quantity purchased. Furthermore, if the tariff is placed on an intermediate good used in the production of an exportable good in the home country, it will increase production costs for domestic firms, reducing their competitiveness in export markets. Finally, to the extent that the populist tariffs suddenly raise new fears about future tariffs, the resulting policy uncertainty will tend to discourage business investments and export market development by exporting firms, since they will be wary of suffering future cost increases and retaliatory market closure due to protection. The business of exporting is in general an expensive undertaking to begin with, as documented by Anderson and van Wincoop (2004), and increased risks of protectionism in the world economy will discourage it. All in all, the irony of populist protectionism, often motivated by nationalist goals of increasing output and well-paying jobs in its import-competing industries, often ends up simultaneously placing countervailing burdens on the competitiveness, output, and often equally well-paying or better-paying jobs of its exporting industries.

Reduced Product Variety, Rent-Seeking, and X-Inefficiency

A number of other factors may compound the cost of the tariff. Consumers may lose additional value from the tariff if it reduces product variety, which often represents a part of the gains from trade (see Amiti 2019). As noted earlier, foreign producers may retaliate, imposing their own restrictions on that country's exports. Exporters in the tariff-imposing country suffer lost export sales to the extent that their displaced foreign sales in one market cannot be seamlessly diverted to other foreign markets. In addition, if domestic producers anticipate the possibility of tariff protection, they have an incentive to expend additional company resources to lobby in favor of the tariff. The lobbying activity thus diverts the firm's resources from "minding the store" with efficient, productive activities (R&D, investment upgrades, worker training, etc.) and directs them toward securing the extra tariff-enhanced profits from the protectionist policy, representing a *rent-seeking* cost of the tariff. Similar rent-seeking costs are possible if the government allows firms to lobby for exemptions from the tariff, typically requiring additional firm resources and costly insider connections to be successful. Protected firms may also be able to increase their price-making market power through the reduction in import competition, allowing them to reduce output and raise prices even higher than the tariff price. In the extreme case the tariff could lead to a domestic monopoly, with additional price increases and deadweight loss. If the tariff reduces the incentives for competitive efficiency among protected domestic firms, they may exhibit lower productivity and higher per-unit costs, a phenomenon referred to as the "X-inefficiency" or "goofing-off" cost of the tariff (Altman 2015).

Tallying the Welfare Cost of the Trump Tariffs

As noted in chapter 4, the series of tariffs introduced by President Trump in 2018 included safeguards tariffs on solar panels and washing machines, Section 232 national security tariffs on aluminum and steel, and three rounds of tariffs specifically targeting China in a unilateral Section 301 action, triggering the US-China trade war. The trade war tariffs escalated further in 2019 (Bown 2019). Several economic studies have estimated the impact of some or all of these tariffs on the US economy (Amiti et al. 2019b; Fajgelbaum et al. 2019; Flaaen et al. 2019; Trade Partnership 2019; Cavallo et al. 2019). The annual cost to US consumers, including deadweight loss and tariff payments, and based on tariffs in effect from 2018 through mid-2019, range from $51 billion to $70 billion. Amiti (2019a) estimates that additional tariffs on China beginning in June 2019 increased the annual US consumer cost to $106 billion. All of these estimates find that the burden of the tariffs fell almost entirely on US private consumers and US import-purchasing firms. All the estimates of the tariffs' aggregate cost to US consumers may be low, as they do not include estimates of transfers from domestic consumers to substitute domestic products. Amiti (2019b) also calculates that foreign retaliation cost US exporters $2.4 billion per month in lost exports, suggesting that an extended trade war would require US exporters to make costly investments in new foreign market development or offshoring in order to avoid the tariffs.

Protection creates additional domestic government financing costs in order to keep the tariffs in place. Trump at first waved off growing concerns about rising prices of imported goods and reduced exports of US exports due to retaliation, telling US farmers, exporters, and import consumers to be patient, as his tariff strategy would force foreign markets to open up and lead to a boom in US exports and economic growth. As the export slump continued, Trump allocated taxpayer-funded compensation to US farmers, a politically valuable constituency, for lost sales, totaling $28 billion from 2018 to the end of 2019. This measure was only partially successful. Like most US agricultural subsidies, large, corporate farms received the lion's share, and most small farmers found that the subsidy payments covered only a small portion of their losses. Trump did not provide compensation for lost export sales in other sectors. Yet he became furious at US motorcycle producer Harley-Davidson, a firm increasingly dependent on retaliation-targeted exports and on steel and aluminum imports, when its management announced that it would have to move some of its production—and jobs—offshore because of the Trump tariffs. Trump threatened the company with additional tariff punishment, assuming evidently that it would try to import its foreign made motorcycles back into the United States.[1] Protectionist policies often involve political sops to mollify selected domestic victims, such as targeted subsidies for favored constituents who suffer economic losses from the restrictions or foreign retaliation. These are financed through the public purse, and politicians try to rationalize them as an act of compassion to redress foreign economic aggression. Populist protectionism goes beyond that political expedient, singling out and publicly shaming individual firms as unpatriotic when they seek a market-driven offshoring arrangement just to remain in business.

More broadly, Trade Partnership (2019) documents a strong decrease in US exports in industries affected by the tariffs, and an overall drop in total US exports since the tariffs began, and estimates a net employment loss in all affected US industries of 935,000 jobs. Flaaen and Pierce (2019) find that the Trump tariffs themselves had a small positive impact on employment in protected manufacturing sectors, but that this effect was more than offset by the negative effects of price increases among US import suppliers due to the tariffs and by foreign retaliation. The net effect of the tariffs on a typical protected US manufacturing sector was significant *decrease* of 1.4% in employment and an increase in end-product prices of 4.1% from 2018 to mid-2019, with a no statistically discernable change in output (Flaaen and Pierce 2019, pp. 20–21). These results have important policy implications, since governments often justify the welfare cost of tariffs by pointing to the benefit of increased employment in the protected domestic sector. In this case, the input cost increases and foreign retaliation subtracted more employment than was created by tariff protection.

Amiti et al. (2019b) also estimate the effect of the tariffs on product variety, a potentially important element of the gains from trade, but concluded that the loss from reduced variety in 2018 was about one-tenth of the value of the rise in prices due to the tariffs.[2] Most of Trump's tariffs in 2018 and 2019 covered more standardized, intermediate industrial products, as the goal in the early stages of his trade strategy was apparently not to target consumers of final goods directly. However, more consumer goods were targeted in subsequent tariff increases after mid-2019 (which are not evaluated in the studies cited here), and costs of reduced variety could rise dramatically if the trade war continued, as Trump was discussing many differentiated products as potential targets of new tariffs in early 2020, including European automobiles and wine. The tariffs apparently did entail rent-seeking costs discussed earlier; however, at least in the form of tariff exclusions, the bureaucratic process of allowing selected import consumers exclusions from paying the tariffs. Firms applied to the USTR for such exemptions, most of which involved industrial inputs from China, especially mechanical appliances, electrical equipment, and instruments. Applicants typically had to follow a slow and nontransparent process of review, with an understaffed exemptions office receiving about 40,000 requests in the first 14 months of the tariffs. Criteria for receiving an exemption officially included whether the product was available exclusively from China (i.e., it is not available in the United States); whether the tariff would demonstrably inflict great harm on the US firm requesting the exclusion; and that the product was not of strategic importance to China's national industrial strategy. The USTR approval rate of tariff exclusion petitions was about 35%, but the final determination did not provide any explanation of the decision, and there was no possibility to appeal (Hufbauer and Lu 2019). De Pillis (2020) documents the case of a small US business owner whose product required a specialized water pump input supplied by a Chinese firm subject to the new trade war tariff. His exemption application was denied with no explanation, despite its consistency with the three criteria for approval. Firms with lobbying links to the White House, in contrast, appeared to have a much higher success rate. Economically, such tariff exclusion red tape provides trade officials with the ability to make sure that the policy achieves specific domestic goals. Objectives may include making sure that domestic firms receiving tariff protection do not suffer domestic customer leakage (a feature that also subject to lobbying influence) and that the tariffs achieve the typical administration goal of increasing employment in basic domestic manufacturing. Otherwise, the system generally gives trade officials the valuable power to play favorites, rewarding political allies and punishing political enemies, and using the system as a tool of industrial policy.

Globalizing the Tariff Cost to Foreign Consumers and Businesses

The economic costs of the Trump trade restrictions to the United States also applied to all other countries that imposed retaliatory measures against the United States. Just as President Trump viewed the trade restrictions as a way to redress the unfair treatment the United States had supposedly suffered at the hands of its trading partners, the trading partners themselves faced political pressure in their own countries to respond in kind. The more closely the retaliation matched the volume and protective level of the Trump tariffs, the more the economic cost on their own economies approached the levels of the United States. One may argue that such retaliation is strategic, giving those countries an advantage in negotiating an end to the initial tariffs. Canada and Mexico, for example, used their retaliatory tariffs as bargaining chips in the USMCA negotiations. The European Union may have had a similar strategy in mind, maintaining its retaliatory measures in anticipation of new threatened tariffs by Trump. The problem in general is that both sides in a trade war tend to view tariffs as armaments directed at the trading partner, whereas their use actually inflicts significant damage on the home country as well. An equilibrium stalemate of mutually imposed tariffs is hardly optimal, and the risk of spiraling escalation and negotiated permanent protectionism is always present. Canada and Mexico, for example, found that removing their retaliatory tariffs in the USMCA negotiations still left them facing new steel and aluminum regional content requirements, as well as contingency voluntary export restraint commitments, in the new agreement. Trade wars therefore have a distinctively populist character, moving previously rules-based trading countries toward economic nationalism, mutual animosity and protectionism. WTO rules were intended to stop such self-destructive behavior, exemplified in the trade wars of the 1930s, and populist trade policy has reopened this Pandora's box.

Another particularly damaging aspect of populist trade policy for the world economy is its tendency to upend expectations of stable trade relations by the sudden announcements of new and unexpected tariffs, reinforced by actions that undermine trade institutions and rules. The increase in policy uncertainty inflicts damage beyond the impact of the trade restrictions themselves, as new investments and trade initiatives face an uncertain policy environment. Figure 8.1 shows the Trade Policy Uncertainty index, which spiked dramatically in 2018 because of the initial Trump tariffs, and then again in mid-2019 when Trump announced new rounds of tariffs against China, escalating the trade war. Not only was Trump imposing tariffs, which under WTO rules can

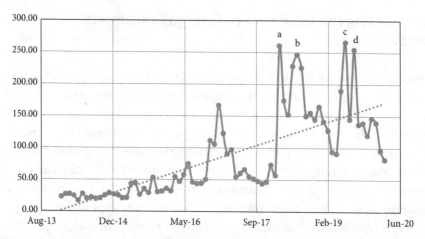

Figure 8.1 Trade Policy Uncertainty Index, January 2014–March 2020
Legend: **a**-US imposes Section 232 global steel and aluminum tariffs; **b**-US imposes first China tariffs; **c**-US raises China tariff levels; **d**-US expands China tariff coverage.
Source: Caldara et al. (2019).

be constrained so as not to disrupt the rules-based trading environment, but he was also violating fundamental WTO norms, practices, and the letter of negotiated trade agreements at the same time. The postponement or cancellation of investments and hiring tied to future trade-based initiatives created knock-on effects in output, income, and consumption, which appeared to decline during this period. The US Congressional Budget Office (CBO 2019, p. 38) estimates that the tariff effects as of mid-2019, combined with the business uncertainty that they created, would reduce real US private investment by 1.3% by mid-2020. Rules-breaking populist disrupters, often seeking to keep political rivals and trading partners in the dark or fearful about future policies, thus create real reductions in economic welfare specifically linked to such uncertainty-inducing behavior. Caldera et al. (2019) develop a model in which the impact of a one-time uncertainty shock takes the form of an initial reduction in investment, followed by a gradual return to investment patterns based on a return to stable expectations. However, a continual renewal of policy uncertainty renews the shock, which the previous shock can amplify. Based on this model, the combined waves of trade policy uncertainty in 2018 and 2019 were predicted to lower global GDP by about 1%, with the effect spread equally among the United States, advanced foreign economies, and emerging market economies. A populist trade strategy that continually seeks to renew trade crisis conditions in a fight against malign globalist trading partners thus risks constantly upsetting business expectations, putting markets in a perpetual state of uncertainty and suppressed investment, including in the populist's own home country. President Trump's trade policy sowed uncertainty in investment markets beyond mid-2019, constantly renewing trade conflicts with new tariffs or threats of tariffs. Some examples of his trade policy aggression included tariff threats against Mexico for its immigration policy, against Brazil and Argentina for alleged currency manipulation, against India for its lack of tariff reciprocity, and against the European Union over Airbus subsidies and its general misdeed of running a trade surplus with the United States. For Trump, trade became a favored method of generating enthusiastic support his populist base, constantly demonstrating his anti-globalist bona fides and economic nationalism to his followers.

The Extended Web of Protectionist Impacts

Tariffs and other restrictions on international business can compound the economic cost of the initial protectionist action and spread their effects to other countries. The following section considers the implications of discrimination in tariff implementation for trade patterns, followed by an example of the damage that tariffs impose on international supply chains beyond the simple welfare analysis discussed in the previous section of this chapter. The discussion then turns to the link between foreign direct investment and trade and the link between immigration and economic growth. The last subsection discusses the impact of populist trade policy on US regional and bilateral trade agreements during the Trump administration, focusing on the USMCA, which replaced the NAFTA.

Discrimination

President Trump's trade war with China raised additional problems because it indulged in discrimination, violating the WTO's most-favored nation clause. Raising tariffs against China alone caused trade diversion by encouraging Chinese firms to relocate their production facilities outside China, redirecting the source of US-bound exports to countries like Cambodia, the Philippines, and Vietnam. While these countries may have benefited from the additional investment, output, and exports due to the diversion, they also faced new threats of protectionist trade restrictions from the United States. Vietnam, for example, has found itself in the crosshairs of Trump's mercantilist ire, as its trade surplus with the United States increased (Hitch 2019). Discriminatory tariffs often create such "whack-a-mole" trade diversion, renewing the protectionist conflict with other countries. A second version of this phenomenon was the illegal transshipment of Chinese goods through third countries, whereby the manufacturer replaced "Made in China" labels with phony certificates and marks of origin. Such practices violated US customs laws, increasing the transactions cost of trade and customs enforcement, while creating new criminal networks of fraudulent trade. Trade policy adherence to the most-favored nation clause would have avoided these problems. US exporters were also victims of the discriminatory aspect of the trade war, as China's retaliatory tariffs against US producers of soybeans, for example, opened the door for other countries to fill the gap and supply soybeans to the Chinese market. As the trade war continued, US exporters feared that their networks of shipment and distribution to the Chinese market would erode, risking a permanent loss with long-standing customers. China also retaliated with yet another act of discrimination: while raising tariffs against United States exports, China simultaneously lowered its tariffs against other countries, which benefitted at US expense as their margin of advantage increased in Chinese markets.

Impact on International Supply Chains

The trade war has shown that foreign retaliation can reduce US exports just as the initial tariffs reduce US imports. As previously described, supply-chain integration of trade markets in the global economy also links import availability with export performance. In this regard, the economic disconnect in Trump's trade policy approach lies in the fact that the global trading environment itself has changed, making it difficult to separate a country's import interests from its export interests. The "great unbundling" of global manufacturing (Baldwin 2016) has allowed production to spread out in supply-chain networks across national boundaries, due to advances in communication, transportation, and technology. These developments have encouraged businesses to engage in foreign investment to build offshore facilities and integrate the various links in their international supply chains in order to maximize production efficiencies. Under these circumstances, a country's tariff walls go through the middle of its own domestic factories. International supply-chain strategies also point to the advantages of deeper economic integration, through foreign investment, related services activities, regulatory harmonization, and intellectual property protection.

From the viewpoint of economic nationalism, supply chains are a danger to a country's sovereignty, since they tie the economy to unwanted foreign influences, and may subject the home country's trade to rules outside its control. One goal of the Trump administration has been to reduce US firm supply-chain linkages to China, although it has also claimed that security and human rights reasons, in addition to other economic issues, lie behind it. For example, under Trump the US government required US firms to receive preapproval for any transactions with certain Chinese firms, including Huawei, whose advanced telecommunications technologies were allegedly a security risk to the United States (Lovely 2019). Whatever the underlying reason, the policy's objective was in part to cause US firms to abandon their manufacturing facilities in China, despite the value of their long-standing supply-chain relationships with international partners. Offshore factories entail investments that cannot be easily recovered once they are abandoned, and the greater the risk that the tariffs will escalate, and the longer the tariffs are expected to remain in place, the more a firm will consider giving up its Chinese production facility. Deng (2019) documents the desperate efforts of a US vinyl flooring manufacturer to adjust to tariffs that escalated from 10% to 25% on inputs from his company's main Chinese supplier, with which it had partnered for 30 years. At lower tariff levels, the resulting price increases could be absorbed or negotiated in a series of small amounts across upstream and downstream links in the supply chain, but higher tariffs eventually forced price increases through the chain to the final consumer, with a commensurate drop in sales. Many discouraged US firms dissolved their Chinese supplier relationships, and those who continued to stick with them had to devote additional firm resources investing in cost-saving measures, product adjustments, and new retail customers. Even so, despite Trump's populist goal of recapturing manufacturing jobs from abroad, few US companies have shifted their Chinese supply-chain investments to the United States, largely because of prohibitive cost factors. It has been more common for production to shift to other Southeast Asian countries, which may also be occurring because of rising costs in China that are independent of the tariff burden. If the main concern is the Chinese security threat, it would have been easier and more transparent for the US government to subject all US foreign investment in China to national security approval, with timeline requirements for withdrawal, an investment treaty strategy for their relocation, and an accountable review process.

Foreign Direct Investment and Immigration

Connected to the supply-chain issue is the populist opposition to bilateral investment treaties (BITs) and investor-state dispute settlement (ISDS) arrangements that make it easier for firms to outsource production to offshore locations. President Trump espoused populist opposition to *outbound* foreign investment, based on the economic nationalist view that US firms should keep their capital and the jobs they create at home. Trump was also opposed to ISDS because protection given to US firms as foreign investors increases their incentives for outbound FDI. As noted, however, supply chains tend to support jobs in the home country through specialization, usually placing higher value-added employment in the home country. Trump did not object, on the other hand, to foreign firms' *inbound* FDI in the United States. His goal appeared to be for US firms to repatriate their investments to the United States, the motivation behind tax incentives for this purpose in the 2017 tax bill. In addition, his tariffs on foreign imports from countries with what he considered to be unfair trade surpluses was intended to force them to increase their inbound FDI and create US manufacturing jobs. In this manner, the protectionist component of FDI restrictions imposes additional economic burdens on the home economy by distorting investment allocation, disrupting supply chains, and rendering the economy less attractive as a base for cost-competitive production.

Finally, labor immigration, both temporary and permanent, is also a component of the globalized economy, playing a significant role in a country's workforce in trade and nontrade related industries. It brings workers with highly specialized skills to advanced industries and less skilled workers to agricultural, construction, hospitality, and food processing industries. Both types of immigration contribute to a country's output and international efficiency through skills acquisition and workforce allocation improvements, but also through the high motivation of many immigrants. In many countries, including the United States and especially Europe, immigrants also supplement aging workforces and contribute taxes to otherwise threatened social security funds. H1-B visas contribute to the composition of the professional workforce, and immigrant entrepreneurs play an important role in innovation, the establishment of new firms, and the creation of new export opportunities to their countries of origin. Trump took a strong stand against most immigration, including a crackdown on approving professional H1-B visas. Immigrants from Latin America, Africa, and Middle Eastern countries were targeted for exclusion on cultural grounds, or on the basis of alleged illegal drug or terrorist activities. Yet even the prospect of allowing the flow of upwardly mobile, professional, and entrepreneurial immigrants that would contribute significantly to GDP runs afoul of populist fears of foreign displacement of American culture and the alleged threat (usually misplaced) to American workers' jobs. The anti-immigrant policies and rhetoric have led to decreases in foreign student applications to US colleges and universities, diminishing the leading US position as a global exporter of educational services, and reducing the incentive for foreign graduates to settle in and contribute to GDP in the United States. A major cost of populism is therefore its protectionist view toward immigration, which is counterproductive to the country's economic interests.

Regional Trade Negotiations and the New USMCA

The most significant populist cost to the United States in terms of trade negotiations was a cost of omission: President Trump's announcement immediately after taking office that the United States was pulling out of the Trans-Pacific Partnership (TPP). While the estimated welfare gains to the United States and the rest of the world of the TPP would have been modest, the framework of a broad regional economic integration agreement would have established new standards in important areas such as state-owned enterprise trading rules. The TPP would thus have been of strategic importance to the United States, since China would presumably have to comply with these rules, shaped largely by the United States, if it wanted to join in the future. Such rules could also have provided a model for changes to the WTO rulebook, helping to resolve dispute settlement controversies on this topic. In addition, the TPP signatories included Japan, the largest US trading partner in the region next to China, and US withdrawal put its exporters, especially in agricultural products, at a competitive disadvantage compared to other TPP agricultural exporters such as Canada and New Zealand. Partly to make up for the omission, the Trump administration negotiated a separate trade agreement with Japan that included some, but not all, agricultural products covered in the TPP, as well as chapters on market access for digital trade and industrial goods. Here the omission was auto trade, the largest portion of Japanese exports to the United States. Normally, any bilateral trade agreement would need to include all major trade categories in order to comply with WTO rules on exemptions from MFN treatment. However, President Trump evidently was planning a separate negotiation on autos with both Japan and the European Union, an $800 billion global export industry, using the threat of new Section 232 national security tariffs, which his Commerce Department had approved for imported autos. This issue was scheduled for negotiation in 2020 (Schott 2019), but never took place. In most trade agreements President Trump tended to focus on individual trade categories of special interest to him politically, rather than bother with the details of a comprehensive agreement. He established this pattern with a renegotiation of the US-Korea trade agreement, which he excoriated during the 2016 presidential campaign as unfair to the United States, threatening to terminate it. Instead, he settled for an increase in the number of US automobiles that Korea would consider importing, and a formal export restraint agreement on steel, which violated WTO rules, as noted in chapter 5. Most of the rest of the original agreement remained unchanged (Gillespie 2018).

The issue of NAFTA, in contrast, required more presidential attention, since he made it a major issue in his presidential campaign. He subsequently came to realize that it was of direct interest to many Trump supporters who would suffer economically if it were terminated, especially in US states bordering Canada and Mexico, and in many other agricultural and manufacturing areas around the country. After 25 years the NAFTA was certainly in need of updating, and despite Trump's frequent threats of canceling the agreement with no replacement, negotiations concluded and final US ratification occurred in January 2020. The new agreement does modestly open Canadian dairy and poultry markets to US suppliers, and liberalizes some customs procedures. In addition, it adds some new provisions for protecting intellectual property and introduces digital trade into the scope of policy disciplines, but does not specify many important aspects of possible policy discretion in this area. The main substantive change is protectionist, and deals with the rules of origin for automobile production in the three partner countries. At President Trump's insistence, all automobile production under the USMCA must now satisfy a North American content requirement of 75%, compared to 62.5% under the NAFTA. There is also an unusual labor requirement, unprecedented in any previous US trade agreement, that 40% of passenger vehicles and 45% of pickup and cargo vehicles manufactured in the three countries be made with labor that is paid a minimum of $16 per hour. The intention of this rule is to discourage labor-intensive auto production in Mexico and shift it toward the United States. It is uncertain how auto manufacturers will adjust to this provision, since the low wages in Mexico suggest a strategy of bypassing this new USMCA rule, at least on some production, and sending noncompliant Mexican-built autos to the United States under WTO-based MFN tariffs instead. However, this incentive raises the possibility of unilateral US increases in auto import tariffs—or other forms of retaliation—in response.

Quantitative assessments of the USMCA's economic impact on the three partner countries tend to agree on most of the new elements of the agreement. The auto rules of origin and wage-floor provisions are responsible for increased auto production costs and most of the economic welfare losses. Using the expiring NAFTA agreement as the basis of comparison, the USMCA decreases US real GDP by about 0.10%, compared to a loss for Canada of 0.40% and for Mexico of 0.79%. A complete elimination of NAFTA, on the other hand, would have increased the US loss by a negligible amount, and increased the losses to Canada and Mexico to 0.49% and 1.09%, respectively (Ciuriak et al. 2019). Another study finds negligible impacts of the USMCA on all three economies, but still finds the new auto rules to be the most damaging aspect of it (Burfisher et al. 2019). A US government study, focusing on US welfare alone, finds modest but positive real GDP gains for the United States of 0.35% based on an optimistic assessment of new data trade impacts (USITC 2019).[3] A bottom-line assessment of the populist cost of the USMCA, however, must go beyond these quantitative assessments and consider the policy uncertainty that remains regarding trade between the United States and its North American partners (Lovely and Schott 2019). President Trump has shown that he feels no compunction about introducing new and unexpected trade restrictions on US trading partners, even if trade agreements officially forbid such measures. His threat of unilateral tariffs on Mexico if it did not change its immigration policy to Trump's satisfaction in August 2019 is an example. Despite the continuation of the original NAFTA dispute settlement arrangement in the USMCA, Trump's view of multilateral rules and arbitration suggest that attempts by Mexico to bypass the new auto content and minimum wage rules could trigger US unilateral retaliatory actions. In addition, even though Canada and Mexico have quantitative exemptions from any future US Section 232 tariffs on automobiles and auto parts, based on USMCA side letters, any new US Section 232 auto tariffs would damage the North American auto industry in general because of the cost impact they would have on auto supply chains and on North American exports to third countries. Digital trade could also spark confrontations regarding taxation and national security restrictions. In the USMCA the United States also introduced a measure allowing a USMCA member to withdraw from the agreement if another member dared to conclude a separate free-trade agreement with a nonmarket economy, such as China. How might the United States interpret that provision if *any* regional or bilateral trade liberalizing measures developed between China and either Canada or Mexico? In short, populism has made the United States an unpredictable and therefore unreliable trading partner. Canada and Mexico, as well as Korea, Japan, and many other countries, had to learn to live with that fact of life during the Trump administration.

Brexit

Brexit, as noted in chapter 6, showed the special problems that the United Kingdom always had as an EU member with regulatory policies that come from Brussels. The general problem in the European Union is that of a democratic deficit, with most decisions made at a distance from voters, is an issue that will require EU governance reforms in order for progress on further integration to be possible. In the United Kingdom, history and long-standing Euroskepticism created a particularly virulent backlash, and the radical path of a chaotic and ill-prepared withdrawal process. A Brexiteer view of the termination of membership in the European Union appears to be that the overwhelming benefit of populism is the sovereignty it restores to the United Kingdom. The cost involves potential losses in EU trade and investment, which can in theory be compensated by a new negotiated relationship with its former EU partners and blue-sky trade agreements with new partners, including the United States and other countries. The cost of populism is the excess of these economic costs above the sovereignty benefits, assuming the absence of additional costs, such as secession by Scotland and Northern Ireland. Estimates of the economic cost alone range from 1.15% to 7.5% of UK GDP (Latore et al. 2019). A more accurate assessment may be possible only as details of the new EU-UK relationship, announced in late December 2020, can be clarified and evaluated.

The costs of Brexit populism, beyond the cost of reversing economic integration in both the United Kingdom and its EU partner countries, include the divisive and inefficient process of the referendum itself. In a sharply divided country on the question, there was no way that a simple up-or-down Brexit vote could have avoided a result without nearly half the population feeling cheated. This would also have been true if remain had won with 52% of the vote, in which case the economic costs would have been avoided (or postponed), but which would have left leave voters seething and spoiling for a new fight on the issue, with divisive populist politics more energized than before. With no framework for compromise or rational comparison of alternatives, a referendum on such an important issue runs the risk outlined by James Madison in the *Federalist Papers No. 10,* warning of a majority faction ("tyranny of the majority") overriding the interests of the minority, especially when their interests are diametrically opposed. The solution for this problem is a deliberative democracy, in which both sides can compromise on more nuanced and qualified legislation that reflects the interests of both sides. A similar problem occurs when a populist leader, acting on behalf of the populist faction alone, seizes control over government institutions and faces no checks and balances, a situation to be discussed at the end of this chapter.

In addition, populism imposes a cost on society, especially with regard to trade, through its interpretation of sovereignty. As a measure of control within a country's borders, absolute sovereignty is possible only with nearly complete isolationism, as in rare and unenviable cases such as North Korea. In a globalized economy trade agreements represent a negotiated balance of shared or pooled sovereignty, as in the proposition "I will offer you access to trade and investment in my market if you allow me similar access to yours." Thus a sacrifice of home market access sovereignty is exchanged for extended sovereignty through access to the partner's market. Leave proponents did not seem to oppose this proposition (although many populists in the United States and other countries do), but underestimated its value as an EU member country. Some may have thought back to the days long before its 1973 accession to the European Union, when British imperial sovereignty guaranteed UK access to its colonies, and later to Commonwealth countries, on favorable terms for the metropole. This bargaining position is no longer possible for the United Kingdom. A more careful approach to recovering sovereignty from the European Union in contested nontrade areas would have allowed a more rational unbundling of the package of sovereignty bargains contained in EU membership, with less economic cost to the United Kingdom. Aside from the divisiveness it created and will sustain, within the United Kingdom, Brexit leaves the European Union without a major voice for trade openness in Brussels. It has also weakened the prospects for further economic and political integration in Europe, although it did provide a needed wake-up call for its political leadership to deal decisively with the democratic deficit.

The Cost of Institutional Erosion

The distinctive and amplifying cost of populism arises from its tendency to damage or even tear down institutions of the allegedly "elitist" order. This section examines various aspects of these costs. It begins with an account of the weakened state of the global trading system, beset with weakened leadership and structural changes in the global economy, as President Trump entered office. In addition, rules on currency manipulation, formerly the subject of strict criteria, review, and negotiations, became the target of Trump's mercantilist approach to international trade. Democratic institutions themselves also became vulnerable to the erosion of checks and balances during his administration, and to his demonization of any and all political opponents.

At the same time, his policy of trade war with China reflected his sense of invincibility in undermining global trading rules, which then extended to his strategy of dealing with the coronavirus pandemic by declaring that it was China's fault, but would nevertheless vanish, seemingly at his command.

The System's Vulnerability

In addition to the economic costs of President Trump's trade restrictions and resulting retaliation and global policy uncertainty, his assault on trade institutions may inflict even greater damage through the erosion of the multilateral system of trade relations, as described in chapter 5. WTO members agreed to trade rules such as nondiscrimination, tariff binding, and peaceful dispute resolution as the best way to create a global public good for all its members to pursue the mutual gains from trade. The principal weakness of the entire postwar GATT-WTO system—which hid in plain sight for decades—was that its success depended on the leadership and commitment of its most prominent members, especially the United States and the European Union. This proposition was tested over the years, with episodes of politically motivated product exceptions from the rules (textiles and clothing), policy exceptions from the rules (protectionist export restraint agreements), and lack of representation (exclusion of developing country interest from the negotiating agenda). The solutions to these problems were often slow, incomplete, and grudging, but ultimately achieved progress and a new consensus in support of the system. Even before the populist challenge to the WTO the organization struggled with its first failed trade negotiation, the Doha Round, and was in need of a renewed commitment to achieve consensus on trade liberalization. Yet in the meantime the members continued to debate this major issue, while maintaining the framework of existing WTO rules for their ongoing trade relations. Trump's populist mercantilism set out to undermine the WTO in a more fundamental way. Mutual respect for WTO rules was replaced with a US-China trade war, subject to unlimited escalation, that has damaged the entire world economy. The United States alienated its longtime trade allies with unilateral steel and aluminum tariffs, on the grounds that its trading partners are enemies threatening its national security. Trump bullied Mexico with arbitrary tariff threats to force a change in its immigration policy. He also shut down the WTO dispute settlement system, with no apparent interest in resolving the underlying issues to restore its functioning as a system of resolving disputes. He also introduced voluntary quantitative export limits on steel with certain countries in the context of the national security tariffs in 2018. These measures were in direct violation of the WTO safeguards clause. In his mercantilist Phase One agreement in the US-China trade war, he introduced a new violation of the GATT's most-favored nation provision, concluding a discriminatory quantitative trade commitment from China requiring its imports from the United States to increase.

It is noteworthy that what might be considered "hard" WTO rules are actually "soft" when a member such as the United States abandons the observed norms of the organization. In some cases this is because of ambiguous language used to achieve consensus on them, but with an understanding that commonly recognized norms of interpretation would guide their application. This was true of GATT Article 21 and the gentleman's agreement for the United States to abstain from immediate unilateral Section 301 retaliation, for example. Similarly, one would have expected that a negotiated agreement to allow the reappointment of AB judges, while contentious, would be prioritized in order to keep the dispute system in operation. Finally, even an apparently hard rule such as the ban on voluntary export restraint agreements becomes soft when a large member openly defies it. When the norms are broken, the system runs the danger of collapse. The damage was compounded by the fact that major trading countries were drawn into the escalating tariff confrontation, further weakening WTO disciplines. The damage to the trading system accrued to each and every country that took part in it.

Currency Manipulation

Another method that the Trump administration used in attempts to undermine WTO rules on tariff binding was through allegations of currency manipulation, which seemed to be a particular obsession of the president. In the United States, such accusations are normally subject to semiannual reviews by the Treasury Department. The reviews include strict criteria that must establish evidence of the foreign country's current account surplus of greater than 3%; persistent foreign central bank one-way purchases of foreign reserves to suppress the home currency's value; and the foreign country's trade surplus with the United States of greater than $40 billion. The Treasury Department has rarely made such a determination since the US Congress passed implementing legislation in 1988 and 2015. It identified China as a currency manipulator in 1994, but not since then. In addition, the existing legislation does not provide for tariffs or other sanctions to punish the violation. Trump attempted to use accusations of currency manipulation against Turkey, Brazil, and Argentina to impose additional Section 232 steel and aluminum tariffs on them when their currencies fell due to economic and financial weakness—that is, for market-based reasons. US Court of International Trade rulings, however, cast doubt on the president's authority to increase tariffs in this manner, and the Trump administration subsequently withdrew most of them (Sikes 2019). Since the beginning of the US-China trade war Trump continued to claim that China was trying to evade US tariffs through currency manipulation, and also wanted additional negotiating leverage to pressure China into a settlement. He had his Treasury Secretary, Steven Mnuchin, declare in August 2019 that China was again manipulating its currency. This claim did not meet the treasury criteria, as China's central bank intervention had actually been supporting its own currency. When it finally ceased its large sale of US dollars in currency markets and the yuan fell, a bogus determination of currency manipulation was announced. The subsequent US-China Phase One agreement in January 2020 revealed the underlying strategy of this move, when the United States withdrew the currency manipulation charge. Yet the agreement itself contained a new bilateral currency manipulation clause, this time empowering the US trade representative's (USTR) office, rather that the Treasury Department, with the final determination of a violation. The apparent objective was to increase the likelihood that a violation would be found, at the president's discretion (Schott 2020). In order to broaden the expanded search for currency manipulation, the Trump administration also issued a new trade law rule in February 2020 that would treat the practice as an illegal foreign subsidy, subject to an investigation by the US Commerce Department and US International Trade Commission, with provisions for punitive countervailing duties (Zumbrun 2020). These agencies are focused on finding foreign unfair pricing practices and domestic injury to specific US industries. They are also more likely to find violations through the "less than fair value" pricing rule and discrete determinations of injury under unfair trade laws than the Treasury Department would be in enforcing the macroeconomic rules in the Congressional legislation, at least if they were followed consistently.

The Cost of Eroding Domestic Institutions

Populism can also affect trade policy through the domestic political process itself. When a populist movement gains the support of the people, identified by cultural, ethnic, racial, religious, or class identity, and focuses their anger against a despised elite, trade policy will often be folded into the policy agenda if it can be linked to the interests of the elite. Since populist rule presumably begins with victory in a democratic election, the issue then turns to whether the populist government will continue to respect democratic elections and democratic political and legal institutions. The politics of a Manichean, good-versus-evil, people-versus-elite populist movement often oversimplifies the sources of anger that fuel its appeal at the ballot box, and once in power, the populist solutions may not be successful. The Achilles heel of a populist government thus often lies in its vulnerability to political forces that may convince a majority that the populist emperor has no clothes, and should be voted out of office. Anticipating its possibly tenuous hold on political power, many populist leaders take steps in office that diminish the ability of the opposition to win elections through diminishing governmental checks and balances regarding executive powers, suppressing freedom of the press and civil liberties, disenfranchising opposition voting blocs, and eroding the rule of law.

Trump's behavior following his defeat in the presidential election of November 2020 bore out these predictions, but the US judicial check on the electoral process prevented him from overturning the vote. While he was behind in the public opinion polls in the runup to the election, he declared that his opponent, Joe Biden, was already rigging the election. Trump took steps to slow postal service deliveries of absentee ballots that would favor Biden and demanded that his Attorney General arrest Biden and other political opponents for various crimes (Cheney 2020). As Biden's election victory was being certified in November and December, Trump refused to concede defeat, declaring that the tally in favor of Biden was proof of a nationwide Democratic Party voter fraud conspiracy, the result of coordinated voting machine tampering, illegal absentee ballots, unregistered voter ballot-box stuffing, and unmonitored vote counting (Yen et al. 2020). Based on these claims, but without credible evidence, he asked Republican state legislatures in key states to replace Democratic with Republic electors for the electoral college vote, and filed dozens of law suits asking state and federal courts to overturn the popular vote in those states, but was rebuffed in each case, and finally by the US Supreme Court (Bruinius 2020). In the end, the US legal system prevailed, the key institution that resisted populist erosion in this case, despite the ability of the US president to nominate federal and supreme court judges. Kyle and Mounk (2018) document the general tendency of populist governments to erode democratic processes, with an empirical study of populist governments in power, drawing on a database identifying such regimes alongside democratic nonpopulist regimes, from 1990 to 2016.[4] Their results conclude that populist rule reduces a country's democracy index by about 10%, all other factors being held constant—a democratic backsliding effect that holds across the board for all types of populist governments. Furthermore, the democratic erosion tends to progress for each successive year the populist government is in power. There is a 13% increased risk in any given year of populist rule that democracy in the country will collapse completely. For these reasons, populist governments tend to stay in office longer, and if they do leave office, they are more likely to do so by being forced out of office rather than through a peaceful transition of democratic elections. The cost of populism to democracy affects trade to the extent that an increasingly authoritarian leader will face fewer and fewer constraints on trade policy, and be freer to restrict trade for the benefit of favored industries, individuals, or other populist agendas.

Populism is thus a warning sign, a symptom of the failure of traditional political representation that points to the danger to liberal democracies. Its impact on public discourse and the political process is jarring, and over time, exhausting. By establishing an anger-driven, tribal division in the electorate, it seeks to diminish the political value of compromise. Once this dynamic takes hold, it tends to drive more and more of the population to extreme positions, at times pushing political opposition to the populist regime toward a mirror-image populist opposition on the other end of the ideological spectrum. In the United States, one type of anti-Trump sentiment has crystallized around left-wing Democratic populists such as early presidential candidates Elizabeth Warren and Bernie Sanders, whose appeal lies in their proclamations, similar to Trump's, that the system is rigged, but in their account by Wall Street interests and plutocrats rather than globalist liberal elites. Ironically, the left-wing and right-wing populist positions on trade are remarkably similar in their economic nationalism, revealing the common populist appeal of trade as an elitist conspiracy of forces inimical to the home country's interests. One need only pick class warfare or culture warfare as the rallying cry. Restoring a functioning global trading will be difficult as long as this protectionist convergence retains its hold on politics in the United States, and especially if it spreads to other countries.

The Wages of Trade War

The trade war with China represented the core of Trump's populist trade strategy during his administration. Based on his campaign rhetoric and his focus on manufacturing jobs and trade deficits, his expectation seemed to be that these measures would be quick and efficient in eliminating the US trade deficit, rejuvenating manufacturing employment, and increasing US economic growth. Trump's own rhetoric appeared to convince him that China would eventually capitulate to his demands, as he declared that "trade wars are good" and "easy to win" against trade surplus countries like China. His view seemed to rest on the assumption that the trade imbalance would cause China to run out of retaliatory import tariff opportunities before the United States would. Left with no other politically acceptable way to respond to these ultimatums, however, China continued to match US tariff escalations as the battle of wills between the two largest economies of the world continued, reaching an uneasy truce with the January 2020 Phase One agreement. In the meantime, US businesses and consumers faced increasing import prices, contrary to Trump's assertion that the foreign exporters would pay for the burden of the tariff. The tariffs and foreign retaliation have generated significant welfare costs for the US economy, which are likely to rise much more if the tariffs persist. US exporters faced reduced market access in China due to retaliation. As noted earlier, Trump attempted to compensate farmers for lost export revenue with $28 billion in subsidies, but even these payments were not enough to prevent 2019 farm bankruptcies from reaching their highest level since 2011(McKeef 2019). Blanchard et al. (2019) estimate that the impact of the trade war alone on US agricultural regions may have led to the loss of five Republican congressional seats (out of a net total of 40 lost) in the 2018 midterm elections.

The trade war left the dubious goal of trade deficit reduction unfulfilled. The US trade deficit worsened during Trump's first two years in office, accelerating after the introduction of his tariff initiatives in 2018. The trade balance is unlikely in any case to respond positively to tariff increases, since such measures do not typically affect the gap between national savings and investment. It is more likely that the president's tax reform bill, which increased the US budget deficit by $1 trillion, was responsible for the worsening balance. As for US-China trade, the bilateral US deficit actually increased from $375 billion in 2017 to 420 billion in 2018, perhaps because of accelerated Chinese exports to the United States in anticipation of the tariffs, in addition to reduced US exports, caused in part by supply-chain effects of the trade war. Whatever Chinese exports were subsequently impeded by the US tariffs also appear to have been diverted in part to other export countries, such as Cambodia, Vietnam, Indonesia, Bangladesh, Mexico, or the Philippines, either legally or illegally (Behsudi 2019).

The overall US economy fared well in Trump's first three years in office, with annual growth averaging 2.5% and unemployment falling from 4.7% to 3.7% through August 2019.[5] The stock market, buoyed by Trump's deregulation and 2018 tax cuts, reached record levels in 2019, but the upward trend slowed after the start of the 2018 tariffs (Long 2019). A growing economy tends to provide a safety net for those suffering unemployment or declines in income, such as those hit by tariff-related layoffs and farm closures. Yet the tariffs apparently stalled US manufacturing employment in particular. A major goal of Trump's trade agenda, according to Peter Navarro's film *Death By China*, had been to increase US manufacturing employment from the current level of 8.5% to 25% of total employment.[6] US manufacturing output and employment had in fact increased in the first two years of Trump's presidency along with the rest of the economy (Frank 2018), but it never significantly increased as a percentage of total employment, and then started to decline shortly after the tariffs began. By late 2019 the US manufacturing sector was in a recession, with decreasing output and stagnant employment growth. The tariffs are likely to have contributed to this decline for several reasons. As previously noted, the hoped-for re-shoring of manufacturing jobs has not occurred, as jobs displaced in China have moved mainly to lower-cost locations in Asia and Mexico. In addition, many US manufacturing jobs are linked with Chinese supply chains, and the tariff-induced cost increases have depressed their competitiveness. Finally, the tariff regime itself, with its uncertain length and continuing escalation, had choked off much of the investment necessary to sustain manufacturing output and growth (see Lee 2019). Beyond the United States, world trade in general was declining as a knock-on effect of the trade war, disrupting global supply chains and casting a shadow on the trading system. The trade war continued to threaten further reductions in business investment, possibly contributing to a sustained global market downturn, and worsening economic conditions in the United States as well.

The festering crisis in trade relations may in fact have increased the world economy's vulnerability to the shock of the coronavirus outbreak in early 2020, which sparked a major global recession. While the triggering shock of the pandemic did not involve trade directly, the US role in the crisis revealed the same populist impulses of unilateralism that President Trump exhibited in his trade policy. Fearful that news of spreading infections would cause a market downturn, damaging his reelection prospects, Trump at first dismissed the crisis as a political hoax engineered by his Democratic opponents and insisted that the virus would quickly disappear. Eschewing cooperation with foreign leaders, he blamed other countries for the problem, another example of populist scapegoating. While China's early cover-up of the disease and European countries' failure to contain its spread were worthy of criticism, Trump's own coronavirus task force failed to develop new testing methods in a timely manner because of failed field tests, manufacturing bottlenecks, regulatory red tape, and faulty reagent components. Many observers viewed this factor, combined with Trump's early denial of the gravity of the crisis, as a significant reason for the undetected spread of the virus in the United States and a contributing cause of the market crash in early March 2020 (Fritze and Jackson 2020). It was also probably the most important reason for his defeat in the November 2020 presidential elections. Trump reinforced his policy of refusing to cooperate with other affected countries by unilaterally announcing a travel ban on European Union countries in response to the crisis, without advance notice or consultation with them, further alienating US allies. The travel ban also threatened to curtail trade traveling by airfreight, including pharmaceuticals, medical supplies, and surgical equipment.[7] There was also a US-China trade war connection with the crisis. US tariffs on Chinese medical and surgical supplies contributed to a shortage of these items in US hospitals, and the Trump administration quietly withdrew the tariffs temporarily in early March 2020. However, after the trade war began China sought out new customers, making it more difficult for US hospitals to regain access to Chinese sources of supply. In addition, other countries fighting the coronavirus were instituting export bans of their supplies (Bown 2020b). Yet the larger impact of this episode is institutional. US international cooperation had previously been a pillar of global disease control, through the World Health Organization and country-to-country ties with medical authorities, an arrangement that benefited the United States as well as other countries. However, the new era of trade wars, national security tariffs against allies, repeated tariff threats, and a lack of coordination, communication, and consultation diminished the ability of affected nations to respond to a serious health crisis. The casualties of populist trade policies include not only global trade relations and economic welfare, but also the broader ability of countries to cooperate on issues and crises of global concern.

Summary

President Trump implemented several new populist trade policies and proposals that restricted trade, imposed economic costs on the United States and other countries, and directly threatened the integrity of the GATT-WTO trading system. The Brexit vote threatened to impose significant long-run collateral damage on the UK economy as it withdrew from European Union integration, and weakened the pro-trade consensus in the European Council. The various costs of these populist policies, including the associated and collateral effects of retaliation, rent-seeking, intimidation, uncertainty, foregone trade agreements, immigration, and weakened cooperation in the coronavirus crisis, are summarized in Table 8.1. Part of the cost takes the form of deadweight loss, inefficient transfers to domestic producers, and uncompensated

Table 8.1 The Cost of Populist Protectionism

Populist Trade Policy	Elements	Incidence	Magnitude
Section 232 tariffs: Steel, Aluminum	Welfare cost of deadweight loss, reduced product variety	US Consumers, firms in supply chains, foreign producers	Welfare cost, net job loss in manufacturing
Section 232 VER agreements: Steel		Rep. Korea, Argentina, Brazil: US steel consuming firms	Welfare cost, anti-competitive effect, violates WTO rules
	Cascading tariffs on steel and aluminum derived products	US firms, consumers of derivative products, supply chains	New series of welfare costs
	Foreign Retaliation	US producers, foreign consumers	Welfare cost, job losses, bankruptcies
	Erosion of WTO Rules	Global trading system	Sparked retaliation, loss of US leadership, respect for WTO agreements
US Section 201 tariffs: Washing Machines		US consumers	Welfare cost
US Section 201: Solar Panels		US panel fabricators, consumers	Welfare cost
US-China Trade War	Tit-for-tat tariffs covering most bilateral trade	US, Chinese import consuming firms, supply chains, consumers	Welfare cost, WTO rules violation, supply-chain disruption
	US tariff exclusions	US importing firms	Rent-seeking, nontransparent bureaucracy
	Discrimination	Chinese producers (3rd country beneficiaries)	Export diversion, fraud, possible knock-on protectionism
	Chinese retaliation	US producers, Chinese consumers	Welfare cost, job losses, bankruptcies
	US transfers to farmers: compensation for retaliatory losses	US taxpayers	Additional financial cost of protection: $28 b
	Medical equipment, supplies	Coronavirus-impacted hospitals, patients	Shortages, higher prices
US-China Phase One agreement	Voluntary import expansion: $200b	China, US	WTO MFN violation, empowers state-owned enterprises
	Dispute settlement	China, US	Bilateral instability; no 3rd party, undermines WTO

Table 8.1 *Continued*

Populist Trade Policy	Elements	Incidence	Magnitude
Trump unpredictability (all trade policies)	Welfare cost of uncertainty: investment, foregone market opportunities	US firms, global supply chains, knock-on effect in global markets	Amplifying effect of continued uncertainty, est. $1 trillion global cost
US blockage of WTO Appellate Body Judges	Quorum of judges not met	Countries appealing DSU panel decisions	Undermines major WTO function
US tariff threat: Mexico	Exaction of policy change on immigration	Mexican policy sovereignty, economy, WTO rules, NAFTA/ USMCA treaty	Erosion of Mexico FDI attractiveness; violation of WTO tariff binding, US treaty commitments
US withdrawal from Trans-Pacific Partnership	Foregone trade, rule-making, leadership opportunities	US export trade, US consumer welfare	Diminished US regional, global influence; lost future US producer, consumer gains from trade
US currency manipulation allegations	US retaliatory tariffs on trading partners	Turkey, Brazil, Argentina, China	US Court rulings limit impact; Trump seeks new presidential authority
US threat of Section 232 auto tariffs	Exaction of concessions on various issues	European Union; possibly other countries	Threat of new trade wars
US removal of GSP for India	Indian trade regime, trade surplus with US	US consumers, Indian exporters	New trade restrictions for GSP countries
Brexit: Loss of economic integration	Exit from single market: trade	UK, EU consumers,	Welfare cost of higher tariffs, less variety
	Exit from single market: investment	UK, EU investment partners	Investment losses
	Exit from common external trade policy	UK as negotiating unit	Weakened trade-bargaining power
	Political cost	Future EU relations; Scotland, N. Ireland	Messy trade divorce Secession from UK?
Brexit: eliminate intra-EU immigration	Backlash against nonpreferred EU citizens	UK labor market	UK labor shortage, loss of competitive workforce
US, UK populist immigration restrictions (general)	Backlash against "undesirable" refugees, immigrants	Labor market, economic growth	Loss of competitive workforce

Memo: Aggregate estimated welfare cost of US Tariffs: $18b annually deadweight loss, plus $16 billion tariff revenue transfer, plus transfer to domestic producers, plus fixed cost of supply-chain disruption (Amiti 2020). US GDP 0.3% annual reduction (Congressional Budget Office 2019). Additional unestimated economic costs include rent-seeking and firm efficiency disincentives.

Including uncertainty effects: 0.5% US GDP reduction, 1.0% Global GDP reduction (Caldera 2019).

Brexit estimated cost: 1.15% to 7.5% of UK GDP, depending on negotiations (Latore et al. 2019) consumer transfers to the government through tariff revenue, which economic studies have estimated (see memo section at the bottom of the table). Additional costs include a large impact of policy uncertainty on business investment and trade activity, which has been estimated to be as high as 1% of annual global GDP, nearly $1 trillion. Other costs are harder to quantify, such as rent-seeking lobbying costs, and the X-inefficiency disincentives for firms. Investment-related cost of protection can be large, and typically stem from supply-chain disruptions. A large portion of the cost of Brexit, for example, is estimated to come from the loss of cross-border investment between the United Kingdom and the EU countries. It is important to note that the cost of protection tends to grow over time, especially in a trade war, where tariffs tend to escalate. In addition, long-term trade restrictions tend to compound the economic costs because they more firmly lock resources into inefficient uses that may be difficult to reverse. Finally, as noted in the discussion of policy uncertainty, earlier unexpected policy actions tend to amplify the impact of renewed uncertainty as policy behavior reveals itself to be increasingly unreliable. Beyond economic costs are the institutional and political costs of disrupted trade relations and rules-breaking, a distinctive feature of populist trade policy in the Trump administration. Brexit may eventually stoke new secession movements in Scotland and Northern Ireland, and both the United Kingdom and the United States may face broader efficiency and trade consequences of populism-induced restrictive immigration policies, which could reduce the supply of labor that contributes to the country's productive capacity and entrepreneurship.

9

The Future Belongs to Globalized Societies

Main Conclusions of the Book

This book set out to examine the impact of populism on trade policies and global trade institutions. A major conclusion of the book is that populism influences trade policy—and in particular trade restrictions—through the deeply embedded human tendency to view the world in terms of insiders and outsiders, especially in times of a perceived foreign threat, the same impulse that motivates xenophobic behavior and war. This view competes with a contrasting human tendency to engage with foreigners in seeking gains from trade, an activity anthropological evidence suggests began 140,000 years ago with the beginnings of human language. Furthermore, populist politics is based on the view that an internal conflict in a country pits the nation's genuine people against the despised elites, and may promote trade skepticism as part of a nativist or anti-globalist ideology, associating elites with malign foreign influences that must be stopped. Anger is a major motivating factor in populism. Trade, through job losses and lower wages, may be a direct source of populist anger, or it may act indirectly through other sources of nativist or economic anger. For example, populist political strategies may link trade with immigrant incursions in the domestic society and their threat to in-group economic, social, and cultural status. Populism is therefore an anthropological, sociological, economic, and political phenomenon.

As a political movement, populism also came to challenge the institutional framework of global trade. The most important single event in the populist inspired erosion of trade institutions was the election of Donald Trump as US president in 2016. He linked US participation in multilateral and regional trade agreements with the dismantlement of US manufacturing, the devastation of communities in Rust Belt regions, and specific countries' alleged theft of US economic welfare through US trade deficits. His condemnation of US trade policy fit squarely into a populist platform that identified globalist elites conspiring to deprive the genuine people of their jobs and way of life. As president he proceeded to implement a populist trade policy of economic

Populism and Trade. Kent Jones, Oxford University Press. © Oxford University Press 2021.
DOI: 10.1093/oso/9780190086350.003.0009.

nationalism, imposing tariffs unilaterally on self-justified national security grounds, initiating an escalating trade war with China, renegotiating trade agreements in order to introduce new protectionist measures, and undermining WTO rules and institutions. In this regard, Trump's populist trade policy has increased the damage to US domestic and global economic welfare beyond the traditional costs of protectionism. A major source of the populist injury was institutional. His tariffs violated several WTO norms and rules that had stabilized trade relations among its members for several decades, weakening the global trading system. His control of US trade policy was largely responsible for the spread of protectionism in the world economy beginning in 2018, through retaliatory responses by many countries to his tariffs, which they regarded as illegal. A related populist element of the institutional damage he inflicted was the uncertainty his rule-breaking created, reducing business investment and related expenditures globally.

Populism also left its mark on trade and trade policy in the Brexit referendum in 2016. Brexit represented a populist revolt by Euroskeptics in the United Kingdom against centralized regulations imposed by the bureaucratic elite in Brussels. While trade was not a central theme of the Brexit campaign, it did contribute to voter dissatisfaction, especially in UK industrial regions. More importantly, severing ties with the European Union inevitably meant severing UK-EU trade and economic integration agreements. Trade became a central feature of the aftermath of the Brexit victory, as the United Kingdom faced the challenge of reconstructing its trade and investment relations from scratch with the European Union and with other trading partners. For the European Union itself, the departure of the United Kingdom weakened the pro-trade coalition in the European Council and pro-trade forces in other EU institutions, and represented part of a broader backlash against further EU integration. Most economic estimates of the impact of Brexit identify significant negative impacts on the United Kingdom, depending on its final degree of economic uncoupling from the European Union.

Populism itself, however, is not inherently protectionist. The implementation of protectionist policies in a populist government depends on the context of the country's populist movement, its governance system, the identity of the elite, the size of its economy, the degree of import disruption linkage to populist anger, ability of the country to overturn existing trade institutions, and the trade ideology of the populist leader. President Trump sought to implement protectionist policies because he had favored protectionism long before he entered politics. He was then able to implement them, even when they violated international rules and departed from long-standing practices, because the United States concentrates the power over many aspects of trade policy in the presidency, and because the United States is the world's largest importer of goods by value. Among other countries, populist governments have tended to have less protectionist policies if they are trade-dependent open economies, which tend to benefit from universal WTO rules and would suffer serious retaliatory damage and isolation from any efforts to break the rules. Populist governments in smaller EU member states also have had less room to pursue protectionist policies in view of the EU common trade policy generally supported by its larger members. Left-wing populist governments and those with high energy export dependency tend to be more protectionist. So-called anti-establishment populist governments, in contrast, tend to favor more open trade policies if their path to power was to oust an existing corrupt and incompetent government.

This final chapter will conclude by considering the prospects for finding ways to overcome the current wave of populism and establish (or re-establish) a global institutional environment that supports multilateral trade liberalization, stable trade relations, and shared economic growth. While populism may be likened in some ways to a fever, an aberration that will have to run its course until it breaks on its own, the populist temptation is likely to persist as a political force as long as underlying populist discontents persist. A remedy, in the author's view, must focus on developing economic policies and institutional support to adapt to the structural and technological challenges of the twenty-first century. These include, at the domestic level, economic adjustment policies and reforms and renewed support and protection of democratic processes. At the global level, they will require institutional leadership and innovative frameworks for multilateral cooperation.

The Populist Challenge

President Donald Trump was defeated in the November 2020 US elections, and most observers anticipate a return to "normalcy" at home and multilateralism in US foreign and trade policy in the Biden administration. However, Trump's brand of populism is likely to persist in the United States and in other countries as a potent political force as long as the disruptions of economic, technological, and social change remain sources of widespread frustration and anger in the United States and other countries. This section begins with Trump's populist manifesto, followed by a rejoinder to the flawed economic theories on which much of it is based. It then delves into the hard work required of governments to address the roots of populist anger in terms of political, legal, and economic reforms, as well as adjustment policies to secure shared economic prosperity and stability for their populations.

Trump's Populist Manifesto

At the United Nations on September 24, 2019, President Trump delivered his international populist manifesto, calling on the rest of the world to join him in national policies based on sovereignty and patriotism:

> The free world must embrace its national foundations. It must not attempt to erase them or replace them . . . Wise leaders always put the good of their own people and their own country first. The future does not belong to globalists. The future belongs to patriots. The future belongs to sovereign and independent nations who protect their citizens, and honor the differences that make each country special and unique . . . At the center of our vision for national renewal is an ambitious campaign to reform international trade. For decades, the international trading system has been easily exploited by nations acting in very bad faith. As jobs were outsourced, a small handful grew wealthy at the expense of the middle class . . . Our goal is simple: we want balanced trade that is both fair and reciprocal. (Trump 2019)

The president's statement begins well but then proclaims that "globalists" are by definition anti-patriotic, impoverishing their populations to enrich themselves alone, with the help of exploitative foreign countries that steal the patriots' wealth by forcing them to import more goods than they export. He goes on to call out certain nations (principally China) as the major disruptive force in world trade, and that WTO rules allowing the disruption require "drastic change." The statement on China is reasonable, and a good starting point for WTO reform. However, he curiously ignores any possibility of following up this statement with proposals to work with US trading partners and WTO members to introduce new global rules, and instead declares proudly:

> To confront these unfair practices, I placed massive tariffs on more than $500 billion worth of Chinese-made goods. Already, as a result of these tariffs, supply chains are relocating back to America and to other nations, and billions of dollars are being paid to our Treasury . . . Hopefully, we can reach an agreement that would be beneficial for both countries . . . We desire peace, cooperation, and mutual gain with all. But I will never fail to defend America's interests. (Trump 2019)

To President Trump, his country—and presumably the rest of the world—are divided between virtuous "patriots" and malign "globalists." His plan for pursuing "peace, cooperation and mutual gain for all" is to disrupt supply chains, impose massive tariffs, and watch the money roll into his treasury—without acknowledging that his own citizens are forced to pay the extra taxes on imports. His goal for the United States is "balanced trade that is both fair and reciprocal," a new global trading order in which the rest of the world is responsible for making sure that the United States never consumes more than it produces, and thus having to import the difference.

A Response to Unilateral Protectionism

This book has documented the populist approach to trade, as represented by President Trump, and has identified several problems and flaws with this approach. First of all, Trump's view is that trade does not allow mutual gains from trade but is a battle waged in the name of economic nationalism, in which those with trade surpluses are the winners and those with deficits are the losers. For this reason, Trump views trade negotiations as distributive (zero-sum) games rather than integrative (mutually beneficial) bargains based on compromise, reciprocal market access, and shared gains from trade for all parties. Furthermore, the Trumpian view is that tariffs will improve a country's trade balance, bring displaced jobs back to the country, increase the country's total welfare and economic growth, and enrich the home treasury at foreign expense. The high net negative cost of protectionism, along with the domestic macroeconomic determinants of the trade balance, shows that none of these propositions is true. After Trump's tariffs began the US trade balance worsened; the tariffs inflicted net job losses on the economy in manufacturing and reduced economic welfare. Domestic prices rose by nearly the entire amount of the tariffs, so that payments to the US Treasury came out of the pockets of private and business consumers of affected imports.

Finally, the populist manifesto implies that countries can pursue "peace, cooperation and mutual gain" through trade restrictions targeted against countries with which it has a trade surplus. Unless Trump views the United States as a global imperial hegemon that can enforce quantitatively determined bilateral trade balances on all its trading partners, the mutual pursuit of such "fair and reciprocal trade," enforced by unilateral tariffs, is internally inconsistent. Bilateral trade balances are determined by each country's domestic macroeconomic forces, not by bilateral tariff regimes, and any system that assumes otherwise is a formula for continual trade wars, a fracturing of the global economy into defensive trading blocs, and the reduction of economic welfare and growth for the world economy. The argument here is that contrary to President Trump's view, patriots can be globalist in their outlook and globalists can be patriots in their home countries. The future in fact belongs to patriotic, globalized societies, each seeking to maximize the welfare of its own citizens through domestic measures to address the challenges of globalization, economic policies to improve country's abilities to gain from trade and investment, and rules-based cooperation with its trading partners. In this manner, all trading countries will gain from trade. This is also the way, to borrow Trump's own words, that "wise leaders . . . put the good of their own people and their own country first."

The prospects for a more enlightened US trade policy after Trump leaves office are not certain. Support for a more open trade regime remains limited in both major US political parties. Republican politicians refused to challenge Trump on his protectionist policies. Traditional support for trade agreements among them may revive after Trump leaves office, although this depends on whether or not the Republican electoral base continues to embrace populism, through either Trump or a new populist candidate who demands similar submission. In addition, most of the progressive (i.e., left) wing of the Democratic party in 2020 were openly protectionist and incorporated left-wing populist views, and the moderate Democratic wing professed mainly mixed views toward trade (see Hufbauer and Jung 2019).[1] In general, most Democratic politicians opposed Trump's arrogation of trade authority and did not advocate leaving the WTO or directly violating WTO rules. At the same time, most remained either skeptical or wary of trade liberalization and openness, and may not be willing to champion a revival of the WTO. Democrats lost many blue-collar, Rust Belt votes in the 2016 presidential election to Trump, and the party is unlikely to proffer an openly pro-trade agenda as long as it perceives such a platform to be politically risky. In the United States, trade therefore remains a potent political issue. In this regard, populism is a warning signal that countries must improve their management of the pain of economic adjustment (Pieterse 2018). In Europe, support for a rules-based trading system is much stronger, but populist movements continued to threaten European integration and its leadership on global trade issues in 2020. The United Kingdom formally exited the European Union in January 2020, when Boris Johnson's initial negotiations with Brussels suggested a hard Brexit outcome for the new UK-EU trade relationship. Populist governments continued in eastern Europe, and populist party influences continued to be significant in Germany, France, and Italy. Populist governments also remained in power in India, Indonesia, and the Philippines and in Latin American countries (Serhan 2020).

Addressing the Roots of Populism Begins at Home

Populism arises within domestic political systems and regional integration agreements such as the European Union. The political framework of both the US and EU systems has contributed to the problem. In the United States, Congress delegated considerable trade policymaking power to the executive branch of government in 1934, and for the next 82 years the US president generally used this power to promote trade liberalization both among the US population and abroad. The role of US presidential discretion was a double-edged sword, however, as a protectionist president came to power in 2016 and proceeded, under the same provisions, to implement unilateral trade restrictions that were unchecked by Congress. This US trade policy framework was democratically enacted, but did not anticipate the damage that a populist, protectionist president could inflict on trade policy, trade relations, and trade institutions. Senator Robert Portman (2019) proposed a partial remedy to the lack of checks and balances in trade policy by requiring increased Defense Department oversight over presidential decisions on national security tariffs, although this provision was not enacted during Trump's term. Ideally *Congressional* oversight would be preferable on this issue, as well as on Section 301 cases, and any other matters where the president can claim unilateral power to impose trade restrictions. There is also a structural problem in the trend in US electoral politics, in that the two-party system has frayed increasingly into left- and right-wing factionalism, decreasing representation of centrist forces that could facilitate compromise on trade and other issues. This state of affairs will have to wait for either populism to wane in importance, encouraging moderation in legislative and presidential politics, or for new political parties to develop, backed by groups perceiving a lack of representation of their interests in the existing two-party system. In the European Union, the issue is one of a democratic deficit on issues of concern to the EU population in all member countries. Democratic institution-building must go beyond the current European Parliament, as many impactful decisions are carried out by the Council and the Commission without adequate deliberation at the national level in member states. It should have been no surprise that accumulated grievances and resentments on a wide range of issues crystalized into an anti-EU vote when given a simple-minded yes/no choice in the Brexit referendum. While more democratic representation may slow down "ever-closer union," it can at the same time forestall such disastrous outcomes.

Within the United States and the EU countries, populism typically reflects social and economic conditions that call for domestic social and economic solutions. Addressing the populist challenge in the future will therefore require initiatives on several fronts to rebuild trust in domestic and international economic institutions. The root causes of populism remain an issue of contention, but the evidence suggests that they include changes in the demographic profile of communities and regions, rapid advances in disruptive technologies, displacement of traditional jobs, and threats to traditional social and cultural status (Pieterse 2018). Economic factors play at times a direct and at times an indirect role in the anxiety over these changes. The political response—or lack of it—determines the resulting nonpopulist or populist government, respectively (Brubaker 2017; Berger 2017). The real problem is that when political institutions fail to keep up with changes in the social and economic environment the society is vulnerable to populist movements, with their attendant dangers of polarization, exploitation by charismatic leaders, and bad policies, including bad trade policies. US trade policy has succumbed to this problem, and there are signs that European Union countries are also considering the same sort of *dirigiste* policies that led to economic stagnation in the 1970s (Zettelmeyer 2019). Such policies are doomed to fail, since they provide economically damaging solutions that do not address the underlying economic anxiety that comes with globalization and rapid technological and cultural change.

The challenge is for governments to reduce the demand for populism at the domestic level through adjustment assistance, retraining, education, labor market reforms, and effective safety net policies (see Ruggie 1982; Hays 2009; Eichengreen 2018, ch. 11). At the same time, governments need to focus on policies that will promote economic growth by improving their workers' abilities to thrive in a globalized and technologically advanced world. European countries have been more inclined than the United States to provide safety nets for job displacement (Eichengreen 2018; Rodrik 2018), but the European temptation to protect "national champions" would decrease the economic flexibility needed to address economic change and provide economic growth. Historically, the underlying triggers for populist movements have included actual or threatened economic dislocation and lost welfare, which tend to heighten widespread perceptions of social and cultural status deprivation caused by immigration and changing ethnic and linguistic demographics. Populism tends *not* to erupt in times of shared economic growth, such as in the period after World War II in the United States and Europe, and it often erupts in times of severe economic stress, such as the financial crisis of 2008. Some of the populist appeal of trade protectionism may therefore dissipate if new legislation can address trade adjustment issues such as education, job skill retraining, healthcare (including portability), interregional job certification, housing, and background checks (Dolan 2016). The declining mobility and flexibility of the US work force in recent years have become major impediments to trade adjustment in the twenty-first century, and political support for trade liberalization will depend on improvements in adjustment policies, labor mobility, and safety nets (Tsyvinski and Werquin 2018). In Europe, labor mobility among member states is an important element of adjustment that remains imperfect, and should not be sacrificed to xenophobic fears. During the first five decades after World War II, GATT participant countries successfully concluded eight rounds of trade liberalization, supported by *domestic* social safety net policies of its major members, a system that became known as "embedded liberalism" (Ruggie 1982). This system has in the meantime become overwhelmed by structural economic changes, and governments will need to implement new and updated social and adjustment policies to protect the interests of workers and manage the adjustment pressures of globalization (Hays 2009). US government trade adjustment assistance programs, in particular, have failed because of excessive red tape, definitions of trade versus nontrade job losses, and a lack of resources. These programs can be improved by extending assistance to all workers suffering job displacement from trade, automation, and technological advancement, and structural changes in market demand (Kletzer and Litan 2001; Jones 2004, ch. 3). The point of adjustment programs is to absorb a part of the transition shock of otherwise permanent wage losses from unforeseen market changes, and help workers shift to new and sustainable employment paths. Protectionist trade policies, in contrast, tend to sustain inefficient investments and place a drag on the economy.

Similarly, the trend in income inequality can be addressed more efficiently and directly through domestic tax reform rather than protectionist policies. Lawrence (2008, p. 17) documents the growing wage-productivity gap among US blue-collar workers since 1980, while Clausing (2019, p. 16) notes that median US household income grew only 16% from 1984 to 2015, while GDP per capita grew by more than 60%. Trade has played a relatively small role in income inequality, based in part on evidence that poorer consumers tend to capture relatively more gains from trade than wealthier consumers through imports (Fajgelbaum and Khandelwal 2016).[2] Technological advancement and its complement—higher education, for those who have access to it—appear to be the main reasons for the growing income gap in the United States, combined with tax policies that favor earnings from capital over labor. Technological advancement replaces labor with automated machinery and processes and is supported by increased global capital mobility, which tends to increase profits from capital investment as it seeks the highest rate of return. International trade certainly plays a role in this phenomenon, by allowing international investments to combine with cheaper foreign labor to produce foreign exports that displace manufacturing jobs in more advanced industrialized countries. In addition, manufacturers in the advanced countries have a strong incentive to adopt and develop labor-saving technologies when faced with increased import competition, which increases output and worker productivity but reduces the number of jobs in the industry.[3] In general, the income distribution problem calls for tax policy reforms that redresses the bias favoring capital, rather than protectionist trade and investment restrictions that reduce economic efficiency and welfare. Clausing (2019, ch. 12) proposes a package of specific tax measures, including increased use of the earned income tax credit for lower income workers, a more progressive tax structure, closing loopholes for international tax avoidance, and equal and more transparent tax rates for various forms of income.

In addition, labor's declining share of income appears to be linked to the increase, across several industrial sectors, in "superstar" firms' degree of market concentration (Autor et al. 2017b). Global superstars include Apple, Google, Amazon, Starbucks, Comcast, and AT&T, which have dominant positions due to varying combinations of proprietary technologies, network economies, mergers and acquisitions, favorable regulations, and superior marketing. As a result, they are also politically powerful. Their impact on income inequality comes from their monopsonistic power in hiring workers and their supernormal profits, which typically accrue to shareholders and senior management rather than workers. Patent law enforcement may also play a role in income inequality, as external patent acquisition by dominant firms of substitute technologies may enhance the firm's market and wage-making power (Hovenkamp and Hovenkamp 2017). The acquisition of patents with no intention of using them may also implicitly suppress innovation, competition, and the introduction of better and lower cost products (Abbot 2016). More generally, the high prices that the superstar firms may be able to charge would also aggravate income inequality by suppressing the real income of consumers (Clausing 2019, pp. 283–286). Furthermore, measures that encourage more innovation and competition will also tend to contribute to increased productivity and economic growth. Pro-competitive regulation and anti-trust policy would be the appropriate channels of government intervention to address the anti-competitive and other damaging economic effects of market-dominating firms.

The foregoing discussion of measures to promote trade adjustment and income equality would apply to any debate over protectionism, not just the populist variety. However, the ability of populism to coopt trade and related economic concerns into a broader set of complaints against alleged elitist misdeeds increases the urgency of ongoing government policies to maintain flexible and forward-looking policies of economic growth, stability, and shared prosperity. A related issue is the lack of government responsiveness and the gap in representation that leads to populist frustration and rejection of the established framework of political parties. Governments therefore must be vigilant in monitoring the signs of disruption, and be ready to implement forward-looking policies to address the problems. In the face of a rapidly changing world, such a society is more likely to embrace the stable politics of compromise and avoid the populist temptation of divisiveness. Maintaining policies to promote a flexible, efficient and growing economy will therefore support not only increasing standards of living across the population, but also political peace as well. If the government does not provide adequate shock-absorber adjustment policies for the disruption, then the anger will be likely to simmer and seek political vengeance, redirecting a divisive populist shock to the entire democratic system.

Rebuilding the Global Trading System

The global trading system was in crisis even before the wave of populism arose in the wake of the financial crisis of 2007–2012. The growing frustration with the consensus rule, the dissatisfaction of developing countries with the agenda, and the lack of effective leadership and cooperation among major member countries left the WTO vulnerable to attacks on its rules by the time they were tested by the Trump administration. Addressing this problem will require reforms not only of the WTO, but also of national trade laws, particularly those in the United States. In the absence of a strong global rules-based trading system, countries will increasingly turn to either unilateral measures or regional trading blocs to carry out their trade agendas.

WTO Norms, Domestic Trade Law, and Unilateralism

Trump's assault on the trading system has made painfully clear that the success of 70 years of the multilateral trading system has always depended more on the *norms*, rather than the letter, of the agreements. Critically, the legitimacy of the system depends on a mutual understanding of the *interpretation and intent* of the rules, and a shared conviction that if everyone abides by them, everyone will benefit. The rules themselves often provide no truly binding constraints on the actions of a WTO member in a position to defy them without an overwhelming threat of forceful and retaliation. There have been times when GATT rules had to bend in order to keep the collective peace, as in the case of the 1955 US carve-out on agricultural protection, the 1974 multifiber agreement to regulate textiles trade, and the proliferation of discriminatory voluntary export restraints (VERs) against trade disrupters. In spite of these derogations from the norms of the GATT-WTO system, negotiations eventually reformed them. There are, however, fundamental underpinnings of the GATT-WTO trading system that are essential for its functioning, and even existence. They provide red lines that set the limits on members' trade policies and practices and define the integrity of the system as a whole. From a strictly legal point of view, the unilateral US national security tariffs, for example, appear not to violate the *letter* of WTO rules, whose wording reflects the desire of countries to retain discretion in their application. Yet the application of this provision over the years reflects both intentions documented in the original negotiations and accepted practices developed over time. Their effectiveness in regulating trade policy behavior therefore depends on a continuing consensus on interpretation. In the original national security exception negotiations, consensus was reached on the meaning of "essential security interests," but the text contains no explicit limit on its scope (Pinchus-Paulsen 2019). This lacuna allowed the United States to assert a new definition of "national security" in terms of employment levels in a self-defined "essential" industry. Another gap between the letter and the meaning of the rules arose in the WTO's tariff-binding provision. Waiving this rule, as the security exception allows under strict conditions, presumes that the countries targeted with such tariffs are at war with (or pose a military threat to) the country invoking this provision. When the United States imposed a new interpretation, it again overturned the institutional integrity of the rules, and the precedent opened a potential Pandora's box of abuse.

The institutional foundation of the WTO also depends on domestic implementing legislation of its rules in the member countries. The US Constitution gives Congress the authority to regulate foreign trade (Article 1, Section 8), but since the 1934 Reciprocal Trade Agreements Act (RTAA), Congress has delegated significant trade policy powers to the US president (see Irwin 2017, pp. 423–443). This landmark act was seen as a remedy to the "log-rolling protectionism" of the 1930 Smoot-Hawley tariffs. The economic benefit of the RTAA was that the president is typically in a better position than Congress to pursue the national interest in trade policy, a view that ironically did not anticipate the economic damage made possible by the concentrated power it would put into the hands of a protectionist president. Both the WTO national security exception, for example, implemented in US Section 232 and the unilateral retaliation provisions of US Section 301 gave the president discretion to apply such trade restrictions without Congressional approval, in the form of national security tariffs on steel and aluminum and the US-China trade war, respectively. The new application of these statutes represented openly protectionist policies without the checks and balances of legislative review. These domestic trade law measures are open to presidential abuse and need to return to the disciplinary purview of Congress.

The Trump administration continued its stubborn policy of unilateral economic nationalism in 2020, his final year in office. The Covid-19 pandemic dominated public policy that year, leading to a mixture of US import tariff reductions and reflexive export restrictions on medical products, described in chapter 8. The United States and European Union traded WTO-authorized retaliatory tariffs over the Airbus-Boeing dispute settlement case, an issue that would carry over to the new Biden administration (Brunsden 2020b). Trump initiated new section 301 threats of retaliatory tariffs against European Union members and other countries in 2020 over digital taxes, threatening to start new trade wars if the Organization for Economic Cooperation and Development (OECD) negotiations were unsuccessful. This was another example of Trump's preference for confrontation and tariff threats, but in the end also another issue for the incoming Biden administration to address (Schwartzenberg 2020). President Biden will also have to decide how to manage the Phase One agreement he inherits from the Trump administration, which after nearly a year showed that China achieved only 58% of its negotiated quantitative targets for imports from the United States (Bown 2020c). The terms of the agreement left most of the trade war tariffs in place and established awkward, WTO-defiant, and probably unworkable managed trade commitments for both China and the United States. The Phase One agreement also left an inherently unstable provision for bilateral dispute resolution in place. In general, Biden entered office inheriting difficult trade issues without the benefit of normal WTO channels or eager trade allies, Trump having alienated most of them during his four-year term. Other decisions awaiting the Biden administration included whether to appoint new WTO Appellate Body judges, and whether to pursue a multilateral approach, rather than a continuation of unilateral trade war, in confronting China over its trade-related subsidy and intellectual property protection policies. Enlisting the support of other WTO members in calling for new disciplines on China would serve to refocus disputes over China's practices properly on WTO systemic remedies, based in large part on the nonviolation provisions of the nullification and impairment "elastic clause." It would also improve the bargaining position of the many WTO members harmed by Chinese trade practices, at the same time reducing the ability of China to retaliate effectively. All countries, China more than others, ultimately have a strong interest in a stable, rules-based trading system. A grand WTO bargain with China on the rules of transparency and the limits of its intervention in trade, investment, and intellectual property markets would go a long way toward resolving a major problem in the global trading system, revitalizing the WTO, and perhaps even helping to break the logjam on general trade liberalization.

Prospects for WTO Renewal

Populist trade policies have wreaked special havoc on the global trading system, but fortunately, as of early 2021, other countries had not followed Trump's lead in abusing the WTO national security exception and other WTO rules. Yet is there any hope that the WTO can restore order and stability in trade relations? Enhancing WTO safety-valve measures, through safeguards reform, would relieve pressure on the use of national security and other measures inconsistent with WTO rules. The current lack of strong leadership in the WTO, however, may also require a rebuilding of international rules consensus through plurilateral agreements among subsets of WTO members, leading perhaps to new patterns of WTO leadership built on issues of common interest. Still, it would be best if a general WTO agreement on reforms, which would require United States approval, would be the best way to repair the global trading system. As noted earlier, the most important element in any revitalized global trading system will be a set of adequate domestic adjustment policies in the member countries, which will be required to reestablish political support for trade among WTO members. A weakened WTO, on the other hand, would push its members increasingly to limited agreements among themselves to settle disputes and promote trade liberalization, particularly through existing and new regional trade agreements. The danger of the regional approach is that world trade could then devolve into a defensive set of exclusive and isolated trading blocs. A more hopeful outcome would arise from a large and open, rules-driven, accession-based trade agreement, which could grow as the network economy of membership increases its value to all the members—in other words, into a new, reconstituted version of the WTO (Jones 2015). The Comprehensive and Progressive Agreement for Trans-Pacific Partnership (CPTPP) is structured in this manner, and if it expanded to include the European Union, China, and especially the United States, many other countries would also want to join. If on the other hand, the United States were to remain aloof, belligerent, and unpredictable in its trade policy, shunning any opportunities for rejuvenating the rules-based system of trade, the US leadership role in global trade would diminish. Throughout the period since World War II, the GATT-WTO system harnessed the willingness of member countries to truck and barter and channeled it into negotiations to expand trade on a nondiscriminatory basis. That impulse still exists, and if the current WTO system fails to fulfill its mandate to provide a forum for trade liberalization, mutually agreed-upon rules and principles, and a reliable system of dispute settlement, it will become necessary to pursue a large and comprehensive new mega-regional agreement with these features that will at-tract new countries to join, motivated by their desire simply not to be left out. Such an agreement, in turn, would then be positioned to expand further and re-build a global trading system.

Final Thoughts

The future belongs to globalized societies that can trade and invest in a stable and open world economy: this is the primary conclusion of this book, and its principal refutation of populist protectionism. But there is a related polit-ical conclusion, based on the recent increases in electoral support for populist parties and candidates at the ballot box. The future also belongs to democratic societies that can address and solve their problems through representative government, deliberation, and the rule of law. This is because populist regimes that develop authoritarian tendencies, from both the left and the right, tend to focus their efforts on retaining control of the government by perpetuating the divisions that brought them to power, delegitimizing the opposition, and suppressing its participation in electoral politics. Aside from undermining democratic institutions, they are also unlikely to undertake any of the efforts needed to reconcile the underlying conflicts that originally divided the elec-torate. Making lasting progress on the difficult and often divisive issues of so-cial and economic change requires an inclusive democratic process that takes into account the interests of the entire population, with deliberation among opposing views and avenues of compromise as moderating forces. Within this political framework, economic reforms and effective adjustment policies can help to address the disruptive effects of globalization, as economic dislocation has historically been a major driver of populist discontent. Yet these measures alone will not be enough. Populist movements, as shown in this book, tend to contain crosscurrents that link and reinforce economic grievances with social and cultural discontents, calling for the reconciliation of these conflicts as well, an issue that goes beyond the scope of what these pages could cover. In this regard, domestic support for a rules-based trading system may depend on broader immigration reform, along with greater efforts at promoting assimilation, social integration, and cultural diversity.

The successful functioning of an expanding, predictable, and peaceful global trade order will therefore depend, in part, on the strength and longevity of the democratic traditions and institutions of countries that lead and champion the system. Democratic societies have proven to be best historically at providing the incentives for commerce, innovation, and growth, but Acemoglu and Robinson (2013; 2019) also argue that democratic institutions themselves will not protect democracy, insisting that active public involvement is necessary to defend it. The integrity of elections, in other words, matters, as seen in the antidemocratic election outcomes in populist countries such as Russia, Belarus, and Venezuela, and in the democratic outcome, with checks provided by the rule of law, in the United States. Aside from maintaining a sustainable trading system, democratic governments will be also be necessary to serve as the basis for international efforts to contain other sources of populist discontent, such as foreign conflicts that generate immigration crises and refugee flows. Building up the domestic political will in democratic countries to support a greater capacity for global cooperation and engagement will be essential, as the many growing problems and crises in the global commons, from global warming to pandemics, increasingly call for global efforts, including a significant role for trade policy. The daunting challenge of managing disruptive change in democratic societies is that it will require newfound trust in democratic processes, domestic political leadership, and the hard work of forging global solutions that must begin at home—and put the populist genie back in its bottle.

Notes

Chapter 1

1. Rovira Kaltwasser et al. (2017) provide a collection of political science essays on populism, and chapters 1–4 offer a discussion of various definitions and approaches to populism from the perspective of this discipline. Gidron and Bonikowski (2013) provide a literature review from this perspective. Ocampo (2019) offers a literature review of the economic analysis of populism.
2. Kyle and Mounk (2018), using data on 45 populist regimes in 33 countries from 1990 to 2018, found evidence that populist governments were more likely than other types of democratic government to damage democratic institutions (by reducing press freedom, amending constitutions to increase executive power, restricting civil rights, etc.) and remain in office for long periods of time.

Chapter 2

1. The following section draws on Jones (2015, ch. 2).
2. See McBrearty and Brooks (2000, pp. 513–517), which dates evidence of distant trade to the middle paleolithic era. See also Oppenheimer (2003, p. 127). Dillian and White (2010) contains several other studies of prehistoric trade. Alonso-Cortés and Cabrillo (2012) examine the association of persuasive and sympathetic linguistic communication with commerce, first addressed as an economic issue by Adam Smith.
3. Neibuhr (1932), in a sharp critique of this aspect of group identity on a massive scale, regarded the aggressive European nationalism of the period between the First and Second World Wars as a manifestation of the tendency for members of the in-group to abandon individual moral behavior and succumb to the collective, immoral mania of the iconic nation and its leaders.
4. History has shown, however, that allure of the gains from more distant trade in exotic and luxury goods, especially in the spice and silk trade that connected Europe with Asia, can outweigh fears of unfamiliar trading partners. See Findlay and O'Rourke (2007, chs. 3–5) and Bernstein (2008, chs. 3–7). Even in this case, however, countries often sought to gain control over both trading routes and the production sources of the exotic goods.
5. The WTO membership stood at 164 countries in early 2021. Twenty-two additional countries were active applicants for accession at that time.
6. Amstutz (2016, ch. 2), provides a brief history and description of the Westphalian system and the principle of sovereignty.
7. See VanGrasstek (2019b, p. 429), who evaluates Donald Trump's trade policies in this light.

8. Trade theory predicts that the country as a whole will gain from trade, since the gains of the winners exceed the losses of the losers. Governments can theoretically promote a coalition of all workers in favor of free trade by redistributing a portion of the winners' gains to the losers, so that all workers (voters) benefit from trade. See Stolper and Samuelson (1941).

9. Coase (1998) remarked that "I find it difficult to ignore the role of stupidity in human affairs."

10. See Rovira Kaltwasser (2018), Mudde (2007), Etzioni (2018), and Oberhauser, Krier, and Kusow (2019).

11. Cheng (2018). President Trump authorized special subsidies to compensate soybean, corn and wheat farmers from lost income from China's retaliatory tariffs. Dornig and Jacobs (2019).

12. Prereferendum mainstream economic estimates are reported in Cadman and Giles (2016). Proponents of Brexit did not promote a protectionist platform, but rather claimed that the United Kingdom, freed from Brussels, would be able to negotiate superior trade agreements on its own. See Heath (2016) and the discussion in chapter 6 of this volume.

13. In the extreme case, an unscrupulous populist leader could use control over his followers, in the context of weak democratic institutions, to capture totalitarian control over the state, as exemplified by Adolph Hitler's 1933 rise to power in Germany. The result is that a voting "correction" is no longer relevant or possible.

14. Among the 17 anti-establishment populist regimes listed in Kyle and Gultchin (2018), seven are linked with post-Communist governments in Eastern Europe, two in Western Europe (both in Italy), four in Latin America, and four in Asia.

15. The Five Star Movement, founded by Beppe Grillo, entered government in June 2018 with 33% of the popular vote, and formed a coalition with the right-wing populist Lega Nord party. It is a political party whose collection of leaders variously represent left-wing, right-wing, and anti-establishment populist positions. In August 2019 the Five-Star-Liga Nord coalition collapsed, requiring the formation of a new government. Subsequently, Five-star has formed coalition governments with other parties (see Economist 2020). D'Alimonte (2019) provides a history of the Five-Star movement's rise to power.

16. Member countries of the European Union with populist governments (as of late 2020: Bulgaria, the Czech Republic, Hungary, and Poland) are tied to a common external tariff and most EU trade regulations, which have generally favored open trade and trade liberalization, especially with regard to regional trade agreements. Chapter 6 of this volume will address issues such as Brexit and the influence of populism on EU trade policy.

Chapter 3

1. Of course, most people need eventually to balance their household budgets with regard to total incoming revenues and outgoing expenditures. Any difference implies either net savings or borrowing by the household. Net household borrowing, like a balance of payments deficit, is typically financed by the willingness of creditors to lend money to the household. The United States finances its deficits in this manner through capital inflows: inbound foreign direct and portfolio investment, foreign holdings of dollars in cash and demand deposits, etc. The productivity of US investments, combined with the role of the dollar as a global reserve currency, make such capital inflows an attractive strategy to foreign

creditors. Deficits can be financed in this manner as long as expected US economic growth and the value of holding dollar assets outweighs any expected decline in the dollar's value in terms of other currencies.

2. In economic terms, the trade balance X-M = (S-I) + (T-G), where S=savings, I=domestic investment, T= tax revenues, and G=government spending. This expression, a basic identity of macroeconomics, is equivalent to the fact that a country's trade balance over a given time period equals the difference between what it produces and what it consumes.

3. A prohibitive, across-the-board tariff that eliminates all imports would tend to constrain the trade balance to zero. The economic reasoning of this outcome is that, starting from a position of trade deficit, the increase in the domestic price level that such a comprehensive tariff would impose on the economy would force a reduction in consumption and an increase in savings, whose utility relative to consumption would rise. Foreign inbound investment would fall, as foreign export earnings of the home currency would decline.

4. The theory of the optimum tariff, in which the tariff results in a net welfare gain to the importing country, depends on the import price elasticity of supply. Full absorption of the tariff by the exporter (and maximum benefit for the importing country) implies an elasticity of zero. For smaller countries, or for countries importing products with numerous alternative export markets, the supply price elasticity approaches infinity, and the entire amount of the tariff will be passed on to the import consumer in the tariff-imposing country. See Corden (1997, pp. 195–200).

5. The pass-through effect of tariffs on prices depends essentially on the size of the importing country, and the price elasticities of import demand and supply in the restricted market. High US import supply elasticities and relatively lower import demand elasticities imply that foreign exporters are willing to maintain their export prices despite reduced US sales, and US importers (perhaps through supply-chain linkages) have few alternatives to the imported goods.

Chapter 4

1. As noted in chapter 1, an elected populist government in power crosses a threshold in its choice of strategy to remain in power. A continuation of classic populist denigration and delegitimization of the elite may lead to an erosion of democratic institutions (Kyle and Mounk 2018).

2. The total US adult population during this period included women and slaves, who did not have the right to vote. Statistics on voter turnout are available back to 1828, when an estimated 57.6% of those deemed eligible voted. See note 10 for information on immigrant voters. Eligible voter turnout increased throughout the period of 1828 to 1860, reaching 81.2% in 1860. Voter turnout for the 2016 US presidential election was 55.5 % and about 67% in 2020.

3. Adams had received 31% of the popular vote compared with Jackson's 41%, while Henry Clay received 13% and William Crawford 11%. However, the popular vote requires the winner to achieve a majority of Electoral College votes: 131 out of 261. In the popular election electoral vote, no candidate won a majority: Jackson 99, Adams 84, Crawford 40, and Clay 38. Provisions of the 12th amendment of the US Constitution required the top three

electoral vote recipients to undergo a deciding vote in the House of Representatives, where each state (no matter what size) had one vote, based on a consensus of its delegation. Clay bitterly opposed Jackson, and although he was excluded from this vote, used his influence to swing representatives in states he won, plus three others, to the Adams camp.

4. Jackson had a personal grudge against the US National Bank, suffering financial setbacks that he attributed to its policies. See Eichengreen (2018, p. 122). Subsequent populist protests against government banking institutions included the Populist Party's bimetallism platform of 1896 and Father Charles Coughlin's proposal to place the Federal Reserve under political control in 1934.

5. Jackson defeated Henry Clay, who had conspired to assure Jackson's defeat in 1824.

6. Trump appropriated Jackson's mantle as a populist president, a connection promoted by Trump's advisor Steve Bannon. Trump's offhand sarcastic remark about the "Trail of Tears" resettlement of Native American tribes sparked controversy (Porter 2019). His choice to embrace Jackson's ethnocentrism and disdain for "unfriendly" court decisions as a role model for his presidency in the twenty-first century ultimately says as much about Trump as about Jackson as a populist.

7. President Trump indicated his admiration for Jackson during a radio interview in 2017, in which he stated that Jackson would have prevented the Civil War if his presidency had occurred later (Rothman 2017). Trump may have been referring to the nullification crisis of 1833, at which time Jackson may have prevented a civil war over the tariff issue. While many Southern secessionists saw tariffs and slavery as twin causes for war against the northern states, the tariff issue could be resolved in 1833 with changes in tariff rates and an unused threat of federal force. The slavery issue between North and South was irreconcilable, however, without a war to decide it.

8. Despite the connotation of ignorance in its name, the origin of a Know Nothing Party came from its secrecy, as its leadership instructed its members, when questioned about their political affiliation, to respond, "I know nothing."

9. Hayduk (2015) notes that many US states throughout the nineteenth century allowed noncitizen resident aliens to vote in local, state, and federal elections, a practice that ended with state and later federal voting citizenship requirements after renewed immigrant surges took place in the late nineteenth and early twentieth centuries.

10. *The Know Nothing Almanac* 1854, p. 23; emphasis in the original, quoted in Betz (2017, p. 340).

11. The Ku Klux Klan, a racist, anti-Catholic, and anti-Semitic organization, arose in the South during Reconstruction and was suppressed by US federal authorities in 1871. It reemerged in 1915, focusing its anti-immigrant activities on arriving Catholics and Jews, mainly from southern and eastern Europe.

12. Eichengreen (2018, p. 7) questions Bryan's status as a populist, since he did not embrace authoritarian and nativist views. Bryan's association with the Populist Party was in any case tentative and short-lived. He chose a nonpopulist as his 1896 vice-presidential running mate, and the subsequent Populist presidential candidate, Tom Watson, did in fact harbor nativist and racist views, as did certain factions of the Populist Party itself (Eichengreen 2018, p. 18–19; Judis 2016, p. 26).

13. The NIRA set up cooperative arrangements among industry, labor and government to avoid open competition and to set fair prices. Many business representatives opposed it on the grounds that it established cartels and fixed prices and wages. See McManus and Helfman (2014, pp. 371–372).

14. Contemporary accounts of Wallace rallies bear a striking similarity to those of Trump rallies 48 years later. See Carter (2000, p. 367).

15. Campaigning outside the two established parties, Nader had no chance of posing a serious threat in his own presidential campaign. However, he won 97,000 votes in Florida in 2000, which probably drew votes away from Democrat Albert Gore, handing victory in that state to Republican George W. Bush by just 600 votes, and tipping the Electoral College vote in Bush's favor. The winner-takes-all Electoral College rule in each state would also play a crucial role in 2016, with small parties playing possible spoilers in close state votes.

16. See Americans for Constitutional Liberty (2019), a pro-Trump lobbying and political organization, in support of a Congressional bill to freeze immigration from "radical Islamic countries."

17. The source of many such theories is summarized in *You Will Not Replace Us!*, by Jean Renaud Gabriel Camus (2018), describing how government elites in Europe are trying to engineer a replacement of the white population there with African and Islamic immigrants. Many white nationalists in the United States adopted this theory.

18. Skonieczny (2018) compares Trump's and Sanders's rhetoric during the 2016 primary campaigns on the trade issue, and concludes that both created similar populist narratives to stir emotional responses among voters.

19. See Stähleli and Savoth (2011) for an analysis of crowd psychology and the populist leader. One account of a participant at a Trump rally likened it to the American high school pep rally, an experience in which the crowd of loyal students showing school spirit would gleefully mock and humiliate a rival high school's athletic team in advance of a game, often culminating in a bonfire with a ceremonial torching of the rival's mascot.

20. Autor, Dorn, Hanson, and Majlesi (2020) also calculated similar counterfactual vote switching in New Hampshire and Minnesota, which Trump lost by small margins, and in Florida and North Carolina, which Trump won by small margins.

21. A detailed account of the many twists and turns in the election, including the details of Trump's razor-thin margin of victory, is beyond the scope of this study. See Badiou (2019).

Chapter 5

1. Participating countries included Australia, Brunei Darussalam, Canada, Chile, Japan, Malaysia, Mexico, New Zealand, Peru, Singapore, and Vietnam.

2. Blustein (2019, ch. 9) disagrees with this conclusion. However, any future US president could decide to renew accession negotiations with the new Comprehensive and Progressive Agreement for Trans-Pacific Partnership (CPTPP), which, without the US, contains amended TPP provisions. In particular, future access negotiations could propose new rules that would apply to state-owned enterprises and other state-level interventions in trade-related activities, a possible future institutional pathway to resolving controversial Chinese trade practices.

3. Anti-dumping and countervailing duty laws are the traditional unfair trade laws jointly administered by the Commerce Department and the US International Trade Commission. It is unusual for the Commerce Department to self-initiate such cases, which usually result from petitions by domestic producers. In retrospect these actions may have served to

build the case for national security tariffs (Section 232) in 2018. See VanGrasstek (2019a, pp. 6–7).

4. The US Court of International Trade granted an immediate injunction against the tariff for the complaining firm, agreeing to review the complainant's claim that Section 232 could not be applied to additional products after the statutory limit for its implementation had expired, among other statutory violations. See US Court of International Trade (2020).

5. Pinchis-Paulsen (2020) notes that the United States position during the original negotiations in 1946 was to allow legal review of the criteria used to justify national security tariffs. In a 2016 WTO dispute case, *Russia—Measures Concerning Traffic in Transit* (WTO 2016a), the United States supported Russia's claim that the national security criteria it used to justify its tariffs were not subject to review, a position that was ultimately rejected by the WTO panel.

6. Brazil and Argentina negotiated voluntary export restraint agreements to replace the tariffs, to be discussed in the following section of this chapter.

7. Regarding Brazil and Argentina, Trump replaced VERs with tariffs in December 2019 (Zumbrun et al. 2019).

8. Reich (2017) notes that WTO dispute cases often take two years or more to resolve. Yet Trump's trade war with China continued through the rest of his presidency, and beyond into 2021.

9. WTO rules on Intellectual property, including trade secrets, are contained in the Trade-Related Intellectual Property (TRIPs) agreement. The Subsidies and Countervailing Measures (SCM) agreement contains rules related to government subsidies. GATT article 10 enumerates transparency obligations. See WTO (1999). The China Protocol of WTO accession contains a number of special "WTO-plus" obligations, applicable specifically to China, regarding forced technology transfer. See WTO (2001).

10. A guiding principle of WTO is that a dispute case must normally identify a specific violation of a negotiated WTO rule. "Non-violation nullification of benefits" in the WTO refers to measures taken by member countries that while technically not in violation of specific WTO obligations, nonetheless deny "reasonably" expected benefits to WTO partner countries based on the results of the measure. Article 26 of the dispute settlement understanding, Article 23 of GATT 1994, Article 23 of the General Agreement on Trade in Services and Article 64 of the Trade-Related Aspects of Intellectual Property Rights provide the main WTO definitions and regulations related to this provision. See also Hoekman and Kostecki (2009, pp. 107–109).

11. Bacchus et al. (2018) note that China faced 41 WTO complaints on 21 separate issues from 2001-2018, resulting in 10 out-of-court settlements and 11 findings against China that led to more Chinese market access, with one terminated case and five still pending as of late 2019.

12. The China-US Phase One agreement WTO agricultural provisions focus on China's measures restricting imports of dairy products, wheat, rice, and corn, as enumerated in agreement chapter 3 (USTR 2020).

13. A WTO dispute case begins with a request for consultations. Approximately two-thirds are settled without official WTO dispute panel review. Of those that go to a dispute panel, approximately 18% are settled or terminated without a panel decision (see Reich 2017). Based on WTO dispute cases that proceeded to a final panel decision (through August 2019) the United States won 91% it filed as complainant, and lost 89% that were filed against it as respondent (Jacobson 2019). In general, countries filing complaints that go to a final panel decision tend to win on the major points of the case, since they

will not pursue the issue on a cost-benefit basis unless they are confident of victory (see Bown and Hoekman 2005).

14. Woodward (2018) reports that Trump, often in fits of anger, repeatedly questioned why the United States remains in the WTO. His advisors then had to talk him down from such a drastic move each time.

15. Lighthizer has indicated that the GATT dispute settlement system was superior to its WTO replacement. See Lighthizer 2017.

16. Even when the United States loses a case, it can be argued that US consumers and firms purchasing imports benefit from the decision. More generally, the existence of third-party review of trade disputes provides a channel for bringing trade conflict into a forum for negotiations and arbitration. The United States, among other WTO members, has availed itself of this process in protecting the market access interests of its exporters.

17. See Swan (2018). The initial draft was titled "The United States Fair and Reciprocal Tariff Act," which acquired the unfortunate acronym FART and encountered a strong backlash from Congress, even among Republicans. In early 2019 the president introduced the revised version of the bill, "The United States Reciprocal Trade Act," directly to the Republican caucus and presented it in his State of the Union address, but the November 2018 election of a Democratic majority in the House of Representatives dampened its prospects for passage.

18. The Swiss formula for tariff reduction, and the zero-for-zero formula for trade negotiations in some industry sectors, exemplify the convergence principle. The Swiss negotiating formula for a country's tariffs is $t_1 = (at_0)/(a+t_0)$, in which a is the ad valorem tariff rate ceiling, t_0 is the initial tariff and t_1 is the final tariff. As a result, higher tariffs fall by more than lower tariffs. See Francois et al. (2006, p. 95).

19. Given the different wage levels represented in a typical auto factory's workforce, the $16 rule appeared to introduce a difficult problem of verification, potentially imposing a significant increase in accounting and monitoring overhead.

20. Curi (2019) reports that Lighthizer was attempting in November 2019 to commit all US auto producers to follow the USMCA content rules on all their US production, even those auto units exported outside North America. This additional provision was not included in the USMCA text at the time. Aside from trying to secure US labor union and Democratic Party support for USMCA, this provision may reflect Lighthizer's fears of erosion of realized US auto content due to the 2.5% imported parts alternative.

21. Trump was successful in insisting on the elimination of the Chapter 11 investor-state dispute settlement provision, which allowed arbitration panel resolutions on complaints brought by foreign investors against government actions by the host country. However, Canada in particular was satisfied with that outcome, based on its record of losing several cases against US investors under the original NAFTA rules.

Chapter 6

1. The *Timbro Authoritarian Populism Index* website provides detailed data on European national parliamentary elections, as well as other information and commentary. See https://populismindex.com/data/.

2. Overall, left-wing parties in Europe had won 10% of the popular vote in national elections in 1981, compared to 1.1% for right-wing populist parties. By 2019 the left-wing populist share had fallen to 6.5%, while the right-wing populist share had increased to 15.5% (Timbro website, https://populismindex.com/).

3. The European coalition to fight the Ottomans, organized through the offices of the Pope, included the Habsburg Empire, several German principalities, and Poland. The French, under Louis XIV, refused to join the European forces, having just grabbed the Alsace region from its Hapsburg rival. European unity even under an existential threat from the Ottoman Empire was elusive.

4. Original EFTA members included Austria, Denmark, Norway, Portugal, Sweden, Switzerland, and the United Kingdom. Finland, Iceland, and Liechtenstein joined later. Most EFTA members eventually joined the Common Market or its successor organizations, the European Economic Community and the European Union, at which point they left the EFTA. As of 2020 only Iceland, Norway, Switzerland, and Liechtenstein remained in the EFTA, all of which have concluded extensive economic agreements with the EU.

5. France, under President Charles de Gaulle, blocked British entry into the Common Market twice, in 1963 and 1967, before his resignation from office in 1969 cleared the way for British accession.

6. The UK also exempted itself from EU provisions regarding EU versus national UK jurisdiction over legal issues regarding labor law, and over certain EU police and criminal legislation. As of late 2019, shortly before Brexit implementation began, the UK had four such EU opt-outs, while Denmark has three, Ireland has two, and Poland had one.

7. Polling after the Brexit referendum showed, however, that the decision to leave had increased approval by UK citizens of the European Union significantly. See European Parliament (2018).

8. The new members admitted in 2004 were the Czech Republic, Estonia, Hungary, Latvia, Lithuania, Poland, Slovakia, and Slovenia, along with Cyprus and Malta.

9. Michael Gove, Conservative Justice Minister and Brexit advocate, quoted in Mance (2016).

10. The UK Parliament finally voted in favor of Brexit in December 2019, but the terms of a post-Brexit trade agreement with the European Union required subsequent negotiation, with a stated deadline of December 2020.

11. GPD measured at market prices. See Eurostat, statistical arm of the European Commission of the EU (https://ec.europa.eu/eurostat).

12. A Norway-type soft Brexit assumes that the United Kingdom would accept free movement of people (unrestricted immigration into the UK by EU nationals) as the price of full EU market access. This scenario is politically dubious, based on the strong opposition among leave voters to EU immigration regulations. A shift away from UK public opposition to this provision would be necessary to enable such a Brexit agreement.

13. An outlier in these results was a study by Minford et al. (2016), assuming a hard Brexit scenario in which the UK eliminates all tariffs unilaterally and trades with the EU under WTO rules, and estimating an increase in UK GDP of 4%. Latore et al. (2019, p. 11) are highly critical of this study because of its assumptions that UK manufacturing and agricultural prices would fall dramatically, and excessively high trade elasticities of demand with respect to trade costs. None of the other studies mentioned come close to the positive GDP effects of the Minford hard-Brexit estimate.

14. The Kingdom of Ireland came under British rule in 1800, and a rebellion for independence eventually led to the establishment of the Republic of Ireland in 1920. As a result, six

northern counties of Ireland, containing a majority favoring continued British rule, were partitioned from the rest of the island and remained with the United Kingdom. Northern Ireland's population reflected the split between a nationalist (largely Catholic) minority favoring reunification with the Republic, and the majority Unionists (largely Protestant) favoring UK rule. Sectarian violence between extremists from both groups flared in 1966, the beginning of "the Troubles" that lasted 32 years, until the Good Friday agreement of 1998 ended open hostilities and established political power-sharing and a fragile peace.

15. These figures represent accumulated losses or gains 1999–2017 (2001–2017 for Greece), based on a comparison of GDP with and without the euro single currency during that time span (see Gasparotti and Kullas 2019, pp. 2–3 for a description of their methodology). The study included only the founding Eurozone members plus Greece, which joined in 2001. Belgium (-€6,400 per capita) and Spain (-€5,000 per capita) lost smaller amounts from Eurozone membership. Greece managed approximately to break even (+€200 per capita), but only because of a credit-fueled consumption boom in the early years, followed by its massive financial collapse in 2009 and subsequent EU bail-outs and austerity measures.

16. The original fiscal rule for Eurozone membership was that countries would maintain an annual budget deficit rule of no more than 3% of GDP, and a total government debt rule of no more than 80% of GDP. These provisions were not strictly enforced, however, and the Greek government concealed its growing budget deficit from scrutiny until after the crisis broke, announcing that the actual 2009 budget deficit, earlier reported as 6% to 8%, was actually 12.7%.

17. Many EU countries, especially Germany, had experienced a similar backlash against foreign immigrants in the 1960s and 1970s. German labor shortages, exacerbated by the cutoff of refugees from East Germany after the 1961 East German closure of its border with the West, drew on millions of *Gastarbeiter* (guest workers) from Greece, Turkey, and Yugoslavia. Many finally returned to their home countries, while others remained and assimilated, with their families, to life in Germany.

18. The Wikipedia page Islamic Terrorism in Europe (https://en.wikipedia.org/wiki/Islamic_ terrorism_in_Europe) provides a chronological list of attacks in Europe since 2000. See also Pinto Arena (2017).

19. The statistics show the unweighted mean and its standard deviation, indicating a large dispersion of protectionism scores among each of the groups. See the following discussion. In addition, each party's score on protectionism and all other issues carries equal weight in the calculation, regardless of the percentage of votes won by the party in the election, or the absolute size of the country's electorate.

20. The right-wing Sweden Democrats, Danish People's Party, Dutch PVV, Finns Party, Estonian Party of Peoples Unity, German ALFA Party, Hungarian Fidesz, and Independent Greeks, as well the left-wing Greek Syzira Party, all expressed some support for the TTIP (Dennison and Pardis 2016, p. 3).

21. Qualified majority voting requires most proposals to achieve support from 55% of the EU membership and 65% of the EU population. After Brexit is finalized, this rule will require support from 15 EU countries with a total population of about 276 million. Based on populist parliamentary representation in EU member countries in 2018 (Timbro database), 15 countries have populist shares above 20%, and together also surpass 65% of total EU population: Germany, France, Italy, Spain, Denmark, the Netherlands, Greece, Slovenia, Austria, Sweden, Latvia, Cyprus, and Slovakia, along with populist governments in Hungary and Poland.

Chapter 7

1. The *Trade Freedom Index* is maintained by the Heritage Foundation, a Washington, DC think tank. Its data base is periodically updated to reflect changes in country scores over time. See https://www.heritage.org/index/trade-freedom to navigate to the data set and for details about the methodology. The tariff component of the index is designed to equal 100 if all tariffs are zero, and a nontariff barrier score, which increases with more restrictive policies, is then subtracted from the tariff component. The Trade Freedom index for Hong Kong and Singapore is 95; for North Korea it is zero.

2. The Fraser Institute is a Canadian think tank based in Vancouver, British Columbia. The *Fraser Economic Freedom* website is found at https://www.fraserinstitute.org/economic-freedom/dataset?geozone=world&year=2018&page=dataset&min-year=2&max-year=0&filter=0&sort-field=freedomToTradeInternationally&sort-reversed=1. The database provides various indexes of economic freedom, and the present regression study uses the Area 4 summary index "Freedom to Trade Internationally." The Methodology tab contains links to Appendices A and B for methodological details. The index ranges in value from zero to 10.0. Singapore scored 9.85 in 1990; Turkey scored zero in 1970.

3. Global Trade Alert (GTA) was initiated by the Centre for Trade Policy Research, a London-based think tank (website at https://cepr.org/), and is supported by the Max Schmidheiny Foundation and the University of St. Gallen, Switzerland (see https://www.globaltradealert.org/about). GTA is a repository of country-by-country trade policy actions, and provides commentary on trade policy trends in periodic reports. It makes its large database accessible to the public at https://www.globaltradealert.org/data_extraction.

4. In the GTA database, harmful (discriminatory) measures either restrict trade directly, through more favorable treatment for domestic products, or through additional bureaucratic or burdensome administrative requirements. They are coded as "red" (certainly harmful) or "amber" (probably harmful). Trade liberalizing measures either remove harmful interventions, actively enhance trade market access, or improve transparency. Information on methodology is available at the data extraction page, https://www.globaltradealert.org/data_extraction. See also Evenett and Fritz (2019).

5. The Center for Systemic Peace is a think tank located in Vienna, Virginia, USA. The main webpage, from which the data for this study was extracted, is located at https://www.systemicpeace.org/inscrdata.html, "Regime Authority Characteristics and Transitions Datasets."

6. Other populism databases limit the categories to left-wing and right-wing. Kyle and Gultchin (2018) use the descriptors "cultural" for right-wing and "socioeconomic" for left-wing. "Authoritarian" is also used to describe right-wing populism. The third Kyle-Gultchin category, "anti-establishment," encompasses cases in which the people oppose an allegedly corrupt elite, dominated by special interests, with a populist agenda of reforms to eliminate the corruption and inefficiency. In practice, this category also includes populist governments that are not easily identified as either right-wing or left-wing in their ideological orientation.

7. See Kaufmann, Kraay, and Mastruzzi (2010). The World Bank Governance Indicators Handbook describes the six variables, indexed from −3 to +3, with higher scores indicating higher quality, as follows: 1) voice and accountability (VA), capturing perceptions of the extent to which a country's citizens are able to participate in selecting their government,

as well as freedom of expression, freedom of association, and a free media; 2) political stability and absence of violence/terrorism (PV), capturing perceptions of the likelihood that the government will be destabilized or overthrown by unconstitutional or violent means, including politically motivated violence and terrorism, and the capacity of the government to effectively formulate and implement sound policies; 3) government effectiveness (GE), capturing perceptions of the quality of public services, the quality of the civil service and the degree of its independence from political pressures, the quality of policy formulation and implementation, and the credibility of the government's commitment to such policies; 4) regulatory quality (RQ), capturing perceptions of the ability of the government to formulate and implement sound policies and regulations that permit and promote private sector development, and the respect of citizens and the state for the institutions that govern economic and social interactions among them; 5) rule of law (RL), capturing perceptions of the extent to which agents have confidence in and abide by the rules of society, and in particular the quality of contract enforcement, property rights, the police, and the courts, as well as the likelihood of crime and violence; and 6) control of corruption (CC), capturing perceptions of the extent to which public power is exercised for private gain, including both petty and grand forms of corruption, as well as "capture" of the state by elites and private interests.

8. Earlier regression runs, not shown here, used a general dummy variable for populist regime observations, and the coefficients for the dummy itself, and associated interaction terms, were insignificant in each case.

9. In a separate set of regressions using a much smaller data set on populist countries alone (not presented here), coefficients for GDP per capita, unemployment, world trade share and current account as a percentage of GDP were all insignificant in all regressions. GDP per capita squared had significantly negative coefficients for Trade Freedom regressions alone, while trade as a percentage of GDP had significantly positive coefficients for Fraser regressions alone. The economic growth variable was significantly positive for Fraser regressions and significantly negative for Trade Freedom regressions.

10. Evenett and Fritz (2019, p. 6) indicate that while the United States has disrupted trade and created global uncertainty with its escalation of tariffs, European Union countries have been responsible for a larger number a major discriminatory trade-related measures, as measured more broadly by the Global Trade Alert statistics, during the populist era of 2017–2020.

11. Kyle and Gultchin (2018) note that several African and Middle Eastern countries with semidemocratic or authoritarian political systems were excluded from the list, along with countries where the populist party may have had significant influence in the government, but nonetheless did not have a populist leader in the highest executive office.

12. ALBA (Alianza Bolivariana para los Pueblos de Nuestra América) included Antigua and Barbuda, Bolivia, Cuba, Dominica, Ecuador, Grenada, Nicaragua, St. Kitts and Nevis, Saint Lucia, Saint Vincent, and the Grenadines, and Venezuela.

13. Mercosur is the South American trading bloc that includes Brazil, Argentina, Paraguay, and Uruguay (Venezuela's participation was suspended n 2016). Bolsonaro himself became a subject of the negotiations due to his policies on the environment and human rights, leading to demands from some EU members to build conditions and monitoring of these issues into the treaty. Its 20-year negotiation was concluded in June 2019, and subsequently faced a potentially long process of ratification.

14. Transparency International is a nongovernmental organization based in Berlin, Germany that advocates for measures to reduce corruption around the world. See https://www.transparency.org/cpi2018#results.

15. The issue was India's food subsidy program, which violated WTO rules. See Bagri (2014).

16. India and the United States subsequently continued to negotiate a possible reinstatement of India's GSP preferences, on a Trumpian reciprocal, dollar-for-dollar basis that would increase US exports to India by exactly the same amount as Indian exports to the United States under the GSP. Such trade value reciprocity was not the original intent of the GSP program. As of late 2020, no agreement had been reached.

17. See Choudhury (2019). RCEP countries include the Association of Southeast Asian Nations (ASEAN)—Brunei, Cambodia, Indonesia, Laos, Malaysia, Myanmar, the Philippines, Singapore, Thailand, and Vietnam—and five of ASEAN's Free Trade Agreement partners—Australia, China, Japan, New Zealand, and South Korea.

18. See chapter 5, note 9. It is likely that Trump administration trade officials advised Russian trade officials on this case.

19. The WTO accession process can be lengthy if the applicant government lacks transparency in its process of trade governance, and if legal and market institutions are poorly developed. Authoritarian governments tend also to take longer, especially if they are not responsive to calls for reforms by the reviewing Working Party. Serbia applied for WTO membership in 2005 and has also applied to join the EU, for which WTO membership as a prerequisite, so its membership process was already at a later stage than was Belarus' in 2020.

20. Slovakia's populist regimes have been variously described as right-wing and anti-establishment, based on their combination of cultural conservatism and anti-corruption rhetoric. The 2019 election of Slovakia's more progressive President Zuzana Čaputová signaled a more moderate immigration stance in that country, but the president's official power is limited (Lindsay 2019). February 2020 elections brought a center-right but culturally conservative populist party to power, led by Igor Matovic. See Associated Press (2020).

21. The Fraser Trade Freedom index is found at https://www.fraserinstitute.org/economic-freedom/dataset?geozone=world&year=2018&page=dataset&min-year=2&max-year=0&filter=0&sort-field=freedomToTradeInternationally&sort-reversed=1. The Freedom to Trade Internationally index components include measures of FDI openness by country and IMF country information on the number of specific capital control measures. See https://www.fraserinstitute.org/sites/default/files/economic-freedom-of-north-america-2019.pdf for methodological details.

22. See the Migrant Immigration Policy index (http://www.mipex.eu/), which provides detailed information about the immigration and assimilation policies of European Union and other countries.

23. The 2019 WTO Annual Accessions Review (WTO 2020) stated that Serbia could be ready to resume working party activity in 2020, with recent reviews emphasizing the need for continuing economic and governance reforms, especially with regard to state-owned enterprises. The next likely occasion for announcing official WTO accession would be the 2022 Ministerial Conference.

24. Neighboring Zimbabwe, under its dictator Robert Mugabe, was also a major agricultural producer and had carried out uncompensated expropriations in the 1990s, resulting in a collapse of its agricultural economy. Land reforms during Zuma's rule in South Africa also showed signs of abandoned cultivation and increased rural unemployment, casting doubt on the ability of populist land seizures to improve the fortunes of previously disadvantaged black farmers.

25. South Africa's Transparency International corruption index fell from 47 to 43 during
    Zuma's term, and its freedom-from-corruption ranking ended at 73rd of 180 countries.
    Its Global competitive index, as measured by the World Economic Forum (http://www3.
    weforum.org/docs/WEF_TheGlobalCompetitivenessReport2019.pdf) fell from 4.41 to
    4.32, ranking 61st among 140 countries.

Chapter 8

1. The CEO of Harley-Davidson, which was targeted by a European retaliatory tariff of 31%
   on motorcycles in response to the US steel and aluminum tariffs, announced that it was
   considering an offshore production site so that it could avoid the tariffs and regain its lucra-
   tive EU market. President Trump accused the company of disloyalty, threatening additional
   tariffs on its motorcycles imported into the United States, apparently unaware that the offshore production would be exclusively for EU customers (Rappeport and Brown 2018).
2. A study by Feenstra and Weinstein (2017) estimated that fully half of the welfare gain to US
   consumers from trade between 1992 and 2005 came from increased product variety. This
   is likely to be the result of increased production specialization in international trade, but
   also, in the US case cited, from the increased liberalization of agricultural goods, such as
   through NAFTA trade in fruits and vegetables.
3. Ciuriak et al. (2019) note that evolving national security, privacy, competition, and tax
   policy regarding digital trade raise questions about the degree to which the USMCA
   provisions in this area can be quantified.
4. There are 45 spells of populist regimes in 33 countries from 1990 to 2018, as identified
   by Kyle and Gultchin (2018). This is the same database used in the regression study of
   chapter 7.
5. During the last three years of the Obama administration, growth averaged 2.3% and unemployment declined from 6.2% to 4.7%. The downward trend in unemployment that had
   started as the financial crisis eased in 2010 (peaking at 9.6%) thus continued throughout
   Obama's second term and into Trump's first three years. See Long (2019).
6. See Peter Navarro (director), *Death by China*, Virgil Films and Entertainment. Narrated by
   Martin Sheen. Producers: Peter Navarro, Joe Zarinko, Michael Addis, Greg Autry. Release
   date 2012.
7. See Amaro (2020). The 30-day travel ban began on March 13, 2020 and included all EU
   member countries, plus the United Kingdom.

Chapter 9

1. Among leading Democratic candidates in the 2020 presidential campaign, incoming
   President Joe Biden is considered generally pro-trade (a view that he is likely to temper in
   order to appeal to blue-collar voters), and Senators Bernie Sanders and Elizabeth Warren
   are trade skeptics (Hufbauer and Jung 2019).

2. Fajgelbaum and Khandelwal (2016) used a sample of 40 countries, including 27 European countries and 13 other, mostly large countries, such as the United States, India, Indonesia, Japan, Korea, Mexico, and Russia. Poorer consumers tend to spend a larger portion of their budget on low income-elasticity traded goods.
3. Lawrence (2008, p. 73) attributes 20% of the relative wage increases for more highly skilled (compared to blue collar) workers to trade.

References

Abbott, Alden F. (2016). "US Government Antitrust Intervention in Standard-Setting Activities and the Competitive Process." *Vanderbilt Journal of Entertainment and Technology Law* 18, no. 2: 225–246.

Abbott, Frederick (2018). "US Section 301, China, and Technology Transfer: Law and its Limitations." Intellectual Property Watch News Service (Geneva, Switzerland), June 7. https://www.ip-watch.org/2018/06/07/us-section-301-china-technology-transfer-law-limitations-revisited/.

Acemoglu, Daron, and James A. Robinson (2001). "Inefficient Redistribution." *American Political Science Review* 95, no. 3: 649–661.

Acemoglu, Daron, and James A. Robinson (2013). *Why Nations Fail: The Origins of Power, Prosperity, and Poverty.* New York: Crown Publishers.

Acemoglu, Daron, and James Robinson (2019). *The Narrow Corridor: States, Societies, and The Fate of Liberty.* New York: Penguin Press.

Ahn, Dukgeun, Koohyun Kwon, Jihong Lee, and Jee-Hyeong Park (2018). "An Empirical Analysis on the WTO Safeguard Actions." *Journal of World Trade* 52, no. 3: 415–459.

Aiyar, Swaminathan S. Anklesaria (2019). *A Reform Agenda for the Next Indian Government.* Policy analysis no. 869. Washington, DC: Cato Institute.

Akin Gump blog (2019). "US Court of International Trade Confirms Limits to Section 232 Action." November 18. https://www.akingump.com/en/experience/practices/international-trade/ag-trade-law/u-s-court-of-international-trade-confirms-limits-to-section-232.html.

Alden, Edward (2017). *Failure to Adjust.* Lanham, MD: Rowman & Littlefield.

Algan, Yann, Sergei Gurieve, Elias Papaioannou, Evgenia Passari (2017). "The European Trust Crisis and the Rise of Populism." Brookings Papers on Economic Activity, Fall: 309–382. Washington, DC: Brookings Institution Press.

Alonso-Cortes, Angel, and Francisco Cabrillo (2012). "From Merchants to Speakers: The Common Origins of Trade and Language." *European Journal of the History of Economic Thought* 19, no. 5: 709–732.

Altman, Morris (2015). "X-Efficiency, X-Inefficiency." In *Real-World Decision Making: An Encyclopedia of Behavioral Economics,* 473–474. Santa Barbara, CA: Greenwood.

Amaro, Silvia (2020). "EU Condemns Trump's Corona Virus Travel Ban, Imposed 'Unilaterally and Without Consultation.'" CNBC, March 12. https://www.cnbc.com/2020/03/12/the-european-union-disapproves-president-trump-travel-ban-amid-coronavirus.html.

Americans for Constitutional Liberty (2017). "Stop the Radical Islamic Invasion of America." Political and Lobbying Organization, Merrifield, Virginia. https://www.conservativeusa.org/issues/stop-radical-islamic-invasion-america.

Amiti, Mary, Stephen Redding, and David Weinstein (2019). "The Impact of the 2018 Trade War on US Prices and Welfare." NBER Working Paper 25672. Cambridge, MA: National Bureau of Economic Research.

Amstutz, Mark R. (2016). *Rules of the Game: A Primer on International Relations.* New York: Routledge.

Anderson, John E., and Eric van Wincoop (2004). "Trade Costs." *Journal of Economic Literature* 42, no. 3: 691–751.

Associated Press (2020). "Slovakia's Populists Win Vote with Anti-Corruption Stance." March 1. https://apnews.com/7c604374a230a71f9a9326c939de9613.

Autor, David H., David Dorn, and Gordon H. Hanson (2016). "The China Shock: Learning from Labor Market Adjustment to Large Changes in Trade." *Annual Review of Economics* 8: 205–240.

Autor, David, David Dorn, Gordon Hanson, and Kaveh Majlesi (2020). "Importing Political Polarization? The Electoral Consequences of Rising Trade Exposure." *American Economic Review* 110, no. 10: 3139–3183.

Autor, David, David Dorn, Lawrence F. Katz, Christina Patterson, and John van Reenen (2017). "Concentrating on the Fall of the Labor Share." NBER Working Paper 23108. Cambridge, MA: National Bureau of Economic Research.

Bacchus, James, Simon Lester, and Huan Zhu (2018). "Disciplining China's Trade Practices at the WTO: How WTO Complaints Can Help Make China More Market-Oriented." Cato Institute Policy Analysis no. 856. Washington, DC: Cato Institute.

Bagri, Neha Thirani (2014). "U.S.-India Agreement on Stockpiles of Food Revives a Trade Deal." *New York Times*, November 13.

Bagwell, Kyke, Chad Bown, and Robert Staiger (2016). "Is the WTO Passe?" *Journal of Economic Literature* 54, no. 4: 1125–1231.

Baldwin, Richard (2016). *The Great Convergence: Information Technology and the new Globalization*. Cambridge, MA: The Belknap Press of Harvard University Press.

Baschuk, Bryce (2020). "Top Trade Negotiator Bullish on Last-Minute UK Trade Deal." *Bloomberg Politics*, December 17. https://www.bloomberg.com/news/articles/2020-12-17/top-u-s-trade-negotiator-bullish-on-last-minute-u-k-trade-deal.

Becker, Sascha O., Thiemo Fetzer, and Dennis Novy (2017). "Who Voted for Brexit? A Comprehensive District-Level Analysis." *Economic Policy*, October: 601–651.

Behsudi, Adam (2019). "Trump Thinks Tariffs Will Add U.S. Manufacturing Jobs. Economic Reality Says They Won't." Today's Workplace, August 26. http://www.todaysworkplace.org/2019/08/26/trump-thinks-tariffs-will-add-u-s-manufacturing-jobs-economic-reality-says-they-wont/.

Berend, Ivan T. (2019). *Against European Integration: The European Union and its Discontents*. New York: Routledge.

Betz, Hans-Georg (2017). "Nativism Across Time and Space." *Swiss Political Science Review* 24, no. 4: 335–353.

Blanchard, Emily, Chad Bown, and Davin Chor (2019). "Did Trump's Trade War Impact the 2018 Election?" CEPR Discussion Paper No. 14091. London: Centre for Economic Policy Research.

Blenkinsop, Philip, and Luke Baker (2020). "EU, China and 15 Others Agree Temporary Fix to WTO Crisis." Reuters Business News, January 24. https://www.reuters.com/article/us-trade-wto/eu-china-and-15-others-agree-temporary-fix-to-wto-crisis-idUSKBN1ZN0WM.

Blustein, Paul (2019). *Schism: China, America and the Fracturing of the Global Trading System*. Waterloo, Ontario: Centre for International Governance Innovation.

Boucher, Jean-Christophe, and Cameron G. Thies (2019). "'I Am a Tariff Man': The Power of Populist Foreign Policy Rhetoric Under President Trump." *Journal of Politics* 81, no. 2: 712–722.

Bown, Chad (2018). "Trump's Steel and Aluminum Tariffs Are Counterproductive. Here Are 5 More Things You Need to Know." Trade and Investment Policy Watch, March 7. Washington, DC: Peterson Institute for International Economics.

Bown, Chad (2019). "The Trade War Is Suddenly Getting Worse." Washington, DC: Peterson Institute for International Economics, August 29. https://www.piie.com/research/piie-charts/trade-war-suddenly-getting-worse.

Bown, Chad (2020a). "Trump's Steel and Aluminum Tariffs Are Cascading Out of Control." Trade and Investment Policy Watch, February 4. Washington, DC: Peterson Institute for International Economics.

Bown, Chad (2020b). "Trump's Trade Policy Is Hampering the US Fight against Covid-19." Trade and Investment Policy Watch, March 13. Washington, DC: Peterson Institute for International Economics.

Bown, Chad (2020c). "US-China Phase One Tracker: China's Purchases of US goods." PIIE Tracker, Update December 23. Washington, DC: Peterson Institute. https://www.piie.com/research/piie-charts/us-china-phase-one-tracker-chinas-purchases-us-goods.

Bown, Chad, and Bernard Hoekman (2005). "WTO Dispute Settlement and the Missing Developing Country Cases: Engaging the Private Sector." Journal of International Economic Law 8, no. 4: 861–891.

Bown, Chad, and Douglas Irwin (2018). "What Might a Trump Withdrawal from the WTO Mean for US Tariffs?" Policy Brief, November 18–23. Washington, DC: Peterson Institute for International Economics.

Bown, Chad, and Jennifer Hillman (2019). "WTO'ing a Resolution to the China Subsidy Problem." PIIE Working Paper 19-17. Washington, DC: Peterson Institute for International Economics.

Bradsher, Keith (2019). "One Trump Victory: Companies Rethink China." New York Times, April 5. https://www.nytimes.com/2019/04/05/business/china-trade-trump-jobs-decoupling.html.

Bruinius, Harry (2020). "Trump Has Asked Judges to Overturn Election. So Far, All Have Declined." Christian Science Monitor, December 10. https://www.csmonitor.com/USA/Politics/2020/1210/Trump-has-asked-judges-to-overturn-election.-So-far-all-have-declined.

Brunsden, Jim (2020a). "US, Japan and EU Target China with WTO Rule Change Proposal." Financial Times, January 14. https://www.ft.com/content/8271be9a-36d6-11ea-a6d3-9a26f8c3cba4?emailId=5e1ef61a3f802e000411ec56&segmentId=2785c52b-1c00-edaa-29be-7452cf90b5a2.

Brunsden, Jim (2020b). "EU Hits US Goods with Tariffs in Airbus-Boeing Dispute." Financial Times, November 9, https://www.ft.com/content/92b23bb8-9def-4aea-983e-80f7ab2ab5cf.

Bruton, Henry J. (1998). "A Reconsideration of Import Substitution." Journal of Economic Literature 36, no. 2: 903–936.

Burfisher, Mary E., Frederic Lambert, and Troy Matheson (2019). "NAFTA to USMCA: What is Gained?" IMF Working Paper 19/73 (March). Washington, DC: International Monetary Fund.

Businesstech (2017). "South Africans Are Not Xenophobic, Says Zuma, as 'Anti-Foreigner' Protests Continue." March 1. https://businesstech.co.za/news/general/161155/south-africans-are-not-xenophobic-says-zuma-as-anti-foreigner-protests-continue.

Businesstech (2018). "How the Zuma Years Killed Foreign Investment in South Africa." October 17. https://businesstech.co.za/news/business/277959/how-the-zuma-years-killed-foreign-investment-in-south-africa.

Cadman, Emily, and Philip Giles (2016). "Economists' Forecasts: Brexit Would Damage Growth." Financial Times, January 3. https://www.ft.com/content/1a86ab36-afbe-11e5-b955-1a1d298b6250.

Caldera, Dario, Matteo Iacaviello, Patrick Molligo, Andrea Prestipino, and Andrea Raffo (2019). "The Economic Effects of Trade Policy Uncertainty." Journal of Monetary Economics, November (online). https://www.matteoiacoviello.com//research_files/TPU_PAPER.pdf.

Campos, Nauro F., Fabrizio Corricelli, and Luigi Moretti (2014). "Economic Growth and Political Integration: Estimating the Benefits from Membership in the European Union Using the Synthetic Counterfactuals Method." IZA DP No. 8162. Bonn: Institute for the Study of Labor.

Camus, Jean Renaud Gabriel (2018). *You Will Not Replace Us!* Plieux, France: Chez l'Auteur.

Carter, Brandon (2018). "Trump: 'If You Don't Have Steel, You Don't Have a Country." The Hill, March 2. https://thehill.com/homenews/administration/376408-trump-if-you-dont-have-steel-you-dont-have-a-country.

Carter, Dan T. (2000). *The Politics of Rage: George Wallace, the Origins of the New Conservatism, and the Transformation of American Politics.* New York: Simon & Schuster.

Chaguaceda, Armando (2019). "Russia and Nicaragua: Progress in Bilateral Cooperation." Global Americans, March 28. https://theglobalamericans.org/2019/03/russia-and-nicaragua-progress-in-bilateral-cooperation/.

Chandran, Nyshka (2017). "We Can No Longer Tolerate These Trade Abuses: Trump Lashes Out at China and Others." CNBC, November 10. https://www.cnbc.com/2017/11/10/donald-trump-speaks-to-asia-pacific-economic-cooperation-in-vietnam.html.

Charnovitz, Steve, and Gary Hufbauer (2020). "Landmark Court Decision Limits Presidential Trade Restrictions." VoxEU Policy Blog, July 28. Center for Economic Policy Research, Washington, DC. https://voxeu.org/content/landmark-court-decision-limits-presidential-trade-restrictions.

Cheney, Kyle (2020). "'Where Are All of the Arrests?': Trump Demands Barr Lock Up His Foes." *Politico*, October 7. https://www.politico.com/news/2020/10/07/trump-demands-barr-arrest-foes-427389.

Cheng, Evelyn (2018). "Soybean Prices Drop to Two Year Low on US-China Trade War Fears." CNBC, June 19. https://www.cnbc.com/2018/06/19/soybean-prices-drop-to-two-year-low-on-us-china-trade-war-fears.html.

Choudhury, Saheli Roy (2019). "India Says No to Joining Huge Asia Pacific Trade Pact." CNBC, November 4. https://www.cnbc.com/2019/11/05/india-says-no-to-joining-the-rcep-pact-involving-major-asian-economies.html.

Clausing, Kimberly (2019). *Open: The Progressive Case for Free Trade, Immigration and Global Capital.* Cambridge, MA and London: Harvard University Press.

Coase, Ronald (1998). "Comment on Thomas W. Hazlett: Assigning Property Rights to Radio Spectrum Users: Why Did FCC License Auctions Take 67 Years?" *Journal of Law & Economics* 41, no. S2: 577–580.

Colantone, Italo, and Piero Stanig (2018). "Global Competition and Brexit." *American Political Science Review* 112, no. 2: 201–218.

Corden, W. Max (1997). *Trade Policy and Economic Welfare*, Second Edition. London and New York: Oxford University Press.

Cox, Daniel, Rachel Lienesch, and Robert P. Jones (2017). "Beyond Economics: Fears of Cultural Displacement Pushed the White Working Class to Trump." Public Religion Research Institute. https://www.prri.org/research/white-working-class-attitudes-economy-trade-immigration-election-donald-trump/.

Crick, Bernard (1968). "Sovereignty." In *International Encyclopedia of the Social Sciences*, vol. 15, ed. David L. Sills. New York: Macmillan Company and the Free Press.

Curi, Maria (2019). "Sources: USTR Wants Auto Companies to Agree All Production Will Comply with USMCA." *Inside U.S. Trade*, November 7.

Ciuriak, Dan, Ali Dadkhah, and Jinliang Xiao (2019). "Quantifying the USMCA." Global Trade Analysis Project annual conference, Warsaw, June. https://www.gtap.agecon.purdue.edu/resources/download/9478.pdf.

D'Alimonte, Roberto (2019). "How the Populists Won in Italy." *Journal of Democracy* 30, no. 1:114–127.

Davis, Bob, and Jon Hilsenrath. 2016. "How the China Shock, Deep and Swift, Spurred the Rise of Trump." *Wall Street Journal*, August 11.

Dean, Adam, and Simo Kimmel (2019). "Free Trade and Opioid Overdose Death in the United States." *SSM-Population Health* 8(May):1–8.

Deng, Chao (2019). "At 25%, Tariffs Have Firms Squirming." *Wall Street Journal*, August 13, p. 1.

Dennison, Susi, and Dina Pardijs (2016). "The World According to Europe's Insurgent Parties: Putin, Migration and People Power." ECFR Flash Scorecard. London: European Council on Foreign Relations.

De Pillis, Lydia (2020). "How Trump's Trade War is Making Lobbyists Rich and Slamming Small Business." ProPublica, January 6. https://www.propublica.org/article/how-trump-trade-war-is-making-lobbyists-rich-and-slamming-small-businesses.

Diamond, Jeremy (2016). "Trump: 'We Can't Continue to Allow China to Rape Our Country.'" CNN, May 2. https://www.cnn.com/2016/05/01/politics/donald-trump-china-rape/index.html.

Dijkstra, Lewis, Hugo Poelman, and Andres Rodriguez-Pose (2018). "The Geography of EU Discontent." Working Paper 12/2018, European Commission. Luxembourg: European Union Publishing Office.

Dillian, Carolyn D, and Carolyn L. White, eds (2009). T*rade and Exchange: Archaeological Studies from History and Prehistory.* New York: Springer.

Dolan, Ed (2016). "Free Trade Under Fire." *Milken Institute Review*, October 19.

Donnan, Shawn (2017). "Trump's Top Trade Advisor Accuses Germany of Currency Manipulation." *Financial Times*, January 31. https://www.ft.com/content/57f104d2-e742-11e6-893c-082c54a7f539.

Dornig, Mike, and Jennifer Jacobs (2019). "Trump Readies New Round of Aid to Farmers Hit by China Trade War." Bloomberg, May 21. https://www.bloomberg.com/news/articles/2019-05-21/trump-farmers-trade-war.

Downs, Anthon (1957). *An Economic Theory of Democracy.* New York: Harper and Row.

Drbohlav, Dušan, and Kristýna Janurová (2019). "Migration and Integration in Czechia: Policy Advances and the Hand Brake of Populism." Migration Information Source Profile, June 6. Migration Policy Institute. https://www.migrationpolicy.org/country-resource/czech-republic.

Economist (2019). "Brexit Boosts Scottish Nationalists." The Economist, December 13. https://www.economist.com/britain/2019/12/13/brexit-boosts-scottish-nationalists?cid1=cust/ednew/n/bl/n/2019/12/13n/owned/n/n/nwl/n/n/na/360436/.

Economist (London) (2020). "Italy's Populist Five Star Movement Is Becoming a More Normal Party." *Economist*, August 20.

Economist Intelligence Unit (EIU) (2019a). *Country Forecast Argentina December 2019 Updater.* New York: Economist Intelligence Unit.

Economist Intelligence Unit (EIU) (2019b). *Country Forecast Turkey November 2019 Updater.* New York: Economist Intelligence Unit.

Eichengreen, Barry (2018). *The Populist Temptation, Economic Grievance and Political Reaction in the Modern Era.* New York: Oxford University Press.

Elsig, Manfred, Mark Pollack, and Gregory Shaffer (2017). Trump Is Fighting an Open War on Trade. His Stealth war on Trade May Be Even More Important. *Washington Post*, September 27. https://www.washingtonpost.com/news/monkey-cage/wp/2017/09/27/trump-is-fighting-an-open-war-on-trade-his-stealth-war-on-trade-may-be-even-more-important/.

England, Andrew (2015). "South Africa's Jacob Zuma Faces Populist Challenge Over Scandal." *Financial Times*, February 11. https://www.ft.com/content/de2074e6-b104-11e4-9331-00144feab7de.

Esserman, Susan, Eric C. Emerson, and Stephanie W. Wang (2018). "Section 232 Update: Expanded Tariffs, Quotas and International Retaliation." *Steptoe*, June 12. https://www.steptoe.com/en/news-publications/section-232-update-expanded-tariffs-quotas-and-international-retaliation.html.

Etzioni, Amatai (2018). "The Rising (More) Nation-Centered System." *Fletcher Forum for World Affairs* 42, no. 2: 29–53.

European Commission (2011). "Attitudes Towards the EU in the United Kingdom: Analytical Report." Directorate-General Communication, Flash Eurobarometer Report #318, March. Brussels: European Commission.

European Commission (2015). "Screening Report, Serbia: Chapter 30, External Relations." Document No. MD 180/15, October 26. https://ec.europa.eu/neighbourhood-enlargement/sites/near/files/pdf/serbia/screening-reports/screening_report_ch_30_serbia.pdf.

European Parliament (2018). "Brexit Effect: Public Opinion Survey Shows That EU is More Appreciated Than Ever." Press release, October 17. https://www.europarl.europa.eu/news/en/press-room/20181016IPR16213/brexit-effect-public-opinion-survey-shows-that-eu-is-more-appreciated-than-ever.

Eurostat. https://ec.europa.eu/eurostat/tgm/table.do?tab=table&plugin=1&language=en&pcode=tps00001.

Evenett, Simon, and Johannes Fritz (2019). *Going it Alone? Trade Policy After Three Years of Populism.* 25th Global Trade Alert Report. London: Centre for Economic Policy Research.

Fajgelbaum, Pablo D., and Amit K. Khandelwal (2016). "Measuring the Unequal Gains from Trade." *Quarterly Journal of Economics* 131, no. 3: 1113–1180.

Fajgelbaum, Pablo D., Pinelopi K. Goldbert, Patrick J. Kennedy, and Amit K. Khandelwal (2019). "The Return to Protectionism." NBER Working paper No. 25638. Cambridge, MA: National Bureau of Economic Research.

Farquharson, Kenny (2019). "Sturgeon Faces a Clash of Wills Against PM Who Breaks Rules." *The Times* (London), December 14.

Faulconbridge, Guy (2018). "In England's Forgotten 'Rust Belt,' Voters Show Little Sign of Brexit Regret." Reuters, August 7. https://www.reuters.com/article/uk-britain-eu-voters/in-englands-forgotten-rust-belt-voters-show-little-sign-of-brexit-regret-idUSKBN1KS0VM.

Feenstra, Robert C., and David E. Weinstein (2017). "Globalization, Markups, and U.S. Welfare." *Journal of Political Economy* 125, no. 4: 1040–1074.

Financial Times (2020). "Brexit Trade Deal Explained: The Key Parts of the Landmark Agreement." December 24. https://www.ft.com/content/bd71fda3-0a34-4b52-ae98-4769848cb628#comments-anchor.

Findlay, Ronald, and Kevin H. O'Rourke (2007). *Power and Plenty.* Princeton, NJ: Princeton University Press.

Flaaen, Aaron, Ali Hortacsu, and Felix Tintelnot (2019). "The Production Relocation and Price Effects of U.S. Trade Policy: The Case of Washing Machines." NBER Working Paper 25767. Cambridge, MA: National Bureau of Economic Research.

Flaaen, Aaron, and Justin Pierce (2019). "Disentangling the Effects of the 2018–2019 Tariffs on a Globally Connected U.S. Manufacturing Sector." Finance and Economics Discussion Series 2019-086. Washington, DC: Board of Governors of the Federal Reserve System. https://doi.org/10.17016/FEDS2019.086.

Formisano, Ronald P. (2008). *For the People: American Populist Movements from the Revolution to the 1850s.* Chapel Hill: University of North Carolina Press.

Foster, Peter (2019). "What Is in Boris Johnson's Brexit Deal, and How Could It Affect You?" *The Telegraph*, December 13.

Francois, Joseph, Will Martin, and Vlad Manole (2006). "Formula Approaches to Liberalizing Trade in Goods: Efficiency and Market Access Considerations." In Economic Development & Multilateral Trade Cooperation, ed. Simon J. Evenett and Bernard M. Hoekman, 89–115. New York and Washington, DC: Palgrave Macmillan and the World Bank.

Frank, Thomas (2018). "Job Gains for the Manufacturing Industry in the Last 12 Months Are the Most Since 1995." CNBC, August 3. https://www.cnbc.com/2018/08/03/job-gains-for-the-manufacturing-industry-are-the-most-since-1995.html.

Frieden, Jeffry, and Stephanie Walter (2017). "Understanding the Political Economy of the Eurozone Crisis." *Annual Review of Political Science* 20: 19.1–19.20. Doi: 10.1146/annurev-polisci-051215-023101.

Fritze, John, and David Jackson (2020). "Response to Trump's Coronavirus Address: Another Market Plunge, Airport Chaos, Anxious Lawmakers." *USA Today*, March 13. https://www.usatoday.com/story/news/politics/2020/03/12/trump-coronavirus-address-nation-roiled-markets-and-politics/5030892002/.

Funke, Manuel, Moritz Schularick, and Christoph Trebesch (2016). "Going to Extremes: Politics After Financial Crises, 1870–2014." *European Economic Review* 88 (C): 227–260.

Gandel, Stephen (2016). "Donald Trump Says NAFTA Was the Worst Trade Deal the U.S. Ever Signed." *Fortune*, September 27. https://fortune.com/2016/09/27/presidential-debate-nafta-agreement/.

Gasparotti, Alessandro, and Mattias Kullas (2019). *20 Years of the Euro: Winners and Losers: An Empirical Study*. Freiburg, Germany: Centre for European Policy.

Gidron, Noam, and Bart Bonikowski (2013). "Varieties of Populism: Literature Review and Research Agenda." Weatherhead Center for International Affairs Working Paper no. 13-0004. Cambridge, MA: Harvard University.

Gil, Marta (2016). "Emotions and Political Rhetoric: Perception of Danger, Group Conflict and the Biopolitics of Fear." *Human Affairs* 26, no. 2: 212–226.

Giles, Chris (2017). "What Has the EU Done for the UK?" *Financial Times*, March 31. https://www.ft.com/content/202a60c0-cfd8-11e5-831d-09f7778e7377.

Gillespie, Patrick (2018). "New US Deal with South Korea: What You Need to Know." CNN Business, March 28. https://money.cnn.com/2018/03/27/news/economy/us-south-korea-trade-deal/index.html.

Gillies, Jamie (2017). "'Feel the Bern': Marketing Bernie Sanders and Democratic Socialism to Primary Voters." In *Political Marketing in the 2016 U.S. Presidential Election*, ed. Jamie Gillies, 97–112. New York: Palgrave-Macmillan.

Gordon, John Steele (2009). "An Inauguration for the People." *Wall Street Journal*, January 20. https://www.wsj.com/articles/SB123241405445996273.

Grove, Jack (2017). "Zuma's Fees Giveaway Is 'Unaffordable Populism' for South Africa." Times Higher Education News (UK), December 28. https://www.timeshighereducation.com/news/zumas-fees-giveaway-unaffordable-populism-south-africa.

Guriev, Sergei (2018). "Economic Drivers of Populism." *AEA Papers and Proceedings* 108: 200–203.

Gvosdev, Nikolas K. (2019). "Is Russia Sabotaging Democracy in the West?" *Orbis* 63, no. 3: 321–333.

Haberman, Maggie (2016). "Donald Trump Says He Favors Big Tariffs on Chinese Exports." *New York Times*, January 7. https://www.nytimes.com/politics/first-draft/2016/01/07/donald-trump-says-he-favors-big-tariffs-on-chinese-exports/.

Hamilton, Robert E. (2019). "Russia's Attempts to Undermine Democracy in the West." *Orbis* 63, no. 3: 334–348.

Harrison, Lowell H., James C. Klotter, Lowell H. H. Harrison, and James C. C. Klotter (1997). *A New History of Kentucky*. Lexington: University Press of Kentucky.

Hartwick, John M. (2010). "Encephalization and Division of Labor by Early Humans." *Journal of Bioeconomics* 12, no. 2: 77–100.

Hayduk, Ron (2015). "Political Rights in the Age of Migration: Lessons from the United States." *Journal of International Migration and Integration* 16, no. 1: 99–118.

Hays, Jude C. (2009). *Globalization and the New Politics of Embedded Liberalism.* New York: Oxford University Press.

Hays, Jude C., Junghyun Lim, and Jae-Jae Spoon (2019). "The Path from Trade to Right-Wing Populism in Europe." *Electoral Studies* 60, August: 1–14.

Heath, Allister (2016). "Economists Have a Century of Failure Behind Them. No Wonder They Back Remain Now." The Telegraph, May 16. https://www.telegraph.co.uk/news/2016/05/18/economists-have-a-century-of-failure-behind-them-no-wonder-they/.

Heise, Michael, and Ana Boata (2019). "Economic Costs of Brexit." *International Economics and Economic Policy* 16, no. 1: 27–30.

Hillman, Jennifer (2018). "Testimony of Jennifer Hillman before the U.S.-China Economic and Review Security Commission hearing on U.S. Tools to Address Chinese Market Distortions." Transcript, June 8, pp. 71–97. https://www.uscc.gov/sites/default/files/transcripts/Hearing%20Transcript%20-%20June%208,%202018.pdf.

Hitch, Alexander (2019). "The Next Battleground in Trump's Trade War: Vietnam." *The Diplomat*, August 16. https://thediplomat.com/2019/08/the-next-battleground-in-trumps-trade-war-vietnam/.

Hoekman, Bernard, and Michel Kostecki (2009). *The Political Economy of the World Trading System: The WTO and Beyond*, 3rd ed. New York: Oxford University Press.

Hovenkamp, Erik, and Herbert Hovenkamp (2017). "Buying Monopoly: Antitrust Limits on Damages for Externally Acquired Patents." *Texas Intellectual Property Law Journal* 25, no. 1: 39–72.

Hufbauer, Gary C., and Euijin Jung (2019). Where Do Democratic Presidential Candidates Stand on Trade? Trade and Investment Policy Watch, March 25. Washington, DC: Peterson Institute for International Economics.

Hufbauer, Gary C., and Zhiyao Lu (2019). "The USTR Tariff Exclusion Process: Five Things to Know About These Opaque Handouts." Trade and Investment Policy Watch, December 19. Washington, DC: Peterson Institute for International Economics.

Irwin, Douglas A. (2017). *Clashing over Commerce: A History of U.S. Trade Policy.* Chicago: University of Chicago Press.

Jackson, Allison (2019). In Swipe at U.S., BRICS Hit Out at Protectionism. Agence France Press news service, November 14. https://news.yahoo.com/swipe-us-brics-hit-protectionism-164932984.html.

Jacobsen, Louis (2018). "How 'Vital to our National Security' Is Steel, Aluminum?" *Politifact*, 9 March 9. https://www.politifact.com/factchecks/2018/mar/09/donald-trump/how-vital-our-national-security-are-steel-aluminum/.

Jacobson, Louis (2019). "Did Trump Turn Around the U.S. Record at the WTO?" *Politifact*, August 16. https://www.politifact.com/truth-o-meter/statements/2019/aug/16/donald-trump/did-donald-trump-turn-around-us-record-wto/.

Jennings, Colin (2011). "The Good, the Bad, and the Populist: A Model of Political Agency with Emotional Voters." *European Journal of Political Economy* 27, no. 4: 611–624.

Johnson, C. Donald (2018). *The Wealth of a Nation.* New York: Oxford University Press.Jones, Kent (1994). *Export Restraint and the New Protectionism.* Ann Arbor: University of Michigan Press.

Jones, Kent (2004). *Who's Afraid of the WTO?* New York: Oxford University Press.

Jones, Kent (2015). *Re-Constructing the World Trade Organization for the 21st Century: An Institutional Approach.* New York: Oxford University Press.

Jones, Kent (2018). "Cuba, Trade Dependency, and the GATT/WTO System." *International Advances in Economic Research* 24, no. 4: 325–338.

Judis, John B. (2016). *The Populist Explosion.* New York: Columbia Global Reports.

Kandel, Maya, and Caroline Gondaud (2019). "Populism, the European Elections and the Future of E.U." *War on the Rocks*, 11 June 11. https://warontherocks.com/2019/06/populism-the-european-elections-and-the-future-of-e-u-foreign-policy/.

Kaufmann, Daniel, Aart Kraay, and Massimo Mastruzzi (2010). "The Worldwide Governance Indicators: Methodology and Analytical Issues." Draft Policy Research Working Paper, September. World Bank, http://info.worldbank.org/governance/wgi/pdf/WGI.pdf.

Kessler, Carson (2018). "Why Harley-Davidson Is Moving Production Overseas." *Fortune*, June 26. https://www.washingtonpost.com/business/2019/08/20/trump-v-obama-economy-charts/.

Kim, Young Mie, Jordan Hsu, David Neiman, Colin Kou, Levi Bankston, Soo Yun Kim, Richard Heinrich, Robyn Baragwanath, and Garvesh Raskutti (2018). "The Stealth Media? Groups and Targets Behind Divisive Issue Campaigns on Facebook." *Political Communication* 35, no. 4: 515–541.

Kirby, Paul (2016). "Turkey Coup Attempt: Who's the Target of Erdogan's Purge?" BBC News, July 20. https://www.bbc.com/news/world-europe-36835340.

Kletzer, Lori, and Robert E Litan (2001). "A Prescription to Relieve Worker Anxiety." Policy Brief 01-2, Peterson Institute of International Economics, March. https://www.piie.com/publications/policy-briefs/prescription-relieve-worker-anxiety.

Kyle, Jordan, and Limor Gultchin (2018). Populists in Power around the World. Report, November 7. London: Tony Blair Institute for Global Change. https://institute.global/insight/renewing-centre/populists-power-around-world.

Kyle, Jordan, and Yascha Mounk (2018). The Populist Harm to Democracy: An Empirical Assessment. London: Tony Blair Institute for Global Change, December 26. https://institute.global/insight/renewing-centre/populist-harm-democracy

Landau, Loren (2015). Populations, Populism and Institutions: Explaining South Africa's Xenophobic Violence. Heinrich Boll Stiftung (Foundation), Capetown, South Africa. Blog posting, June 2. https://za.boell.org/en/2015/06/02/populations-populism-and-institutions-explaining-south-africas-xenophobic-violence.

Latore, Maria, Zoryana Olekseyuk, Hidemichi Yonezawa, and Sherman Robinson (2019). "Brexit: Everyone Loses, But Britain Loses the Most." Working Paper 19-5, March. Washington, DC: Peterson Institute for International Economics.

Lawler, Dave (2020). "Belarus Dictator Lukashenko Says He'll Leave Post After New Constitution." *Axios*, November 27. https://www.axios.com/belarus-dictator-lukashenko-step-down-constitution-bb9cee66-4366-4814-b9f5-1ba9ec955b9e.html.

Lawrence, Robert Z. (2008). *Blue-Collar Blues: Is Trade to Blame for Rising US Income Inequality?* Policy Analysis in International Economics no 85 (January). Washington, DC: Peterson Institute for International Economics.

Lawrence, Robert Z. (2018). "Five Reasons Why the Focus on Trade Deficits Is Misleading." Policy Brief 18-6. Washington, DC: Peterson Institute for International Economics.

Ledoux, Joseph (2003). "The Emotional Brain: Fear and the Amygdala." *Cellular and Molecular Neurobiology* 23, no. 4/5: 727–738.

Lee, Don (2019). "Manufacturing Is Now Officially in Recession, Despite Trump's Vow to Boost Industry." *Los Angeles Times*, October 11. https://www.latimes.com/politics/story/2019-10-09/despite-trump-vow-manufacturing-in-recession.

Lee, Yong-Shik (2019). "Three Wrongs Do Not Make a Right: The Conundrum of the US Steel and Aluminum Tariffs." *World Trade Review* 18, no. 3: 481–501.

Lennon, Olena, and Aemin Becker (2019). "Belarus at the United Nations: An Analysis of Belarus's Global Policy Alignment Following the Maidan Revolution in Ukraine." *Demokratizatsiya: The Journal of Post-Soviet Democratization* 27, no. 3(Summer): 319–348.

Lighthizer, Robert (2017). "U.S. Trade Policy Priorities: Robert Lighthizer, United States Trade Representative." Interview, September 18. Center for International and Strategic Studies, Washington, DC. Transcript at https://csis-website-prod.s3.amazonaws.com/s3fs-public/publication/170918_U.S._Trade_Policy_Priorities_Robert_Lighthizer_transcript.pdf.

Lindgaard, J. (2018). "EU Public Opinion on Turkish EU Membership: Trends and Drivers." FEUTURE Online Paper no. 25, October. Cologne, Germany: University of Cologne. https://feuture.unikoeln.de/sites/feuture/user_upload/Online_Paper_No_25_final.pdf.

Lindsay, Frey (2019). "Will Slovakia's New Progressive President Change Anything on Migration?" *Forbes*, April 25. https://www.forbes.com/sites/freylindsay/2019/04/25/will-slovakias-new-progressive-president-change-anything-on-migration/#38e807854192.

Loch, Dietmar, and Ovidian Cristian Norocel (2015). "The Populist Radical Right in Europe: A Xenophobic Voice in the Global Economic Crisis." In *Europe's Prolonged Crisis*, ed. Virginie Guiraudon, Carlo Ruzza, and Hans-Jörg Trenz, 251–259. Palgrave Studies in European Political Sociology. London: Palgrave-MacMillan.

Loewenstein, George (2000). "Emotions in Economic Theory and Economic Behavior." *American Economic Review* 90, no. 2 (May): 426–432.

Long, Heather (2019). "The Trump vs. Obama Economy, in 15 Charts." *Washington Post*, August 20. https://www.washingtonpost.com/business/2019/08/20/trump-v-obama-economy-charts/.

Lovely, Mary E. (2019). "The Cost of Another US-China No-Deal Deal." Trade and Investment Policy Watch, October 15. Washington, DC: Peterson Institute for International Economics.

Lovely, Mary E., and Jeffrey Schott (2019). "The USMCA: New, Modestly Improved, But Still Costly." Trade and Investment Policy Watch, December 17. Washington, DC: Peterson Institute for International Economics.

Luhby, Tami (2016). "Yes, 'President Trump' Could Kill NAFTA, But It Wouldn't Be Pretty." CNN Business, July 6. https://money.cnn.com/2016/07/06/news/economy/trump-nafta/index.html.

McBrearty, S., and A. Brooks (2000). "The Revolution That Wasn't: A New Interpretation of the Origin of Modern Human Behavior." *Journal of Human Evolution* 39, no. 5: 453–563.

McGee, Luke (2019). "The UK Will Never Get the US Trade Deal It Wants." CNN Business, November 6. https://www.cnn.com/2019/11/06/business/brexit-us-uk-trade-donald-trump-boris-johnson-intl-gbr/index.html.

McKeef, Clive (2019). "US Stock Market at Record, But Farm Bankruptcies at Highest Since 2011." *Market Watch*, November 19. https://www.marketwatch.com/story/us-stock-market-at-record-but-farm-bankruptcies-at-highest-since-2011-2019-11-16.

McManus, Edgar J., and Tara Helfman (2014). *A Constitutional History of the United States*, Concise Edition. New York: Routledge.

Magni, Gabriele (2017). "It's the Emotions, Stupid! Anger About the Economic Crisis, Low Political Efficacy and Support for Populist Parties." *Electoral Studies* 50 (December): 91–102.

Mance, Henry (2016). "Britain Has Had Enough of Experts, Says Gove." *Financial Times*, June 3. https://www.ft.com/content/3be49734-29cb-11e6-83e4-abc22d5d108c.

Mansfield, Edward D., Diana C. Mutz, and Devon Brackbill (2016). "Effects of the Great Recession on American Attitudes Toward Trade." *British Journal of Political Science* 49, no. 1: 37–58.

Maurice, Eric (2015). "Visegrad States Meet on Refusal of Refugee Quotas." *EU Observer*, September 4. https://euobserver.com/migration/130115.

Mayda, Anna Maria, and Dani Rodrik (2005). "Why Are Some People (and Countries) More Protectionist Than Others?" *European Economic Review* 49, no. 6 (August): 1393–1430.

Mead, Walter Russell (2011). "The Tea Party and American Foreign Policy: What Populism Means for Globalism." *Foreign Affairs* 90, no. 2 (March/April): 28–44.

Minford, P., S. Gupta, V. Le, V. Mahambare, and Y. Xu (2016). *Should Britain Leave the EU? An Economic Analysis of a Troubled Relationship*, 2nd ed. Cheltonham, UK and Northampton, MA: Institute of Economic Affairs and Edward Elgar.

Mount, Ian (2016). "Trump Says It Might Be Time for the US to Quit the WTO." *Fortune*, July 25. https://fortune.com/2016/07/25/donald-trump-free-trade-wto.

Mudde, Cas (2007). *Populist Radical Right Parties in Europe*. Cambridge: Cambridge University Press.

Navarro, Peter, director (2012). *Death by China*. Virgil Films and Entertainment. Narrated by Martin Sheen. Producers: Peter Navarro, Joe Zarinko, Michael Addis, Greg Autry.

Nechepurenko, Ivan, and Anton Troianovski (2020). "After Vote That Many Called Rigged, Challenger to Belarus Leader Leaves." *New York Times*, August 11. https://www.nytimes.com/2020/08/11/world/europe/belarus-election-Svetlana-Tikhanovskaya.html.

Niebuhr, Reinhold (1932). *Moral Man and Immoral Society*. New York: Scribner's.

Norris, Pippa, and Ronald Inglehart (2019). *Cultural Backlash: Trump, Brexit and Authoritarian Populism*. Cambridge, UK: Cambridge University Press.

North, Douglass (1991). "Institutions." *Journal of Economic Perspectives* 5, no. 1: 97–112.

Nossiter, Adam, and Jason Horowitz (2019). "Bannon's Populists, Once a 'Movement,' Keep Him at Arm's Length." *New York Times*, May 24. https://www.nytimes.com/2019/05/24/world/europe/steve-bannon-european-elections-paris.html.

Nowrasteh, Alex (2019). "Terrorists by Immigration Status and Nationality: A Risk Analysis, 1975–2017." Policy Analysis No. 866, May 9. Washington: Cato Institute.

Oberhauser, Ann M., David Krier, and Abdi M. Kusow (2019). "Political Moderation and Polarization in the Heartland: Economics, Rurality, and Social Identity in the 2016 U.S. Presidential Election." *Sociological Quarterly* 60, no. 2: 224–244.

Ocampo, Emilio (2019), "The Economic Analysis of Populism: A Selective Review of the Literature." Universidad del Cema, Buenos Aires, Argentina, Working Paper no. 694, May. https://ucema.edu.ar/publicaciones/download/documentos/694.pdf.

Oppenheimer, Stephen (2003). *Out of Eden: The Peopling o the World*. London: Robinson.

Patunru, Arianto A. (2018). "Rising Economic Nationalism in Indonesia." *Journal of Southeast Asian Economies* 35, no. 3: 335–354.

Payosova, Tetyana, G. C. Hufbauer, and J. Schott (2018). "The Dispute-Settlement Crisis in the World Trade Organization: Causes and Cures." Policy Brief 18-5. Washington, DC: Peterson Institute for International Economics.

Petersmann, Ernst-Ulrich (2019). "How Should WTO Members React to Their WTO Crises?" *World Trade Review* 18, no. 3: 503–525.

Pierce, Justin R., and Peter K. Schott (2020). "Trade Liberalization and Mortality: Evidence from US Counties." *American Economic Review: Insights 2020* 2, no. 1: 47–64.

Pieterse, Jan Nederveen (2018). "Populism Is a Distraction." *New Global Studies* 12, no. 3: 377–386.

Pietromarchi, Virginia (2019). "With Salvini Gone, What's Next for Italy's Immigration Policy?" *Aljazeera*, September 10. https://www.aljazeera.com/news/2019/09/salvini-italy-migration-policy-190910121122318.html.

Pinchis-Paulsen, Mona (2020). "Trade Multilateralism and U.S. National Security: The Making of the GATT Security Exceptions." *Michigan Journal of International Law* 41, no. 1: 109–194. https://repository.law.umich.edu/mjil/vol41/iss1/4/.

Pinker, Steven (2011). *The Better Angels of our Nature: Why Violence has Declined*. New York: Viking.

Pinto Arena, Maria do Céu (2017). *Islamic Terrorism in the West and International Migrations: The "Far" or "Near" Enemy Within?* Research paper no. 2017/28. Robert Schuman Centre for Advanced Studies, San Domenico di Fiesole, Italy, May.

Pitman, George R. (2011). "The Evolution of Human Warfare." *Philosophy of the Social Sciences* 41, no. 3: 352–379.

Podobnik, Boris, Ivona Skreblin Kirbis, Maja Koprcina, and H. E. Stanley (2019). "Emergence of the Unified Right- and Left-Wing Populism: When Radical Societal Changes Become More Important Than Ideology." *Physica A* 517: 459–474.

Portman, Robert (2019a). "Portman Delivers Remarks on Need to Reform National Security Tariff Process, Protect American Jobs." Press Release, February 8. https://www.portman.senate.gov/newsroom/press-releases/portman-delivers-remarks-need-reform-national-security-tariff-process.

Portman, Robert (2019b). "Q&A: Sen. Portman talks Section 232 Legislation, China and WTO Reform." *Inside U.S. Trade*, November 11.

Putzhammer, Fritz (2018). Globalization, Trade and Populism in Germany. Global Economic Dynamics Focus Paper, Bertelsmann-Stiftung (Foundation), Guetersloh, Germany. https://www.bertelsmann-stiftung.de/fileadmin/files/BSt/Publikationen/GrauePublikationen/MT_GlobalizationTradeAndPopulismInGermany.pdf.

Rappeport, Alan, and Stacey M. Brown (2018). "Trump Threatens Harley-Davidson, Saying it 'Surrendered.'" *New York Times*, June 26. https://www.nytimes.com/2018/06/26/business/trump-harley-davidson-tariffs.html.

Reich, Arie (2017). "The Effectiveness of the WTO Dispute Settlement System: A Statistical Analysis." Florence, Italy: European University Institute Working paper LAW 2017/11.

Rho, Sungmin, and Tomz, Michael (2017). "Why Don't Trade Preferences Reflect Economic Self-Interest?" *International Organization* 71, no. S1 (April): S85–S108.

Rico, Guillem, Marc Guinjoan, and Evan Anduiza (2017). "The Emotional Underpinnings of Populism: How Anger and Fear Affect Populist Attitudes." *Swiss Political Science Review* 23, no. 4: 444–461.

Riley, Bryan (2020). "Fact-Checking Peter Navarro's Latest Broadside." National Taxpayers Union Foundation Blog, 14 January 14. https://www.ntu.org/foundation/detail/fact-checking-peter-navarros-latest-broadside.

Rodrik, Dani (2018). "Populism and the Economics of Globalization." Journal of International Business Policy 1, no. 1 (June): 12–33.

Rothman, Lily (2017). "President Trump's Question About the Civil War Was Answered by Abraham Lincoln." *Time Magazine*, May 1. https://time.com/4761335/trump-jackson-lincoln-civil-war/.

Rovira Kaltwasser, Cristobal (2018). "Studying the (Economic) Consequences of Populism." *AEA Papers and Proceedings* 108: 204–207.

Rovira Kaltwasser, Cristobal, Paul A. Taggart, Paulina Ochoa Espejo, and Pierre Ostiguy (eds.) (2017). *Oxford Handbook of Populism*. New York: Oxford University Press.

Ruggie, John (1982). "International Regimes, Transactions and Change: Embedded Liberalism in the Postwar Economic Order." *International Organization* 36, no. 2: 379–415.

Runje, Leon (2018). "Challenges to Democracy: The Origins of Protectionist Populism in Europe." *Interdisciplinary Description of Complex Systems* 16, no. 3-B: 446–451.

Salmela, Mikko, and Christian Von Scheve (2017). "Emotional Roots of Right-Wing Political Populism." *Social Science Information* 56, no. 4: 567–595.

Savage, Charlie (2019). "The President's 'Emergency' Tariffs on Mexican Goods, Explained." *New York Times*, June 6. https://www.nytimes.com/2019/06/06/us/mexico-tariffs.html.

Schipani, Andres, Benedict Mander, and Bryan Harris (2019). "South American Tensions Threaten Mercosur Trade Deal." *Financial Times*, December 4.

Schlesinger, Jacob M. (2018). "Trump Forged Trade Ideas in in 1980s—and Never Deviated." *Wall Street Journal*, November 16, p. A1.

Schlesinger, Jacob M. (2019). "Will the U.S. Bring Down the WTO?" *Wall Street Journal*, November 30, p. C5.

Schott, Jeffrey (2018). "For Mexico, Canada and the United States, a Step Backwards on Trade and Investment." Trade and Investment Policy Watch, October 2. Washington, DC: Peterson Institute for International Economics.

Schott, Jeffrey (2019). "Reinventing the Wheel: Phase One of the US-Japan Trade Pact." Trade and Investment Policy Watch, September 27. Washington, DC: Peterson Institute for International Economics.

Schott, Jeffrey (2020). "The US-China Currency Deal Will Provoke New Trade Tensions." Trade and Investment Policy Watch, February 7. Washington, DC: Peterson Institute for International Economics.

Schultz, Florence (2019). "How Strong Is Right-Wing Populism after the European Elections?" *Euractiv*, June 4.https://www.euractiv.com/section/eu-elections-2019/news/how-strong-is-right-wing-populism-after-the-european-elections/.

Schwartz, Nelson D., and Quoctrung Bui. 2016. "Where Jobs Are Squeezed by Chinese Trade, Voters Seek Extremes." *New York Times*, April 25.

Schwartzenberg, Andres B. (2020). "Section 301 Investigations: Foreign Digital Services Taxes (DSTs)." Congressional Research Service Update, Report no. IF11564, December 10. Washington: Congressional Research Service, https://crsreports.congress.gov/product/pdf/IF/IF11564.

Searle, John (2005). "What Is an Institution?" *Journal of Institutional Economics* 1, no. 1: 1–22.

Şenyuva, Özgehan (2018). "Turkish Public Opinion and the EU Membership: Between Support and Mistrust." FEUTURE Online Paper no. 26 (October). Cologne, Germany: University of Cologne. https://feuture.uni-koeln.de/sites/feuture/user_upload/Online_Paper_No_26_final.pdf.

Serhan, Yasmeen (2020). "Populism Is Morphing in Insidious Ways." *The Atlantic*, January 6. https://www.theatlantic.com/international/archive/2020/01/future-populism-2020s/604393/.

Sikes, Devin (2019). "US Court of International Trade Confirms Limits to Section 232 Action." *Mondaq Business Briefing* blog, November 25. https://www.mondaq.com/unitedstates/international-trade-investment/867364/.

Skonieczny, Amy (2018). "Emotions and Political Narratives: Populism, Trump and Trade." *Politics and Governance* 6, no. 4: 62–72.

Stähleli, Urs, and Eric Savoth (2011). "Seducing the Crowd: The Leader in Crowd Psychology." *New German Critique* 38, no. 3: 63–77.

Stamouli, Nektaria (2017). "Greece: A Case Study in Capital Controls." *The Greek Crisis*, June 15. http://www.greekcrisis.net/2017/06/greece-case-study-in-capital-controls.html.

Stanley, Ben (2017). "Populism in Central and Eastern Europe." In *The Oxford Handbook of Populism*, ed. Cristobal Rovira Kaltwasser, Paul Taggart, Paulina Ochoa Espejo, and Pierre Ostiguy, 140–160. Oxford: Oxford University Press.

Stolper, Wolfgang, and Paul A. Samuelson (1941). "Protection and Real Wages." *Review of Economic Studies* 9, no. 1: 58–73.

Swan, Joanathan (2018). "Exclusive: A Leaked Trump Bill to Blow Up the WTO." *Axios*, July 1. https://www.axios.com/trump-trade-war-leaked-bill-world-trade-organization-united-states-d51278d2-0516-4def-a4d3-ed676f4e0f83.html.

Swanson, Ana, and Peter Eavis (2020). "Trump Expands Steel Tariffs, Saying They Are Short of Aim." *New York Times*, January 27. https://www.nytimes.com/2020/01/27/business/economy/trump-steel-tariffs.html.

Taggart, Paul (2017). "Populism in Western Europe." In *The Oxford Handbook of Populism*, ed. Cristobal Rovira Kaltwasser, Paul Taggart, Paulina Ochoa Espejo, and Pierre Ostiguy, 248–263. Oxford: Oxford University Press.

Tralac (2019). "South Africa: A 2018 Trade and Investment Profile." Tralac Trade Law Center, Stellenbosch, South Africa, February. https://www.tralac.org/documents/publications/trade-data-analysis/2672-south-africa-2018-trade-and-investment-profile-february-2019/file.html.

Trump, Donald (2016). "Remarks on Trade." *Time*, June 28. http://time.com/4386335/donald-trump-trade-speech-transcript.

Trump, Donald (2017). "Inaugural Address." January 20. Washington, DC: The White House.

Trump, Donald (2019). "Address to United Nations General Assembly." September 24. https://www.whitehouse.gov/briefings-statements/remarks-president-trump-74th-session-united-nations-general-assembly/.

Trump, Donald J. and Hillary Clinton (2016). "First Presidential Debate, 25 September." Transcript, *New York Times*, September 27. https://www.nytimes.com/2016/09/27/us/politics/transcript-debate.html.

Tsyvinski, Aleh, and Nicolas Werquin (2018). "Compensating Welfare Losses from Economic Disruptions." *Vox CEPR Policy Portal* blog, July 9. https://voxeu.org/article/compensating-welfare-losses-economic-disruptions.

Turak, Natasha (2019). "Turkish Central Bank Needs to Be 'Fully Independent', IMF's Europe Director Says." CNBC, April 15. https://www.cnbc.com/2019/04/14/turkish-central-bank-needs-to-be-fully-independent-imf-europe-chief.html.

Upadhyay, Brajesh (2019). "Modi Visit to US: Trump Appearance Signals Importance of India." BBC News Washington, September 20. https://www.bbc.com/news/world-us-canada-49760165.

US Congress (2019). United States Reciprocal Trade Act. January 24. https://duffy.house.gov/sites/duffy.house.gov/files/wysiwyg_uploaded/BILL%20-%20USRTA.pdf.

US Court of International Trade (2020). Huttig Building Products, Inc. et al. v. U.S. et al., case number 1:20-cv-00045 (Section 232 Steel and Aluminum Derivative Product Tariffs). Filed 4 February. Complaint document. https://www.thompsonhinesmartrade.com/wp-content/uploads/sites/783/2020/02/PrimeSource-Building-Products-CIT-Section-232-Amended-Complaint-Feb-11-2020.pdf.

US Department of Commerce (2018). The Effects of Imports of Steel on the National Security: An Investigation Conducted under Section 232 of the Trade Expansion Act of 1962, as Amended. January 11. Washington, DC: US Department of Commerce.

US Trade Representative (USTR) (2017). Summary of Objectives for the NAFTA Renegotiation. July 17. Washington, DC: Office of the US Trade Representative. https://ustr.gov/sites/default/files/files/Press/Releases/NAFTAObjectives.pdf.

US Trade Representative (USTR) (2019). Agreement between the United States of America, the United Mexican States and Canada. May 30 text, signed November 30, 2018. https://ustr.gov/trade-agreements/free-trade-agreements/united-states-mexico-canada-agreement/agreement-between.

US Trade Representative (USTR) (2020). Economic and Trade Agreement between the Government of the United States of American and the Government of the People's Republic of China. Office of the United States Trade Representative. January 15. https://ustr.gov/sites/default/files/files/agreements/phase%20one%20agreement/Economic_And_Trade_Agreement_Between_The_United_States_And_China_Text.pdf.

Van der Waal, Jeroen, and Wellem de Koster (2018). "Populism and Support for Protectionism: The Relevance of Opposition to Trade Openness for Leftist and Rightist Populist Voting in the Netherlands." *Political Studies* 66, no. 3: 560–576.

Van Eck, Jan (2018). "Turkey: Currency Collapse, Nepotism and the Portent for Gas." Oilprice.com, September 12. https://community.oilprice.com/topic/3478-turkey-%C2%A0-currency-collapse-nepotism-and-the-portent-for-gas.

VanGrasstek, Craig (2019a). "The Trade Policy of the United States Under the Trump Administration." EUI Working Paper RSCAS 2019/11. Florence: European University Institute.

VanGrasstek, Craig (2019b). *Trade and American Leadership*. Cambridge: Cambridge University Press.

Vaudano, Maxime, and Agathe Dahyot. "Elections européennes 2019: comment ont voté les 82 eurodéputés français depuis 2014?" *Le Monde*, May 10. https://www.lemonde.fr/les-decodeurs/article/2019/05/10/europeennes-2019-comment-ont-vote-les-deputes-europeens-francais-depuis-2014_5460395_4355770.html#ancre_commerce.

Viviani, Lorenzo (2017). "A Political Sociology of Populism and Leadership." *Società Mutamento Politica* 8, no. 15: 279–303.

Volkens, Andrea, Werner Krause, Pola Lehmann, Theres Matthieß, Nicolas Merz, Sven Regel, and Bernhard Weßels (2019). The Manifesto Data Collection. Manifesto Project. Version

2019b. Berlin: Wissenschaftszentrum Berlin für Sozialforschung. https://doi.org/10.25522/manifesto.mpds.2019b.

Wadsworth, Jonathan, Swati Dhingra, Gianmarco Ottaviano, and John van Reenan (2016). "Brexit and the Impact of Immigration on the UK." Centre for Economic Performance (CEP) Brexit Analysis No. 5. May, London School of Economics.

Warburton, Eve (2018). "Inequality, Nationalism and Electoral Politics in Indonesia." *Southeast Asian Affairs* (Singapore) 2018: 135–252.

Westen, Drew (2007). *The Political Brain: The Role of Emotion in Deciding the Fate of the Nation.* New York: Public Affairs.

Weyland, Kurt (1999). "Neoliberal Populism in Latin America and Eastern Europe." *Comparative Politics* 31, no. 4: 379–401.

White House (2019). "Remarks by President Trump in a Meeting with Republican Members of Congress on the United States Reciprocal Trade Act." January 24. https://www.whitehouse.gov/briefings-statements/remarks-president-trump-meeting-republican-members-congress-united-states-reciprocal-trade-act/.

White House (2020). "Proclamation on Adjusting Imports of Derivative Aluminum Articles and Derivative Steel Articles into the United States." January 24. https://www.whitehouse.gov/presidential-actions/proclamation-adjusting-imports-derivative-aluminum-articles-derivative-steel-articles-united-states/.

Woodward, Bob (2018). *Fear: Trump in the White House.* New York: Simon & Schuster.

World Trade Organization (WTO) (1998). United States: Sections 301–310 of the Trade Act of 1974—Panel Report—Action by the Dispute Settlement Body. Dispute Settlement Case DS152. Geneva: WTO, https://www.wto.org/english/tratop_e/dispu_e/cases_e/ds152_e.htm.

World Trade Organization (WTO) (1999). *The Legal Texts: The Results of the Uruguay Round of Multilateral Trade Negotiations.* Cambridge: Cambridge University Press.

World Trade Organization (WTO) (2001). "Report of the Working Party on the Accession of China." Document WT/ACC/CHN/49. https://docs.wto.org/dol2fe/Pages/SS/directdoc.aspx?filename=Q:/WT/ACC/CHN49.pdf&Open=True.

World Trade Organization (WTO) (2012). Trade Policy Review: Ecuador. Secretariat Report. Geneva: WTO Secretariat.

World Trade Organization WTO (2016a). Russian Federation: Measures Concerning Traffic in Transit, filed by Ukraine. Dispute Settlement Case 512. Geneva: WTO, https://www.wto.org/english/tratop_e/dispu_e/cases_e/ds512_e.htm.

World Trade Organization (WTO) (2016b). Trade Policy Review: Russian Federation, Secretariat Report. Geneva: WTO Secretariat.

World Trade Organization (WTO) (2018a). Trade Policy Review: Bolivia. Secretariat Report. Geneva: WTO Secretariat.

World Trade Organization (WTO) (2018b). Trade Policy Review: Israel. Secretariat Report. Geneva: WTO Secretariat.

World Trade Organization (WTO) (2018c). United States: Safeguards Measures on Washers, filed by Republic of Korea. Dispute Settlement Case DS546. Geneva: WTO, https://www.wto.org/english/tratop_e/dispu_e/cases_e/ds546_e.htm.

World Trade Organization (WTO) (2020). "WTO Accessions: 2019 Annual Report by the Director-General." Document WT/ACC/36 (WT/GC/207). February 21. https://docs.wto.org/dol2fe/Pages/SS/directdoc.aspx?filename=q:/WT/ACC/36.pdf&Open=True.

Wu, Mark (2016). "The 'China, Inc.' Challenge to Global Trade Governance." *Harvard International Law Journal* 57, no. 2: 261–324.

Yen, Hope, Ali Swenson, and Amanda Seitz (2020). "AP FACT CHECK: Trump's Claims of Vote Rigging Are All Wrong." *New York Times*, December 3. https://apnews.

com/article/election-2020-ap-fact-check-joe-biden-donald-trump-technology-49a24edd6d10888dbad61689c24b05a5.

Zettelmeyer, Jeromin (2019). "The Return of Economic Nationalism in Germany." Policy Brief 19-4, March. Washington, DC: Peterson Institute for International Economics.

Zukowski, Arkadiusz (2017). "Land Reform in the Republic of South Africa: Social Justice or Populism?" *Werkwinkel* 12, no. 1: 71–84.

Zumbrun, Josh (2020). "New Trump Rules Will Allow Tariffs Against Currency Manipulation." *Wall Street Journal*, February 4. https://www.wsj.com/articles/new-rule-lets-u-s-companies-fight-currency-manipulation-11580831245.

Zumbrun, Josh, Paulo Trevisani, and Amrith Ramkumar (2019). "Trump to Levy Tariffs on Brazil, Argentina." *Wall Street Journal*, December 3, p. A1.

Index

For the benefit of digital users, indexed terms that span two pages (e.g., 52–53) may, on occasion, appear on only one of those pages.

Tables and figures are indicated by *t* and *f* following the page number